LA SOCIEDAD

LA SOCIEDAD

Guardians of Hispanic Culture
Along the Río Grande

Text by
JOSÉ A. RIVERA

With the assistance of
Rogelio Briones, Michael Atencio, *and* Daniel Salazar

Photographs by Daniel Salazar

UNIVERSITY OF NEW MEXICO PRESS
Albuquerque

Library of Congress Cataloging-in-Publication Data
Rivera, José A., 1944–
La sociedad : guardians of Hispanic culture along the Río Grande / text by José A. Rivera ;
With the assistance of Rogelio Briones, Michael Atencio, and Daniel Salazar ;
photographs by Daniel Salazar.
p. cm.
Includes bibliographical references and index.
ISBN 978-0-8263-4894-4 (cloth : alk. paper)
1. Sociedad Protección Mutua de Trabajadores Unidos. 2. Fraternal organizations—
Southwestern States. 3. Hispanic Americans. I. Title.
HS1510.S6656R58 2010
369'.368079—dc22
2010014705

DESIGN AND COMPOSITION
Barbara Haines
TEXT IS MINION PRO 10/13.75

CONTENTS

FOREWORD

As a young boy growing up in Placitas, New Mexico, I remember attending burials of elders who had passed away in our community. I was very much impressed by the perfect respect exhibited by the members of La Sociedad de Protección Mutua de Trabajadores Unidos[1] during the ceremonies they performed at the gravesite. The *hermano* who delivered the eulogy and read the *resoluciones de condolencia* did it in such a way that it produced goose bumps on those of us in attendance. All of the society members wore a *siempreviva* leaf, an evergreen representing fraternity, pinned next to the *devisa* on their clothing. As the formation of members walked around the grave, each hermano placed his leaf on the coffin of the departed member and then bid his last farewell: "Hermano, descanse en paz" (Brother, may you rest in peace).

I also remember the anniversary dances at the meeting hall of local Council No. 14, an affiliate of La Sociedad located nearby at El Rito, New Mexico. The members started the dance by entering the hall in formation and singing the official La Sociedad hymn. It was very moving to hear those strong baritone voices all in unison:

¡Juremos ser LIBRES	Let us pledge to be FREE
Y viva la UNION!	And long live the UNION!
¡Que viva la LIGA	Long live our LEAGUE
DE MUTUA PROTECCION!	OF MUTUAL PROTECTION!
Defendemos su Bandera	We defend her Flag
Con nuestras Fuerzas y Unión	With all our Strength and Unity
Defendemos su Bandera.	We defend her Flag.

I recall that the dances used to be announced in the community by what was called *"sacar el gallo,"* where a horse-drawn wagon led a parade of society members and musicians, usually a guitar and a violin and sometimes an accordion, playing the polkas and *corridos* of the times. This was done on Saturday morning to announce social events such as La Sociedad's local anniversary program to be held later in the day followed by a public dance in the evening. At the dance, the band was set up on a makeshift stage at the front of the meeting hall, and the walls on both sides were lined with wood-crafted benches. These benches were reserved for the young girls and their mothers. The men gathered and stood inside the main entrance of the hall, from where they would come out to escort female partners onto the dance floor. Because it was not good etiquette to stand up a suitor, the taking out of a good dancer or attractive partner became like a first-come, first-dance contest. Consequently, the young men made a beeline to dance with the most popular girls.

I remember that women did not pay to come into the dance, but neither did the men. The method of collection was done during the dance. The band would pause in the middle of a dance piece, and members of La Sociedad who were assigned as *bastoneros* would come out on the dance floor and collect a dime from each male dancer. This was done for every dance, so the gentleman who danced all night had to have a pocketful of dimes. The rules of chivalry were enforced by the chief bastonero. No one was allowed to smoke while dancing, and the men were not allowed to dance with their hats on. Women had to be walked back to their sitting places. Men who refused to abide by the rules were politely escorted outside. When men greeted one another, they would tip their hats or remove them completely if they shook hands. This respect between gentlemen is still promoted and encouraged by the *hermandad* of the society and is very much part of our heritage that needs to be preserved.

My family has been involved in La Sociedad for four generations: my grandfather, Tomás Campos; my father, Victor Trujillo; myself; and my own son, Lucas Trujillo Jr. Together, we have more than one hundred years of fraternity. In my case, I formerly served as an officer of the Concilio Superior, and since 2001 I have served as the president of the Cuerpo Legislativo Superior. The rich heritage portrayed in this book is truly an integral part of our Hispanic culture and a legacy for our youth and children. Rogelio Briones, president of the Superior Council from 2001 to 2005, took the initiative in 1993 to make it possible that our history be recorded so that it may never be forgotten; it will always be there for us and for posterity. As superior president, Hermano Rogelio became highly knowledgeable about the history of the society and the depth of commitment by local council members as he traveled to and participated in their community meetings and anniversaries. During the documentary survey for the book, he served as the production manager, and, along with Daniel Salazar, he conducted field surveys of the local councils and recorded the oral histories of the officers and elders.

Daniel Salazar is a photographer-artist from Denver, where he is a dedicated member of Council No. 7. In the 1990s, he eagerly took the lead in conducting a survey of images to prepare for the centennial anniversary scheduled for the year 2000, and he later expanded the survey to include the additional photos needed for this book. In the process, Daniel amassed a unique collection of photographs depicting council members, meeting halls, and general conventions of delegates, and he finished the documentary with a survey of the community landscapes of the places where local councils are located. His photographs are featured throughout the book. Our fellow members express gratitude to Daniel for his generosity in sharing the many photos that tell the story of La Sociedad and preserve our fraternal history in images.

Michael Atencio, Council No. 19 in Alamosa, Colorado, contributed to the oral history collection by relating accounts of the women's auxiliaries in Antonito at a time when his grandmother was an active member and a dedicated treasurer. Likewise, his grandfather was a longtime member of La Sociedad and served as secretary of the local council in Ortiz, Colorado. Michael himself served as the *portero* of the Superior Council at the time the documentary survey was under way and later as superior vice president. During the book's production phase, he convened meetings at Trinidad State Junior College in Alamosa and collected photographs of Antonito and other important historic sites from the archives of the Colorado Historical Society. Finally, José Rivera is a member of Council No. 57 in Nambé, New Mexico, and teaches community and regional planning at the University of New Mexico, where he also conducts research at the Center for Regional Studies. We thank him for writing the book's narrative text and for preparing and editing the manuscript for submission to the University of New Mexico Press.

Lucas O. Trujillo Sr.
President, Cuerpo Legislativo Superior, 2001–2010

PREFACE

T HE FIRST PUBLICATION TO DOCUMENT the origins and early history of La Sociedad was a book by José Timoteo López titled *La Historia de La Sociedad Protección Mutua de Trabajadoes Unidos*. José Timoteo López was born in the small farming community of Ortiz, Colorado, in 1899, and became a member of Council No. 5 in Ortiz at the age of eighteen; he later transferred to Council No. 2 in Capulín, Colorado, where he was a merchant and post-master. He started the book project in 1951 with modest objectives: to pre-serve the memory and motives of the founders, inspire the youth, and compile notes about the history and accomplishments of the society, calling his manu-script, "Los Datos Históricos de la SPMDTU." A few years later he realized the importance of preserving the information he had collected and took steps in 1958 to publish the manuscript largely with his own resources. By this time, he was residing with his wife and nine children in Ogden, Utah, where he was an active member of Council No. 61, serving as the council secretary in the 1950s and early 1960s.

La Historia covers La Sociedad's history for the first half of the twentieth century and remains significant for preserving the early steps taken by the founders to organize the society in 1900. As López details, the book describes the chronology and sequence of when local councils were established in the tristate area of Colorado, New Mexico, and Utah. Most important, it shares what little we know about the life of the honorable Celedonio Mondragón, founder of the society. The book has been out of print for more than a gen-eration, but current members appreciate its significance. They hold it in high regard for the recognition it has brought the society, and members who own copies of *La Historia* treasure them as much as the Código Ritualístico and other society documents.

In the year 2000, the members commemorated the society's centennial anniversary. This event spurred the officers of the Concilio Superior to once again document its history, as inspired by Hermano José Timoteo López. At the time, I served as the superior president of "La Mutua," as we often call our society to show our respect and recognize the bonds we have to each other. A sense of urgency that had always been present on the periphery now engulfed us, for we knew that it was imperative that we "dust off" the idea of accomplishing a documentary because earlier attempts at a film project had not come to fruition in the 1980s. The median age of society members in the year 2000 was about sixty years or older. Many of the officers and members had joined as young adults, following in the footsteps of their *padres*, *tíos*, and *abuelos*, and once initiated into the society, most of them had retained their memberships for life. The leaders who had championed La Mutua all these decades were "pasando a mejor vida" (passing on to a better life), as surviving members often say in tribute to deceased brothers and sisters. We sensed that if we did not act immediately, we would lose the human and physical resources that have made La Sociedad so unique.

Many hermanos who had been instrumental in moving the organization to the twenty-first century were gone but not forgotten for their loyalty and significant contributions. Memorable individuals include: Frank López Sr. from Nambé, New Mexico, who, along with other executive officers, was responsible for ensuring that the organization remained financially solvent while it was governed by the regulations of the Colorado Insurance Commission; Vianes Trujillo from Ojo Caliente, New Mexico, who served for many terms on the Superior Council until he was unable to drive to Antonito for the meetings; Manuel Fernández from Salt Lake City, Utah, who was a member of many prominent national Hispanic organizations but nonetheless regarded La Sociedad as the most important of his affiliations; and Juan López from Denver, who willed himself to remain an active member of the Superior Council despite the distances he had to travel to attend the meetings at the home office in Antonito, Colorado. Samuel Mascareñas from Salt Lake City served as a Superior Council officer even though he, too, had to travel to the meetings in Antonito, mostly at his own expense. Elías Rascón, a member of Council No. 19 of Alamosa, Colorado, was a multitalented person: a musician and singer of *alabados* as well as a fascinating storyteller. His most extraordinary accomplishment was that he had memorized verbatim all of La Sociedad's ritual ceremonies. Hermano Elías had such a command of the Código Ritualístico that if any member made an incorrect reference to this code of conduct, he would prompt the member very politely with the correct and precise language.

Concerned that many more hermanos would pass away, the Superior Council officers determined that there was no time to waste in preserving La Sociedad's history and significance. We were fearful that its history would be lost to future generations if steps were not taken to interview longtime members before they passed on or as local meeting halls were closed or fell into disrepair, which had already happened in the case of some of the councils. We also wanted to have a way of honoring the struggles of the founders and the other elders who had sustained the society from generation to generation since its founding in 1900. Our motive was to paint a portrait of the society, its elders, meeting halls, records, and conventions and thus to preserve the significance of the society for appreciation by our youth and future generations of members.

With initial funding from Adobe de Oro and Concilio de Artes and with a supplemental award later from the EN FOCO New Works Fellowship Program, we launched the project in 1993 with a pictorial history of La Sociedad. Together, Daniel Salazar and I embarked on a photographic survey of La Sociedad as a method for capturing the material culture and the intangibles that up to the present have held the society together: solidarity, a sense of place, and closeness to the land. Our aims for the survey were multifaceted: recognize La Sociedad's history and its connections to the *hispano* culture of the region; document the councils that are still functioning; interview the elders who held and continue to hold vital information about the history of the society in their communities; and capture in photo images the society's "geography," from the quintessential villages of northern New Mexico to the agricultural towns of the San Luis Valley in southern Colorado (by this time, the councils previously existing in Utah were no longer active).

At first, our strategy was simply to photograph the members and the remaining meeting halls of every council in Colorado and New Mexico. In Colorado, the Superior Council of Antonito and the councils in Chama and La Garita owned properties with *salas* that were still in use or had been used in the recent past for meetings and community social events. The New Mexico councils were the most numerous, but some of the buildings had fallen into private ownership; we prioritized photographing these historic buildings first. A private individual from California had just purchased the meeting hall in Costilla; we fortunately were able to photograph this building before it was remodeled into a residence. Ojo Caliente, New Mexico, also presented a challenge. The location where the council's building once stood is already a parking lot for a local country store, but several photographs of this building were taken prior to demolition and are now part of the documentary collection, as are the meeting halls in Cerro, Ranchos de Taos, Nambé, and El Rito, New

Mexico. We made subsequent visits to these communities in 2005 to photograph the landscapes of these remarkable places for inclusion in this book. Our final images for the book were taken at the 2006 biannual convention in Ranchos de Taos as well as at the 2008 convention in Denver.

The initial collection of the photographs by Daniel Salazar premiered in a commemorative exhibition curated by the Museo de Las Américas in Denver, entitled Keepers of Culture—The 100th Anniversary of the SPMDTU, from June 2 to August 12, 2000. The exhibit received press coverage by the local media and was well attended by both society members and the general public. Many of the photographs from the exhibition are presented in this book and convey in images the society's essence: faces and symbols of spiritual fraternity, memories of earlier times, intergenerational bonds, member participation at the adobe meeting halls, survival of a people, and a sense of ownership and belonging. The exhibit's success prompted us to move forward with the expansion of the documentary into a book. To help us gather additional information, the Center for Regional Studies of the University of New Mexico supported the collection of oral histories and video recordings at local council meetings and at the general conventions. The oral histories were transcribed, and much of the information obtained directly from longtime members is featured in this book: reflections, anecdotes, and memories of local activities. On behalf of all La Sociedad officers and members, we acknowledge the efforts of the center's director, Dr. Tobías Durán, for approving the funding that made possible the research and the publication of our book. Without his enduring support, from inception to submission of the final manuscript, it would never have been completed and published.

In retrospect, we acted wisely by documenting the years leading up to the one hundredth anniversary and into the first decade of the twenty-first century. In the course of the project, La Sociedad lost several prominent members, including Tomás Romero. From 1969 to December 2005, Hermano Tomás had served as Superior Council secretary-treasurer, thirty-six years. Most organizations rarely experience that kind of continuity for such a key position of trust and leadership. Hermano Tomás was not only a most trustworthy and impeccably honest secretary-treasurer, but also La Sociedad's most knowledgeable historian. The position he held was by appointment, made exclusively by the Superior Council's president and elected officers every two years following the general conventions and installation of officers. Tomás Romero was appointed as the secretary-treasurer continuously by eight different administrations. For a time, he also served as president of Council No. 19 in Alamosa, from 1969 through 1972 and again in 1980. To honor his memory, society

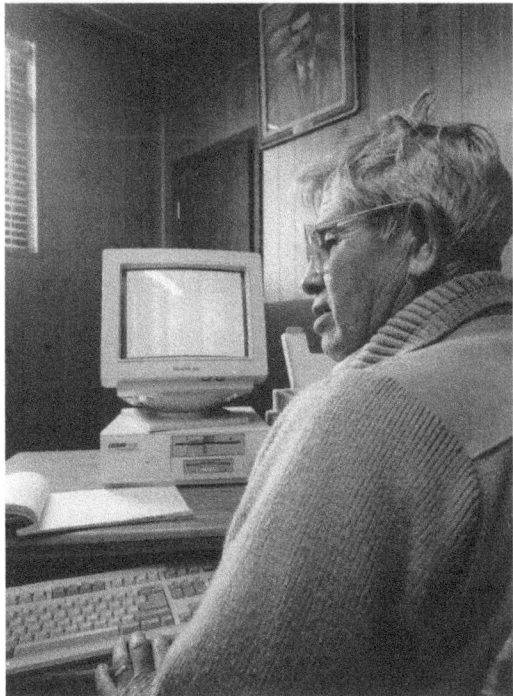

Figures 1 and 2. Tomás Romero served as the secretary-treasurer of the Concilio Superior from 1969 to 2005 and was widely respected for his honesty and loyalty. Courtesy of Daniel Salazar, 1993.

officers and members dedicated the 2006 biannual convention at Ranchos de Taos in his honor. Other longtime servants of the organization who passed away while the documentary project was in progress include the exemplary member and orator Juan Olivas. He was the driving force in Council No. 31 of Chama, Colorado. When he spoke at the conventions, his words had a profound impact on the other members. His loyalty and dedication to La Sociedad were much admired. Hermano Juan passed away in December 2002. We also lost Pancracio Romero of Ranchos de Taos Council No. 18, one of the true "godfathers" of the organization. He was instrumental in directing the society when it offered life insurance benefits, and, along with Esequiel Salazar, Frank López Sr., and Tomás Romero, he helped to safeguard the insurance reserves and keep the society financially solvent during the many years he served as Superior Council president. He was a member of the society for more than half a century, joining in 1946, and he continued as a respected member until 2004, when he died.

Finally, no one will forget Juan de Vargas, a former president of local Council No. 18 at Ranchos de Taos. Hermano Juan will be remembered for the constant smile that defined his vivacious personality and that explains—in addition to his storytelling style and sense of humor—why he was beloved by everyone. His positive attitude about life epitomized his belief in La Mutua, as stated in the Código Ritualístico: "La vida no es después de todo tan pesada como la juzgamos" (After all is said and done, life is not as much a burden as we may judge). Juan de Vargas passed away in 2005. We were fortunate to have interviewed Hermano Juan while he was the *consejero* of Council No. 18, and we have included some of his oral history reflections here. We dedicate this book to all of the members, named and unnamed, who committed themselves to La Sociedad's goals and remained steadfast members until they departed from this life. Que en paz descansen (may they rest in peace).

Rogelio Briones
President, Superior Council, 2001–2005

ACKNOWLEDGMENTS

W E EXPRESS OUR MOST SINCERE GRATITUDE to the members of La Sociedad who generously contributed oral histories, photographs, and other information for use in this book and who allowed us to interview them. Their personal stories, reflections, and memories gave an interpretive meaning to the project that is not possible from secondary sources and documents. We also recognize and credit José Timoteo López, María Mondragón-Valdez, Gregory A. Hicks, Devon G. Peña, Frederick Sánchez, Virginia McConnell Simmons, and the others whose works we have cited regarding the historical context that gave rise to the formation and development of La Sociedad. In addition, we acknowledge the unique documents and memorabilia of the women's auxiliaries provided by Ruben Archuleta, a member of Council No. 1 in Antonito, Colorado, now living in Pueblo, Colorado. Anselmo Arellano shared his excerpts of Spanish-language newspapers with accounts of *mutualista* societies and the business affairs of La Sociedad's founder, the honorable Celedonio Mondragón, during the crucial period of the early 1890s. Manuel D. Salazar, archivist of the Colorado Society of Hispanic Genealogy and member of Denver Council No. 7, added important details about the Mondragón family of Conejos County. We also credit Arnold Valdez for his floorplan drawings of the Superior Council in Antonito when the building was undergoing nomination as a historic property and for describing the architectural features of the Sala Superior and the construction of local meeting halls.

Once the draft manuscript for the book was completed, several volunteers read the chapters and provided many helpful revisions: Frank López Jr., former president of Council No. 57 in Nambé, New Mexico; María Jesús Buxó i Rey, anthropology professor at the University of Barcelona in Spain; Phillip B. Gonzales, professor of sociology at the University of New Mexico (UNM); and

FIGURE 3. Manos. The clasping of outstretched hands symbolizes the bond of fraternalism among SPMDTU members. This carving of the SPMDTU emblem was made in 1928 by José Lauriano López, then a member of Capulín Concilio No. 2. Courtesy of Daniel Salazar, 1999.

historian Thomas F. Glick of Boston University. We are also indebted to UNM professor Enrique Lamadrid and his son, Armando, for proofing the documents that we translated from Spanish into English. Ann Massmann, Donald Burge, and Nancy Brown-Martínez assisted numerous times with the handling and lending of La Sociedad Records from the manuscript archives at the Center for Southwest Research, University Libraries, UNM. Miguel Gandert formatted some of the archival and digital photos to conform with the technical requirements of publication. In addition, this book about La Sociedad would not have been possible without the support of Dr. Tobías Durán, director of the UNM Center for Regional Studies. From the outset, he encouraged our work and found ways of providing financial assistance during the research

FIGURES 4 AND 5 (*combined*). Concilio Superior Meeting Hall, Main Street, Antonito, Colorado, listed in the State Register of Historic Properties, Colorado, and the National Register of Historic Places, U.S. National Park Service. Courtesy of Daniel Salazar, 2004.

FIGURE 6. The Honorable Celedonio Mondragón, 1863–1923, founder of La Sociedad. This portrait is the most frequently used in newspaper articles that describe the SPMDTU's origins. Framed prints of the photo are displayed on the front wall of the Concilio Superior head-quarters office and at local council meeting halls. Courtesy of Daniel Salazar, 2004.

phases of the documentary survey, the collection of oral histories and transcriptions, and the writing of the chapters. Last, we thank UNM Press editor Clark Whitehorn for his numerous suggestions as the book developed from the early drafts to the final manuscript. His feedback was always timely, on point, and constructive.

José A. Rivera
Professor of Community and Regional Planning and Research Scholar,
Center for Regional Studies, University of New Mexico

INTRODUCTION

LA SOCIEDAD PROTECCIÓN MUTUA DE TRABAJADORES UNIDOS (SPMDTU or La Sociedad, Society for the Mutual Protection of United Workers) was one of hundreds of Hispanic mutual aid societies that flourished in the American Southwest from 1880 to 1930, a period of rural industrialization coincident with significant changes in the region's political economy and in the competition for the control of natural resources. The broad purpose of this book is to examine the SPMDTU as a case study of collective action in the context of a pluralistic American society, rapid social change, and the dynamics of mobilization for cultural survival. Chapter 1 focuses on the social and economic conditions that gave rise to the SPMDTU in 1900 and on the values that have bonded its members across generations: self-reliance, cooperative traditions, and a common heritage as a land-based people. These themes are rooted in the economic history and politics of the upper Río Grande, but they hold universal appeal in depicting the struggles of a people when confronted with a changing environment and how the practice of mutual aid helped them find solutions to daily life problems and the preservation of a culture.

Chapters 2 and 3 describe the origins, growth, and development of the SPMDTU, culminating in the centennial anniversary in the year 2000 and the biannual conventions from 2002 to 2008. The cultural values of association and the material benefits and incentives offered to members have sustained the organization for more than a century. Will La Sociedad survive into the remaining decades of the twenty-first century? Chapter 4 addresses this central question and describes the significance of the SPMDTU as a case study of mutual aid with lessons of sustainability that can be shared with other regions of the world undergoing population growth and diversity, stresses on the environment, and competition for scarce resources.

1

Founded on November 26, 1900, at Antonito, Colorado, La Sociedad celebrated its one hundredth anniversary at the meeting hall of the Superior Council on September 2, 2000. The Superior Council continues to function as the society's executive body and approved the research for the publication of this book. In addition to the chapters, the book features oral histories by elder members, historical accounts from local newspapers and secondary sources, documentary photography, analysis of organizational records, and examples of women's auxiliaries. The interviews in appendix 1 capture the personal histories of longtime members with their reflections, memories of past events, the values perpetuated by the society, and their common goal of helping members in need. The book also features ethnographic data alongside the scores of images that depict the SPMDTU's visual and architectural history, its local council meeting halls where members gather, and the community landscapes of the places where the society was born and has lived. Major events such as the centennial anniversary and subsequent general conventions are also documented. Shortly after the centennial, the Superior Council entered into an agreement with the Center for Southwest Research at the University Libraries of the University of New Mexico to archive the organizational records as a way of preserving the society's history. A selected group of SPMDTU documents and the women's auxiliaries are excerpted and included in appendix 2.

To the membership, the name "La Sociedad" evokes a sense of community, much like a place-name conveys an attachment across neighbors and families who live there. When speaking in their heritage Spanish language, past and current members of the society use this name most often over all others, alternating it at times with "La Mutua" or with the initials SPMDTU. One special quality of La Mutua is that people from the community, in this case members of each local council, join the society for life and not as a passing association or source of temporary material assistance. The members are also cognizant that these relationships of fraternity have survived for more than a century since the founders first wrote the Reglas Mutuas (rules of mutual aid) at Antonito, Colorado, in 1900.

La Sociedad has withstood the test of time and has more than survived: it endures for the core values expressed in the organization's motto, "Fraternidad, Ilustración y Progreso" (Fraternity, Enlightenment, and Progress). As a fraternal society, it has shown resiliency not often associated with other ethnic group organizations that collapsed or simply faded away once they fulfilled their missions. Over time, La Sociedad has adapted to changing conditions, and even though it no longer offers the major incentive of financial relief, the members hold on to the traditions of the culture that perpetuate a sense of place embedded in the social history of the Río Grande, a region where people self-identified as *la gente de nuestro pueblo* (the people of our homeland) during the founding decades of the SPMDTU.

Themes of the Book

The substantive goal of this book is to recover the origins, development, and functions of La Sociedad as presented in the narrative chapters as well as in the oral histories and key documents excerpted in the appendixes. As a whole, the book constitutes an institutional biography for the broad audience of readers in the twenty-first century interested in the preservation of diverse cultures and the principles of mutual help that transcend the history of any particular ethnic group or region. The case study of La Sociedad can also serve as a reference work by scholars interested in comparative theoretical analyses along a wide range of inquiry. Thus far, very little scholarship has been written about the SPMDTU except for the sources noted here. For example, the classic study of Mexican American mutual aid societies by José Amaro Hernández devotes a chapter to the religious brotherhoods (*los hermanos penitentes*) of New Mexico, but there is no mention of the SPMDTU anywhere in the book. David Gutiérrez, in his book on the ethnic politics of Mexican Americans and Mexican immigrants, devotes some attention to working-class mutual aid societies, but he focuses on enclaves located in California, Texas, and Arizona, with only a passing reference to rural New Mexico and southern Colorado. A more recent book by Thomas A. Krainz includes Costilla County used as one of six Colorado counties to study the implementation of Progressive Era welfare, but, like Hernández, Krainz also focuses on the charitable works of the religious penitents of the upper Río Grande with no reference to the SPMDTU.[1] The basis of the La Sociedad's organization was distinct in the upper Río Grande homeland, which oddly appears to be the reason for omission by many scholars but at the same time affords us an opportunity to document and preserve the history of mutual aid in a unique geographical region in the Americas.

THE HISPANO HOMELAND

In the mountains and mesas of northern New Mexico and southern Colorado, a land-based Indo-Hispano village culture persists against all odds. For over four centuries, these isolated ranching and farming communities have survived the rigors of frontier life in the farthest corner of the Spanish kingdom, generations of raiding by nomadic tribes, rebellions, wars and conquest, the vagaries of weather, dispossession of community lands, and desperate poverty. But they have done more than simply survive. A distinctive culture has developed in the region that remains a dynamic and defining presence today. And after centuries of continuity and adaptation, rural villagers have acquired a powerful sense of belonging, a rooted knowledge and reverence for their homeland that has become rare in the modern world. (Atencio, Of Land and Culture, *1.)*

La Sociedad: Guardians of Hispanic Culture Along the Río Grande brings to light the achievements of an institution that has endured and thus far has maintained the continuity of a regional culture in the upper Río Grande of Colorado and New Mexico that is different from other Hispanic enclaves in the United States and the Americas. At the same time, the book conveys to all readers the universal lessons of human struggles for self-preservation and the retention of culture. For this larger meaning, *La Sociedad* focuses on five broad research topics:

1. The roots, core values, and the social organization of mutual aid independent of government assistance or public welfare programs.
2. The structure, governance, and leadership of a traditional mutual aid society that has persisted and adapted over time.
3. The pooling of resources to provide material benefits and services as well as social functions vital to community cohesion during cycles of economic restructuring.
4. The expression of cultural identity and solidarity under conditions of rapid social change and turbulence in the environment.
5. The lessons of community building for replication in other multicultural regions of the world in times of competition for resources, political transformations, and uneven development.

This case study of a specific mutual aid society can also be used to compare the SPMDTU to other forms of social-welfare relief and voluntary participation in American society. Most other ethnic-based mutual aid societies were established to help immigrants adjust to a new way of life in an adopted culture with the goal of incorporation into the mainstream. La Sociedad, in contrast, was not organized as part of any ambition or drive for inclusion. Quite the opposite, it evolved naturally from the social structure of cooperation for economic and social security of an agrarian people who confronted the realities of a cash economy and other forces of modernity imposed on them, in particular a foreign way of administering resources essential for their survival—land, water, and timber in the forests.

From the outset of Spanish and Mexican land grant concessions, settlement patterns in the upper Río Grande had followed the needs of a preindustrial culture based largely on a subsistence economy of extended kinship groups, clustered residences, and mutual networks of cooperation and assistance that bonded the community. Reciprocity became the key element of daily existence, as evidenced by the establishment of the *acequias de común* (communal irrigation systems) and other early forms of social organization linked to *cofradías*, Catholic penitential brotherhoods that performed acts of charity in the community and buried the deceased. "La gente de nuestro pueblo" were often members of both the acequias and the cofradías, and many of these same villagers also joined *las mutuas* such as the SPMDTU, which at one time consisted of sixty-five local councils ranging from Fort Collins in northern Colorado to Salt Lake City in Utah and as far south as Las Cruces, New Mexico.

To the members of the SPMDTU, "La Sociedad" has a double meaning of identity: the Concilio Superior, representing the entire regional membership, and the local councils at the community level, named by place and number, as in "Ranchos de Taos, Concilio No. 18." The members belong to a council named after their own community and given a number commissioned by the Superior Council in sequence according to the new council's founding date. Per this tradition, contemporary members align and continue to identify with their respective councils when they attend local society meetings and when they serve as delegates at the biannual general conventions: Antonito Concilio No. 1, Denver Concilio No. 7, and Alamosa Concilio No. 19 in Colorado; Placitas Concilio No. 15 in the El Rito Valley, Ranchos de Taos Concilio No. 18, and Nambé Concilio No. 57 in New Mexico. These six local councils have survived, along with the Concilio Superior, headquartered on Main Street in Antonito, a landmark listed on both the Colorado Register of Historic Properties and the National Register of Historic Places. As described in later chapters, this central meeting hall symbolizes the unity of the members across the upper Río Grande region and, after completion of a major restoration program currently in progress, may hold the key to the SPMDTU's role for decades into the future.

The Bonds of Solidarity

The practice of mutual aid is a universal and ancient phenomenon. Social cooperation and reciprocity surfaced during the early forms of human organization mainly to provide for basic needs, protect the vulnerable, and maintain the thresholds of daily survival. In prehistoric society, kinship groups banded together in their struggles for protection and to gain access to food and shelter as they worked collectively to solve common problems. When the quality of life improved, it was often attributable to the group's solidarity and the informal rules as to what was beneficial for the clan or tribe as a social unit—relationships of mutual support described by Peter Kropotkin as the origins of ethical progress and the main factor of human evolution. In Kropotkin's analysis, trade guilds in the medieval cities of Europe widened the benefits of mutual support to circles of association beyond that of a single kinship group or tribe. The guilds functioned not only as production and marketing agents for the members, but also as voluntary social welfare collectives. These self-governing brotherhoods were meticulous as to the duties to be assumed by their members, and these traditions persisted into the late eighteenth century. When a member experienced misfortunes, such as the loss of a ship or a burned house, the rest of the brethren had to come to his aid. During times of a serious illness, the rules required fellow members to keep watch until the brother was out of danger, and if the member died, the guild was obligated to bury the deceased brother and provide for his widow and children.[2]

In a similar fashion, the cofradías of medieval Spain, in addition to serving a religious function, provided social and economic relief for their members in times of crises and other misfortunes. The cofradías were voluntary sodalities organized to pay homage to a patron saint, perform acts of charity in the Christian manner, and conduct burial services for deceased members. The members often belonged to the same trade or occupation, and, as a sodality, they followed a common code of conduct set forth in their *ordenanzas* (rules and regulations) not only to maintain the standards of their industry, but to aid their brothers in times of economic need, leading in some cases to the formation of *gremios*, or trade associations. By the seventeenth century, several types of Spanish cofradías had evolved to include *hermandades de socorro* (brotherhoods of mutual aid) with formalized schedules of payments and benefits for members' social and economic security.[3] Absent a centralized state to take care of the working-class people's social needs, the common people themselves gradually took responsibility and formed their own cooperatives and mutual aid organizations. These concepts of *mutualismo* would rise again in late-nineteenth-century Spain and in the Americas as people fended for themselves and established autonomous institutions for preservation and economic survival.

Immigrant Societies in the United States

In the United States, ethnic immigrants from Europe and other regions developed mutual aid organizations soon after they arrived on the east coast and later when some relocated to large midwestern cities. The Scots Charitable Society of 1657 is often recognized as the first mutual aid group in the eastern colonies. Historians, however, cite the nineteenth century as the period that evidenced the greatest development of mutual aid and fraternal societies in the United States. The rapidly changing living conditions of the Industrial Revolution motivated immigrants to establish their own organizations to help accommodate individuals and families to a new way of life in America by providing social outlets, charitable works, and economic security. Lacking external funding, these early societies operated with limited resources and provided only the most basic of services: temporary lodging and meals, sick benefits, home visitations, interest-free loans, and burial funds to surviving widows.

Philadelphia, Chicago, and New York City were among the urban areas where ethnic mutual aid organizations proliferated. All three cities were major centers of employment for immigrants seeking economic opportunity, liberty, and, in some cases, religious freedom. In Philadelphia, German Jews arrived during the latter part of the eighteenth century, and shortly after 1802 a Hebrew German society formed its own congregation and organized benevolent and educational activities around the synagogue—initiatives that successive waves of Jewish immigrants took up in other cities. In 1851, Bavarian Jews in Chicago established the Hebrew Benevolent Society, organized a cemetery association, and purchased land as a burial ground. The object of this organization was similar to that of other societies: "To provide in time of health for each other; for times of need and sickness . . . ; and also to pay the last duty and homage in what must fall to all living." By 1872, Russian Jews in New York City had established twenty-nine congregations of their own, along with numerous self-education societies, night schools, newspapers in Yiddish, trade unions, and mutual aid organizations.[4]

To assist fellow immigrants with adjustments to a changing environment, many ethnic societies expanded their burial fund programs and developed more formalized insurance benefit programs similar to the first mutual insurance lodge organized by John Jordan Upchurch at Meadville, Pennsylvania, in 1868. Upchurch was a Mason who organized the Ancient Order of United Woodmen for working-class neighborhoods based on the principles of fraternalism, good citizenship, and human dignity. Soon after its founding, the order developed a plan of affordable life insurance and extended these benefits to railroad shop workers through a system of lodges—a system that later became a model for other fraternal benefit societies. The early mutual aid societies organized around fraternal insurance in the United States included the German Order of Harugari (1869), Free Sons of Israel (1871), Polish National Alliance (1880), Independent Order of Svithiod (1881), Lithuanian Alliance of America (1886), Alianza Hispano-Americana (1894), Sons of Norway (1895), Russian Brotherhood Association (1903), and the Slovak Catholic Sokol (1905).[5]

Fraternal benefit societies along the Upchurch model offered a variety of social, educational, and life insurance programs to immigrants as they assimilated into the urban neighborhoods of a new society. These networks of assistance were often large, as in the case of the Greek immigrants in Massachusetts. By 1912, the Pan Hellenic Union had organized twenty branches statewide. Organizations by and for other immigrant groups also emerged in the commonwealth. Springfield, Massachusetts, for example, was home to twelve separate societies for Italians, each one connected to a town or region in Italy. The Lithuanians developed sixty mutual benefit societies. Polish, French, German, Hebrew, Swedish, Belgian, and Finnish cooperative associations also flourished in Massachusetts at the turn of the twentieth century.[6]

Black Americans likewise developed mutual aid societies, particularly during the Reconstruction era and into the late 1890s. Rooted in the church and the helping traditions of the black extended family, benevolent associations and fraternal orders for blacks provided a variety of social services to their members in times of distress, such as sick benefits, emergency relief, burial funds, and pensions to widows and orphaned children. Utilizing their own resources, many of these societies organized educational and other social improvement programs in the urban enclaves: schools, literary societies, libraries, and debating clubs. By 1889, Philadelphia was home to eighty black mutual aid societies, a number that grew to more than one hundred a decade later. In the rural South, because the commercial insurance companies did not market their policies to low-income communities, blacks were compelled to develop their own programs of disability and life insurance, which ultimately led to the establishment of the first black insurance companies.[7]

Mutualism in the Hispanic Southwest

The American Southwest was home to scores and then hundreds of mutual aid societies among Mexican American populations at the turn of the twentieth century, from 1880 to 1930. This period was an era of rapid economic and political change, especially in the territories of the upper Río Grande that encompassed the San Luis Valley of Colorado and northern New Mexico. Known in the vernacular Spanish as "mutualistas," these organizations included a wide range of voluntary associations based in rural villages, mining boom towns, and rapidly expanding agricultural districts: religious penitential brotherhoods, burial fund societies, Catholic mutual aid unions, secular fraternal insurance lodges, literary and debate societies, social clubs, and hybrids of these forms. Despite their variety in size, composition, and location, these societies were founded on the common principle of *ayuda mutua*, a mutual help response to the harsh realities of survival during periods of social change and economic difficulty.[8]

The early mutualistas in the upper Río Grande region were first established in the agrarian villages of New Mexico and later extended to the agricultural and mining towns in the San Luis Valley of Colorado, where hispanos from north-central New Mexico migrated in search of seasonal wage labor. During the 1880s and 1890s, many hispano workers from the mountain villages of New Mexico relocated to employment centers in Colorado while maintaining family ties with their home communities in New Mexico—labor migrations that would continue for many generations. Here they joined other hispanos who had settled the San Luis Valley since the mid–nineteenth century, a generation or more before the arrival of Anglo-Americans from Texas, Oklahoma, and Missouri. The people of the San Luis Valley, too, had roots in the Taos basin and in New Mexican villages from which their ancestors had originated, dating to Spanish colonial times in the seventeenth and eighteenth centuries.

Newcomer Anglo-Americans arrived in the 1870s and 1880s and began to homestead parts of the upper Río Grande, bringing with them a new set of legal, political, and economic institutions—the aftermath of the conquest of the region following the Mexican-American War of 1846–48. The U.S. economy of mercantile capitalism operated on a cash and credit basis, meaning that the agropastoral people of the upper Río Grande basin had to exist at both levels: maintain a foothold on their ancestral farmlands for survival during economic downturns and earn income to purchase everyday necessities by migrating from their places of origin to areas where wage employment was more plentiful. For the most part, these adaptive behaviors succeeded. The native hispanos resisted pressures to assimilate into Anglo culture, and for many decades they preserved their cooperative institutions and managed to retain control over their agrarian economy and natural resources.[9] Subsistence agriculture, the extended family structure, and other local institutions buffered downturns in the cash economy, providing mutual support, cultural solidarity, and a system of reciprocal assistance. The family ranchos in *el país* were mortgage free, and they served as safe havens for young adults and their families as they migrated to the employment centers and then returned when seasonal jobs ran out or the mines closed down. The traditional villages functioned as refuges for hispano families from one economic cycle to another, reinforcing the attachment to the upper Río Grande as a homeland, a concept of *querencia* that has persisted for more than four centuries.[10]

To cope with the economic and technological changes of Anglo-American modernization, the native hispanos participated in the wage labor economy wherever jobs could be found. They also mobilized collectively to defend their property interests and help families in times of hardship, decades prior to the inception of governmental intervention or other public welfare programs. Mutual aid societies were popular in both the villages of origin and the centers of seasonal employment, permitting the natives to stall assimilation and retain major elements of their culture: a folk Catholic religion, the Spanish language, and cooperative traditions of village self-help. In scores of boomtowns, hispano miners and railroad workers formed mutualista societies, seventeen in the Territory of New Mexico between 1885 and 1912 and eight branches of a single Colorado organization, the Sociedad Protección Mutua de Trabajadores Unidos.[11]

Many of the mutualistas originated as burial-assistance societies in response to the fact that commercial life insurance was not affordable in the region's agrarian communities and mining towns. The hispano villagers were subsistence agropastoral farmers with limited access to cash resources or investment capital, and the majority of the population spoke only Spanish, the native language. During the latter part of the nineteenth century, the upper Río Grande was still a frontier, mostly with a few small towns serving as trade centers, each surrounded by dozens of outlying farm and ranch villages and no municipal services or other governmental assistance. There were no income-maintenance programs, no workman's compensation, and no social security benefits, as came later during the Great Depression of the 1930s.[12]

As conditions changed in society and the economy, the mutualistas that started as burial societies gradually incorporated other functions commensurate with the changing needs of the members and their families: payments for loss of wages in times of illness or injuries at the workplace, low-cost insurance for health disabilities, and emergency relief and loans when confronted with economic misfortunes. In other cases, the mutualistas also sponsored literary and debate clubs for the enlightenment and educational advancement of members, most of whom had not completed high school. Some societies were organized as lay religious brotherhoods under the auspices of the Archdiocese of Santa Fe, such as La Unión Católica de San José y San Andrés in 1893 near Springer, New Mexico. Other societies were founded on the broad principles of union and fraternity and offered a range of social, educational, recreational, and economic security benefits—such as La Sociedad Unión y Fraternidad Mexicana in the barrio of Chihuahuita (Roswell, New Mexico) in 1902 and La Unión Protectiva founded in Santa Fe in 1916.

The majority of these traditional mutualistas eventually expired or were supplanted by other programs of assistance in part due to the advent of the modern welfare state: county-administered relief, the federal Social Security Act, the introduction of public-works employment, and the cash-assistance programs of the New Deal during the middle and late 1930s. Villagers' rural outmigration to the urban centers of the West after World War II also led to the decline of many of the societies, a process that also brought about a shift to more modern forms of voluntary association such as the League of United Latin American Citizens (LULAC), the GI Forum, and other civil rights organizations that still function and serve the broader Hispanic community.[13]

From among the hundreds of mutualistas that proliferated in the upper Río Grande, only a few organizations have survived into the twenty-first century. Akin to the religious cofradías and the acequia associations in the area of water management, some Hispanic mutuas continue to govern their own affairs and maintain the regional culture. In rural communities, faith-based societies address the needs of local parishes and perform charitable works much like before. For example, the Unión Católica del Sagrado Corazón de Jesús of Nambé, New Mexico, organizes prayer services, provides voluntary labor for the upkeep of the church, plans the annual patron saint procession, and holds vigil over the exposed Blessed Sacrament on a monthly schedule. For charitable works in the community, the members operate a charity fund called the Fondo de Caridad, provide clothes to the needy, and administer the Fondo de Defunción, or Death Benefit Fund, to pay for local members' funeral services, a practice since the founding of the society in 1916.[14]

Some of the members of the Unión Católica del Sagrado Corazón de Jesús also belong to SPMDTU Council No. 57 in Nambé, a tradition from earlier times when dual membership was common across different forms of mutualistas. La Sociedad continues to sponsor local councils in northern New Mexico, the San Luis Valley of Colorado, and the urban chapter in Denver. These *concilios locales* adhere to the common Código Ritualístico (Code of Rituals) for the conduct of their meetings; they follow prescribed ceremonies to honor deceased hermanos at funerals; and they continue to provide social services and charitable functions in their communities. In keeping with the requirements of the SPMDTU Constitution, the Superior Council convenes a general convention every two years and maintains the meeting hall and headquarters office in Antonito, Colorado. Rural outmigration of hispanos from the villages, the introduction of federal social security and public-assistance programs, and access to commercial life insurance eventually reduced the SPMDTU's scale and membership. More than a century after its inception, however, it endures and conducts its business in the regional Spanish language much as the founders and their ancestors did over multiple generations. The occasion of a funeral serves to remind the members of the core values that helped form the society: "I think one of the things that we forget and the older members stress it a lot is: que nos tratamos con amor, we treat each other with love and respect. It is a good way, when you finally pass away—se muere uno. It's beautiful to have somebody; somebody is going to come in to pay his or her last respects. I have had the privilege to do that with a few hermanos that have passed away, and it is simply beautiful" (Rogelio Briones, Council No. 19, Alamosa, Colorado).

FIGURE 7. Juan Olivas in front of the Chama Concilio No. 31 meeting hall. Courtesy of Daniel Salazar, 1999.

FIGURE 8. Elfirio Espinosa in front of the Cerro Concilio No. 43 meeting hall. Courtesy of Daniel Salazar, 1999.

FIGURES 9 AND 10. Ben Gallegos in front of the Ojo Caliente Concilio No. 13 meeting hall and a close-up of its mural. Courtesy of Daniel Salazar, 1997.

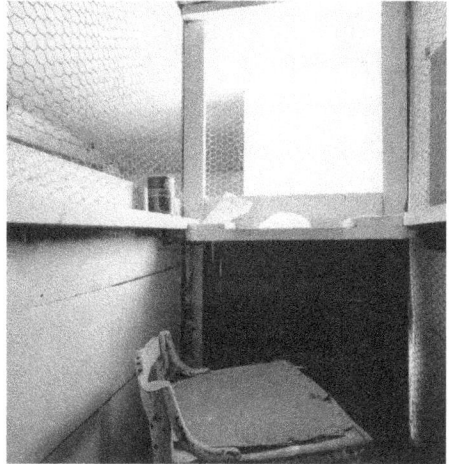

Figures 11–13. La Garita Concilio No. 16 meeting hall. The photos depict the facade on the gabled end of the large building, the main room of the interior, and a ticket booth near the entrance. The concilio was used as both a meeting hall for the members and a venue for public dances and other social events. Courtesy of Daniel Salazar, 1993.

FIGURE 14. El Rito Concilio No. 14 meeting hall. Courtesy of Daniel Salazar, 1997.

FIGURE 15. Nambé Concilio No. 57 meeting hall. Courtesy of Daniel Salazar, 2004.

FIGURE 16. Costilla Concilio No. 12 meeting hall. Courtesy of Daniel Salazar, 1997.

FIGURE 17. Ranchos de Taos Concilio No. 18 meeting hall, wire fence and landscape view from hilltop. Courtesy of Daniel Salazar, 2004.

CHAPTER ONE

A Cultural and Economic History of the Upper Río Grande

T HE MAJORITY OF HISPANIC MUTUAL AID SOCIETIES were organized to perform charitable works and conduct burial services in the local community along the lines of the religious penitent brotherhoods. In addition, there were a few that organized in the defense of land and water rights when Anglo-American cattle companies and other investors from "*los estados*" (the United States) to the east entered the upper Río Grande in the 1870s and 1880s seeking to profit from the land, labor, minerals, and other natural resources there. During this era of economic industrialization, the railroad and its associated industries played a catalytic role in the development of the region, making possible the shipment of large quantities of livestock, alfalfa, and other fodder crops to midwestern and eastern markets. The rise in the Anglo-American population, coupled with the imposition of a new legal-administrative system of land ownership, set the stage for resource use conflicts between the native hispanos and the English-speaking newcomers, especially in the case of the community land grants that had been issued to them by Spanish and Mexican authorities. Despite provisions in the 1848 Treaty of Guadalupe Hidalgo with Mexico that property rights of former Mexican citizens would be protected, the U.S. Congress failed to confirm the vast majority of hispano land grant claims, and most were eventually partitioned, stolen by fraudulent schemes, or reverted to the public domain.

To resist encroachment and protect their natural resources, hispano communities in New Mexico and Colorado organized mutual benefit and protective associations. For example, in 1888, the acequia irrigators of Cerro in Taos County formed La Asociación de Mutua Protección y Mutuo Beneficio de la Plaza de Cerro de Guadalupe (Association for the Mutual Protection and

Mutual Benefit of the Town of Cerro de Guadalupe) to defend their agricultural lands, water rights, and mountain pastures:

> The objects of this association shall be: Mutual protection and mutual
> benefit so that united we may be able to assert, defend and take care of
> the rights and privileges that for more than thirty-seven years we have
> enjoyed in the waters of the Ritos del Latir in Taos County, N. Mex.,
> as much for the irrigation of our lands, as for domestic purposes; hav-
> ing constructed ditches from the sources of said Ritos de Latir, which
> are four in number; . . . as also to procure for ourselves legal titles to the
> lands possessed and occupied by each one of the associates herein for
> more than thirty-seven years, in and about the town of Cerro de Gua-
> dalupe, N. Mex., as also to defend our rights to mountains and graz-
> ing ranges, which in the same conformity as above we have enjoyed;
> and . . . to secure for ourselves and for our children the rights we may
> have acquired and now enjoy on our agricultural lands, our homes and
> the right to the use of the aforesaid waters, commonly by us.[1]

Fourteen years later, hispano farmers and ranchers of the Costilla Valley, north of Cerro, formed an alliance of their own, La Asociación Defensiva de los Pobladores de los Terrenos del Río de Costilla (Defensive Association of the Settlers of the Lands of the Río de Costilla). In their founding constitution of 1902, the settlers united to protect and defend their land and other property rights along the Río de Costilla against claims by foreign land-development companies attempting to evict them from "La Merced de la Sangre de Cristo" (Sangre de Cristo Grant):

> Nosotros los pobladores de La Costilla, cuidadanos de Los Estados
> Unidos, residentes del Condado de Taos en el Territorio de Nuevo
> México, con el fin de formar una alianza firme y constante para defen-
> der en unión y armonía fraternal nuestros hogares y propiedades
> raíces que por tantos años hemos tenido bajo nuestra posesión conti-
> nua quieta y pacífia sin perturbación alguna: nos hemos constituído
> y organizado en un cuerpo político e incorporado bajo la ley general
> de corporaciones del Territorio de Nuevo México. . . . El objeto de esta
> Asociación será la defensa unida y protección mutua de los asociados
> en sus hogares, derechos (de) propiedad y dominio que los pobladores
> aquí asociados han adquirido en los terrenos del Río de la Costilla. . . .
> [E]stos terrenos actualmente reclamados por companías extranjeras a

nosotros pretendiendo y reclamando ser dueños del terreno bajo una pretendida merced dada en 1843 a Luis Lee y Narciso Beaubien.[2]

[We the settlers of the Costilla, citizens of the United States of America, residents of the County of Taos in the Territory of New Mexico, with the purpose of forming a constant and firm alliance to defend in union and fraternal harmony our homes and real properties that for so many years we have had under our possession continuous, quiet and peaceful without any perturbation: we have constituted and organized in a political group and incorporated under the general law of corporations of the Territory of New Mexico. . . The object of this Association will be the united defense and mutual protection of its associates in their homes, property rights and domain that the settlers herein associated have acquired in the lands of the Río of Costilla. . . . these lands actually claimed by strange companies to us pretending and claiming to be the owners of the land under a pretended grant given in 1843 to Luis Lee and Narciso Beaubien.]

In the nearby San Luis Valley of Colorado, hispanos established the SPMDTU in 1900 to help workers during times of unemployment, illness, and injuries at work; to assist widows and orphans in the event of a member's death; and, importantly, to unite the working class against discrimination in the modern industries emerging in the region. In addition to unskilled wage laborers, some of the initial members were farmers and sheepmen who operated small-scale ranches and engaged in the informal economy of bartering and self-subsistence. Like their neighbors in nearby Costilla and Cerro, these residents of the San Luis Valley united in support of the powerful words stated in the preamble of the society's constitution: "Para protegerse contra las injusticias de los tiranos y de los déspotas, de los usurpadores de la ley y de la justicia, de los ladrones de vidas, honras y propiedades" (To protect each other against the injustices of tyrants and despots, the usurpers of law and justice, and those who steal our lives, honor and property).[3]

Chapter 2 details the social and economic forces that led to the rise of the SPMDTU in 1900 and how it expanded from its origins in the San Luis Valley into a tristate mutualista. In the meantime, the rest of this chapter outlines the background of community land grants in New Mexico and southern Colorado, the competition for the control of natural resources after the introduction of the railroad economy, and the resistance by hispanos with property rights on the Sangre de Cristo Grant as a case example of the land struggles and conflicts that erupted in the region. The chapter concludes with a summation of how *la cultura de ayuda mutua*, culture of mutual aid, fostered the evolution and development of La Sociedad and other mutual protection organizations in the upper Río Grande.

Community Land Grants

The first Hispanic settlements in Colorado were founded in the San Luis Valley, concentrated in the present Conejos and Costilla counties.[4] Up until 1861, most of southern Colorado had been part of the New Mexico Territory, but in that year the U.S. Congress established the Territory of Colorado. By the time of separation, the San Luis Valley had already been settled by New Mexican families under a common history as La Provincia del Nuevo México, one of the northern borderlands of New Spain dating to the first Spanish-Mexican colony founded in 1598 at the confluence of the Río Grande and the Río Chama. Other settlements were gradually established along the tributaries of both rivers to the north, west, and east due to population growth and the need for additional lands for cultivation of crops and the grazing of livestock. During the 1830s and 1840s, a few pioneers living in El Rito Valley and the Taos basin concluded that water shortages on the small land parcels they had been farming could no longer sustain their extended families. To develop land farther to the north, they ventured to the San Luis Valley in search of the resources they had customarily utilized elsewhere in the upper Río Grande: woodland forests for timber to construct homes, corrals, and sheds and to use for firewood; rivers and streams to divert for the irrigation of agricultural crops; and grazing lands for the pasturing of horses, sheep, goats, and other livestock.[5]

The lands to the north were located in an alpine valley along the headwaters of the Río Grande and two of its most bountiful tributaries: the Río Conejos and the Río Culebra. Some of these streams had been explored centuries earlier by Spanish expeditions when the region was under the domain of migrating Utes and Jicarilla Apaches.[6] To fortify these northern borders, the Spanish and subsequently the Mexican governors issued *mercedes*, or grants of land, to settlers as incentives to occupy the land and establish permanent colonies in the Río Arriba of New Mexico and later within the San Luis Valley.[7] In 1833 and again in 1842, a group of hispanos from Taos, El Rito, and Abiquiu petitioned for the use of the Conejos Grant, a large tract of land along the Conejos River, intending to utilize the resources communally, as had been the case in scores of Spanish and Mexican grants in other parts of Nuevo México. The boundaries of the land grant straddled the Río Grande north and south near its headwaters and to the eastern side of the San Juan Mountains encompassing 2.5 million acres. After an unsuccessful attempt in 1833, eighty-three heads of families eventually were placed in possession of the land in 1842. Following the customary provisions as a colony grant, their goal was to build permanent settlements along the Conejos River: "The tract shall be cultivated and never abandoned, and he that shall not cultivate his land within two years or that shall not reside upon it will forfeit his rights; land to be reassigned to another; pastures and watering places shall be in common for all the inhabitants. . . . Towns founded shall be walled around and fortified and settlers must move there at once and build shelters for protection of their families."[8] In the years after the 1842 proclamation, the settlers at Conejos began to cultivate the lands in compliance with their second petition to the prefect of New Mexico's northern district in Taos, Juan Andrés Archuleta, but again they repeatedly met with resistance and were dislodged by the Moache Utes, Jicarilla Apaches, and Navajos, who trampled their fields and forced their retreat to New Mexico before villages could be built and fortified, a phase that was not accomplished until later, around 1854.[9]

On the eastern side of the San Luis Valley, Narciso Beaubien, the son of Charles Beaubien—a Frenchman from Quebec who had married into the Lovato family of Taos—and Stephen Louis Lee, a fur trader under the employ of the elder Beaubien, were awarded the 1,038,195-acre Sangre de Cristo Grant in 1843, situated along the Río Culebra of present Costilla County and extending south into the Río de Costilla watershed in Taos County. In accordance with Mexican law, the land grant would have to be partially settled within the first two years after its approval by the governor of New Mexico. In 1845, hispanos from Taos attempted to occupy and farm the land along the streams, but these plans were abandoned because the area had not yet been pacified. Upon the death of Narciso during the Taos Rebellion of 1847, Charles Beaubien acquired his son's half of the grant and purchased the other half in 1848 from the Stephen Louis Lee estate with the intention of once again recruiting settlers to establish agricultural colonies, as had been recited in the original petition for the grant.[10]

The Provincia del Nuevo México, meanwhile, was placed under the control of General Stephen Watts Kearny and his Army of the West at the conclusion of the war between the United States and Mexico (1846–48). Once the province was under U.S. occupation, the American regime established Fort Massachusetts at the southern base of Sierra Blanca in 1852 (the fort was later relocated closer to San Luis, Colorado, and renamed "Fort Garland") and set out to pacify the Ute Indian frontier. The Treaty of Guadalupe Hidalgo had entitled the Mexican people, now U.S. citizens, to occupy permanently the land grants of the San Luis Valley. To perfect their claims, the natives obtained deeds from Beaubien to help him develop parts of the Sangre de Cristo Grant, and in a document recorded in 1863 Beaubien granted them usufructuary rights in *la vega* (a commons meadow) of the valley floor to pasture milk cows, horses, and mules, and to use the natural resources of *la sierra* (forested uplands in the Culebra Range) for livestock grazing in the spring, hunting, and the harvesting of timber products.[11]

Meanwhile, additional hispanos from the Taos Valley and other parts of New Mexico had migrated north and succeeded in building homesteads along the rivers, creeks, and other sources of water. Along the Río Culebra alone, seven villages and more than a dozen acequia irrigation systems were established between 1850 and 1860: Viejo San Acacio, San Luis de la Culebra, San Pablo, San Pedro, San Francisco, Chama, and Los Fuertes. By the summer of 1864, these settlers on the Sangre de Cristo Grant were producing high-quality wheat by means of irrigation, and many families lived in relative comfort. West of San Luis, hispanos from Abiquiu, El Rito, Ojo Caliente, and other New Mexican villages on the lower Río Chama settled additional plazas on the Conejos Land Grant. Between 1854 and 1867, the communities on the western side of the San Luis Valley included Guadalupe (Conejos), San José, San Rafael, Rincones, San Juan, and Los Sauces.[12]

In 1861, by act of Congress, the Territory of New Mexico ceded the San Luis Valley to the new Territory of Colorado, and in 1868 the U.S. military relocated the Utes to southwestern Colorado and Utah, facilitating the development of mining in the San Juan Mountains on the western side of the valley. Hispanos expanded their acequia settlements into a network of villages with outlying farmsteads and ranches as they cultivated new fields, constructed diversion dams and irrigation ditches, built permanent dwellings, and raised livestock. By the late 1870s, they occupied much of the arable land in the San Luis Valley. A decade later, however, the settlers began to confront Anglo homesteaders, land speculators, and cattlemen newly arrived from Texas and other states who were crowding them and competing for their landholdings.[13] The railroad reached Alamosa to the north of Conejos in 1878. For the first time, rail transportation linked the region's agrarian culture to the national economy and created new opportunities for trade, commerce, and tourism, and in the process it dramatically increased Anglo immigration to both Colorado and New Mexico.[14]

Driven by the potential for economic gain induced by the building of the railroad, speculators, foreign investors, and lawyers began to challenge the legal

FIGURE 18. Monte Vista Depot, Colorado, c. 1900–1910. The arrival of a passenger train into the Monte Vista Depot along the Denver and Rio Grande Railroad line marked a new era of industrialization that brought with it an influx of newcomers to the San Luis Valley. Courtesy of the Colorado Historical Society, Denver and Rio Grande Collection, Scan no. 200005692.

status of the Spanish and Mexican land grants with the aim of displacing the natives in order to sell off tracts of lands to newcomers and land-development companies. The opportunity for exploitation of lands was advertised as far away as London. In 1869, English capitalist William Blackmore noted to potential investors that the completion of the Union Pacific Railroad was destined to make the resources of the Territory of Colorado accessible to European emigrants in part due to the "low price of resident labour." Blackmore's famed report was based on surveys of the minerals and natural resources to be found within the Sangre de Cristo Grant in the Trinchera and Costilla tracts of southern Colorado and Taos County in New Mexico, making possible, he proposed, a wide range of manufacturing plants such as sawmills, brick factories, flouring mills, distilleries and breweries, woolen mills, tanneries, and potteries. Although the contributors to Blackmore's report recorded the presence of hispano settlers already farming along the rivers and streams of "San Luis Park," they regarded these natives as "chiefly ignorant, degraded Mexicans" who held "strange customs [and] are a degenerate and priest-ridden race." The aim of displacing the natives was clear:

> The soil is fertile, equal to any in Colorado, as is shown by the crops raised at San Luis, Culebra, and other settlements. . . . The population, which I estimate at about two thousand, or less, are contented, happy, and prosperous, and increasing rapidly by influx from New Mexico. The opening of the mines will call in an American community. . . . I think that as soon as the tract is open for settlement, and through proper influences, there will be an immense influx of our people, and that the Mexicans will be gradually crowded out. At present nothing could be more painful to them than to be obliged to leave their beautiful settlements.[15]

Competition for Natural Resources

THE CONQUEST AND AFTERMATH

The cycle of conquest brought a new legal system to New Mexico in 1846 with different legal concepts. The Anglo-American system of jurisprudence imposed on New Mexico by the U.S. occupation was the vehicle for wrestling control of the land grants from many of their Hispano owners. (Ebright, "New Mexican Land Grants," 15)

Soon after the railroad reached Alamosa in 1878, Anglo-Americans, Mormons, and immigrants of European ancestry occupied the western side of the San Luis Valley in the towns of Del Norte, Monte Vista, and Alamosa, as well as along the southern side in La Jara, Manassa, and Sanford. Some of the newcomers developed large irrigation projects in order to establish commercial agricultural ventures on lands formerly part of the Conejos Grant.[16] The new railroad transportation system enabled the livestock industry to ship cattle and sheep to eastern markets in larger quantities and more efficiently than in the past. Despite assurances from the U.S. government that the 1848 Treaty of Guadalupe Hidalgo would protect the property rights of former Mexican citizens, Anglo-American law often exploited the native farmers as stockmen from West Texas encroached on the natives' traditional land grants to expand their own livestock and ranching enterprises. From the Llano Estacado on the east, Anglos in the range cattle industry entered the Canadian River basin and soon acquired vast sections of the Maxwell and Las Vegas land grants in the Territory of New Mexico. One claim alone encompassed forty-five million acres located in the eastern half of New Mexico as well as parts of Colorado, Oklahoma, and West Texas on the pretension of establishing settlements on the "Arkansas Colony Grant," a land-grab scheme that eventually failed. On the north along the Colorado Rockies, Anglo cattlemen crossed the Continental Divide into the San Luis Valley and the San Juan basin, where they encountered scores of hispano agropastoral villages already nestled in the creek and river valleys.[17]

From the 1870s onward, speculators, lawyers, judges, politicians, and bankers formed alliances and acquired large portions of the Spanish and Mexican land grants by paying nominal sums or employing other stratagems of questionable legality.[18] In the process, hispano settlers who had cleared the land, built homes and irrigation ditches, brought the land under cultivation, and been the first to engage in livestock ranching were treated as squatters and faced eviction if they did not buy their lands back from these landholding companies.[19] In cases where hispanos occupied and farmed small holdings outside of community land grant boundaries, many were dispossessed of their rights by unscrupulous newcomers who filed claims in compliance with Anglo property laws written in English that the original settlers knew little about and did not understand. This practice increased during the 1880s, when Anglo ranchers sought additional land and water resources for the grazing of their cattle.[20] Hispanos with small flocks of sheep competed with Anglo cattlemen for the pastures in the high mountains, resulting in conflicts that at times escalated into violence. Some of the hispano sheep growers eventually lost their flocks to repay loans and subsequently became sheepherders for the larger ranchers in the valley.[21]

VIOLENCE ON THE RANGE

At first sheep grazed in the high mountains without much competition, but by 1900 these ranges were becoming overgrazed. Also, as cattle were driven to summer pastures in the mountains by the turn of the century, conflicts between Anglo cattlemen and Hispanic sheepmen became serious. From time to time there were beatings and murders or the scattering of livestock. (Simmons, San Luis Valley, 260)

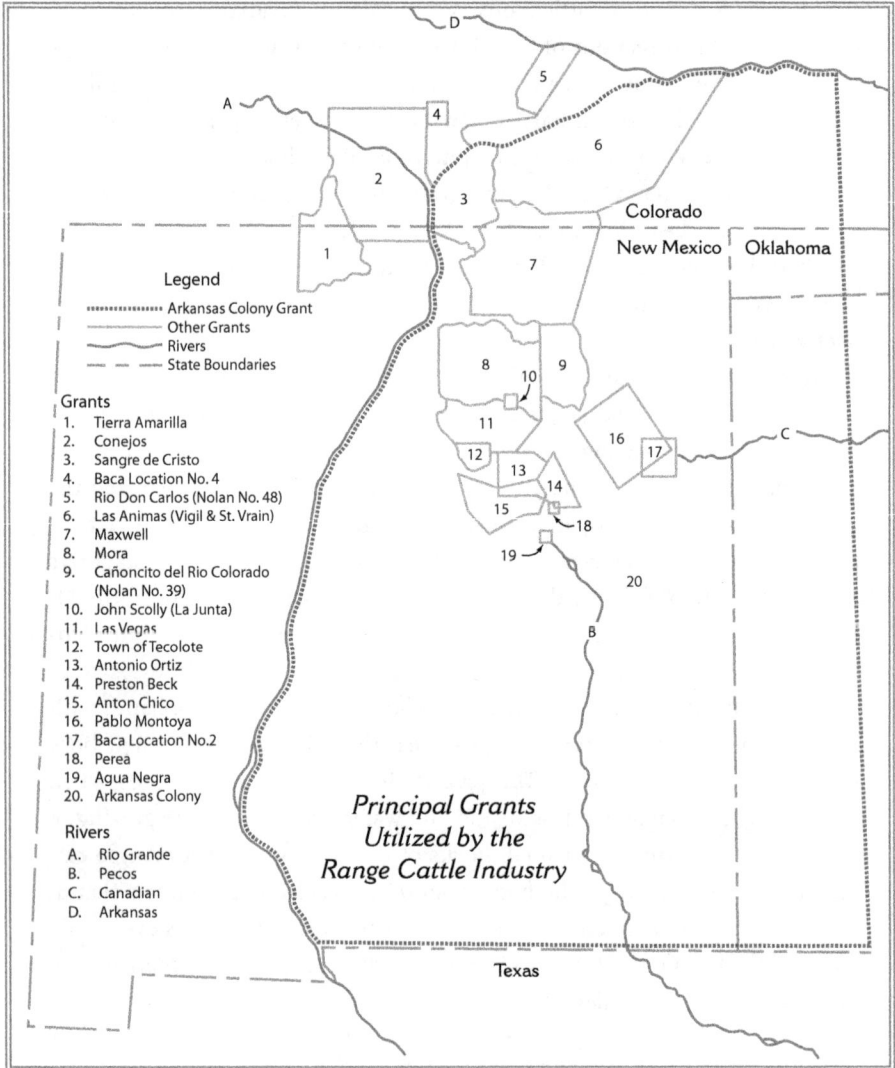

FIGURE 19. Map of New Mexico and Colorado land grants, c. 1880. Despite legal protections under the Treaty of Guadalupe Hidalgo between the United States and Mexico in 1848, Anglo-American speculators, lawyers, and landholding companies formed alliances to divest the native hispanos of their land in order to develop a range cattle industry within twenty grants along the Río Grande valley. Adapted from Westphall, *Mercedes Reales*, 155.

Other land pressures resulted from the Homestead Act of 1862 when the federal government began offering public lands for agricultural development to Americans from other regions who were willing to relocate in the western states. In 1872, the U.S. Congress amended the Homestead Act and a few years later passed the Desert Land Act of 1877, both of which clouded titles to the existing lands owned and occupied by the resident hispano population of the American Southwest. Competition for lands intensified hostilities between Anglo newcomers and native hispanos. Speculators acquired multiple 640-acre parcels, despite the law that allowed only one parcel per person, and consolidated them into larger holdings for development. Land-ownership patterns changed even more rapidly when some of the newcomers resorted to fraudulent schemes and blatant intimidation. In his aptly titled work *Foreigners in Their Native Land*, historian David J. Weber concludes: "Yankees used coercion and violence to divest the Hispanos of their private claims."[22]

In addition to Anglo homesteaders from neighboring states and cattle companies owned by eastern investment groups, immigrants from Europe were attracted to the lands and mineral resources of the area, especially those within the fertile San Luis Valley. Economic opportunities were made possible by, among other factors, the ready markets for agricultural goods in the mining sector. English, German, and Swedish immigrants took up farms and established new colonies alongside those of tenant farmer Mormons who had recently arrived from the southeastern states and themselves were growing in numbers.[23] Conflicts with the agropastoral hispano communities erupted over the barbed-wire fencing of land grant areas, the construction of large irrigation systems and reservoirs by private canal- and land-development companies, the drilling of thousands of artesian wells, the increased withdrawal of water from the Conejos River and La Jara Creek, and the conveyance of land titles to the Anglo homesteaders, Mormon colonies, and other immigrant groups who settled in the San Luis Valley.[24]

Competition for natural resources was compounded by an increased demand for water within many of the new industries. Water administration gradually shifted away from control by the community acequia systems in both the New Mexico and Colorado territories. In New Mexico, new laws governing water development replaced customary practices, and the modern water codes often favored large-scale irrigation projects financed by eastern promoters who invested in the territory's economic growth, thus clashing with the needs of hispano subsistence farmers who had lived off the land for hundreds of years.[25] Similarly, between 1880 and 1896 in the San Luis Valley of Colorado, the Travelers Insurance Company acquired and irrigated thousands of acres for commercial farming, depleting flows in the Río Grande at the expense of 65,000 acres farmed in the middle Río Grande, which downstream users eventually had to abandon.[26] Access to common lands in the Sangre de Cristo and other land grants were curtailed or severely restricted as landholding companies financed by banks and investors from New York, London, and Amsterdam fenced off the mountain ranges adjacent to the hispano villages.[27]

The U.S. government was not any more compassionate than the private companies in its land dealings with hispano farmers and ranchers living on the Spanish and Mexican grants. Unlike the land claims in Texas and California, where grant titles were settled or confirmed by Congress in an expeditious manner, land titles in New Mexico and Colorado were subjected to a cumbersome system of claims investigation and special court proceedings. In 1854, Congress created the Office of Surveyor General of the Territory of New Mexico to investigate the legal basis of each land grant and to recommend to Congress whether it should be patented.[28] Understaffed, unfamiliar with Spanish and Mexican land laws, corrupted, and insufficiently funded, the Office of the Surveyor General had by 1880 examined only 150 land claims from among more than 1,000 in New Mexico.[29] In an attempt to accelerate the process of the unsettled claims, Congress established the Court of Private Land Claims in 1891. This intervention, however, served only to increase the hispanos' property losses. The Court of Private Land Claims did not conclude its work until 1904 and by this time had confirmed to hispano claimants in New Mexico, Colorado, and Arizona less than 6 percent of the total acres at stake, only 2,051,526 out of 35,491,020 acres. In regard to the San Luis Valley of Colorado, the court rejected the Conejos Grant of 2.5 million claimed acres with a negative ruling handed down in 1900 in part because the 1833 document awarding the original land grant could not be found. The Sangre de Cristo Grant had been approved by the Office of the Surveyor General in 1856 but was sold by Charles Beaubien and his partners in 1863–64 and later was divided into the Trinchera and Costilla estates by holding companies formed to develop and sell the land to emigrants from Europe.[30]

The greatest land losses in the upper Río Grande occurred after the Court of Private Land Claims initially approved the common lands claimed by hispano petitioners of the San Miguel del Bado Grant along the Pecos River in northeastern New Mexico. This favorable outcome was reversed in 1897 by the U.S. Supreme Court in the landmark case *United States v. Sandoval et al.* (167 U.S. 278). Here, the surveyor general argued that the *ejidos*, common lands, in the land grants had been the property of Mexico and not of the local community and thus should remain as public domain under U.S. jurisdiction.[31] Contrary to international law, the Supreme Court concurred and ruled that these common lands were not retainable by local communities and instead passed to the United States as the successor state after Mexican cession. Subsequent to the Supreme Court's decision, some of the open lands formerly owned in common by land grant heirs at San Miguel del Bado were thus made available for homesteading by agencies of the federal government.[32]

Hispanos and Indian pueblos alike found themselves encroached upon from all directions and were restricted to a land base inadequate to the needs of their villages. Unconfirmed communal lands became federal public lands and were subsequently opened for development by homesteaders. In addition, land and cattle companies fenced off huge tracts of the open range during a rapid expansion of the commercial livestock business. To stimulate economic development, the federal government granted railroads large sections of public lands with forty to fifty miles on each side of the rail tracks as rights-of-way they could lease to raise revenue. In addition, the Forest Reserve Act of 1891 withdrew large portions of the public domain from community land grants to create the Santa Fe National Forest in 1892 and the Carson and Cibola National Forests in 1904, and millions of acres were granted to the New Mexico Territory for the support of public education.[33]

With land losses throughout the region but the availability of jobs in the new industries, hispanos became a significant part of the low-wage working class. The American cash economy necessitated their entrance as migrant and seasonal workers into the labor markets in mining, timber harvesting, ranching, railroad building and maintenance, and commercial agriculture. The requirements of economic survival forced many hispano subsistence farmers and sheep ranchers to relocate and obtain jobs laying railroad tracks for the Denver and Rio Grande Railroad south of San Antonio Junction into New Mexico and west into the San Juan Mountains during the late 1870s until the line was completed in 1880. Railroad stations were eventually built in Tres Piedras, Embudo, Española, and other New Mexico locations, resulting in the nickname "the Chile Line" for the railroad.[34] Additional employment sources included the Platoro mine near the headwaters of the Río Conejos and regional factories such as the Beet-Sugar Factory that opened in Monte Vista in 1911. Other hispano workers migrated farther out to the more productive mines of Cripple Creek west of Colorado Springs, the sugar beet refineries in Grand Junction and Fort Collins to the north, and later the mining camps of Bingham Canyon in Utah.[35]

San Antonio Junction became a thriving shipping center as the Denver and Rio Grande Railroad built company housing around its depot, soon followed by the establishment of a post office, a hotel, saloons and gambling houses, a newspaper, and other businesses along Railroad Street.[36] New streets were platted, and the town of Antonito was incorporated in 1889 near the original site of San Antonio Junction. Antonito grew with the railroad and quickly became the major rail link in the San Luis Valley connecting Santa Fe, Durango, and Silverton with Denver. The depot provided passenger and shipping services and housed the local office of the Western Union telegraph. By the turn of the century, Antonito had become an economic trade center for the shipping of produce, livestock, ore and other minerals, timber, commercial goods, mining supplies, and general freight. Newcomers from outside the region arrived to work in the railroad depot or to establish and operate mercantile stores, boarding houses, restaurants, and hotels and saloons. Most of these early businesses were owned by residents of German, Irish, and northern European ancestry.[37] Some of these merchants acquired enough wealth to expand their investments into land development, commercial farming, and ranching in competition with the farms and ranches of the native hispano settlers.

Along with the railroad industry, mining operations also impacted the economy and labor force of the San Luis Valley. Following the mineral explorations of the 1860s, mining camps began to appear in the 1870s and 1880s each time silver and gold ores were discovered at Summitville, Stunner, Platoro, Creede, and other locations well into the turn of the century. These mining districts attracted an influx of laborers by the hundreds and then thousands into the camps, boomtowns, and cities in the region. Some miners were northern Europeans, Italians, and Irish; at most of the early mining camps, however, hispanos were the largest component of the labor force.[38] As unorganized workers in the mining, agricultural, and railroad sectors, hispanos took the brunt of labor abuses, exploitation, and wage discrimination. Their employment was subject to seasonal fluctuations and substandard wages, especially in the commercial agricultural economy.

Spurred by the railway system, agricultural production in Colorado increased dramatically between 1890 and 1912. The South Platte Valley in the Denver area was home to the Great Western Sugar Company. Operating with the latest available equipment for the production and harvesting of sugar beets, Great Western contracted with farmers in the Arkansas Valley of Colorado and in other areas throughout its factory districts in the south. To ensure a supply of stoop labor for thinning and cutting operations, Great Western hired agents from 1912 to 1916 to recruit laborers in the rural villages of southern Colorado, New Mexico, and parts of Texas.[39] Large numbers of workers

FIGURE 20. Main Street, Antonito, Colorado, c. 1910–20. Following its incorporation as a town in 1889, Antonito developed into a regional trade center providing commercial services in the modern economy, such as a post office, mercantile
stores, hotels and saloons, and gasoline stations. Courtesy of the Colorado Historical Society, Denver and Rio Grande Collection, Scan no. 200005312.

FIGURE 21. Platoro Mining District, Fourth of July Parade, 1913. Located on the
eastern slope of the San Juan Mountains, the Platoro mine in Conejos County was
a major source of employment for hispanos from the San Luis Valley, but like the
workers in other mining operations, the native labor force in this sector was
subjected to exploitation, substandard wages, and discrimination. Courtesy of
the Colorado Historical Society, Denver and Rio Grande Collection, Scan no.
200005157.

were hired from Colorado's Conejos and Costilla counties and from adjacent counties in New Mexico to meet the labor demands during this period of expansion, but then the mechanization of farm equipment and competition from Mexican migrant laborers during and after World War I depressed local wages and resulted in long periods of unemployment.[40]

The industrialization of the region in parallel with the commercialization of agriculture brought prosperity and attracted mercantile capitalists to the fledgling towns and economic centers of the San Luis Valley such as Antonito, La Jara, Monte Vista, and San Luis. Hispanos did not own many businesses, despite their status as the majority population. Instead, large numbers of hispanos left their subsistence family farms and were absorbed into the cash economy as rail yard laborers, miners, freight haulers, sheepherders, cattle ranch hands, seasonal agricultural workers, and wage workers in the service and retail industries. Travelers and Anglo-American writers who had made the first contact with the hispanos of the upper Río Grande in the mid–nineteenth century had earlier described the natives in pejorative terms, stereotyping Mexicans as inferior to the Anglo-Saxon peoples—an image that lasted throughout the rest of the century and later. The Treaty of Guadalupe Hidalgo of 1848 extended American citizenship to Mexican citizens who continued to reside in the conquered territory, but the notion of Anglo-Saxon supremacy pervaded the area with regard to both Mexico and the newly formed Territory of New Mexico.[41] In 1866, just a few years after the U.S. Congress ceded a part of New Mexico to create the Territory of Colorado, the oldest newspaper of the region reflected the antihispano prejudice and blatant racism: "The counties of Conejos and Costilla are settled, principally, by New Mexicans, a mongrel race, half Spanish and half Indian."[42]

Land Struggles and Resistance

SANGRE DE CRISTO GRANT

The Mexican people who had settled on Beaubien's grant were farming their plots of land, had rights to water from streams through their irrigation ditches, and were grazing their livestock and cutting timber on land which they did not own but to which they had right of access during Beaubien's ownership. When the new land company took over, the Mexicans were told that the original settlers would receive quitclaim deeds to their property but not timber and grazing rights. (Simmons, San Luis Valley, 148)

During the 1870s, hispano landowners confronted harassment and litigation against them when the United States Freehold & Emigration Company proposed development plans for the Costilla Estate to be located in the southern half of the Sangre de Cristo Grant. This section of the land grant included the original hispano settlements at Viejo San Acacio, San Luis de la Culebra, San Pedro, San Francisco, and others in the vicinity, where villagers had use rights to the vega pastures in the commons and to the natural resources of the wooded uplands that later came to be known as the mountain tract, or "la sierra." U.S. Freehold had been organized in 1869–70 as the successor owner of the grant, after purchase of most of the one million acres from the Beaubien family and other partners by William Gilpin, the first and by now former governor of the Territory of Colorado.[43] Encouraged by a geological report indicating the presence of gold, silver, copper, and other valuable minerals, as well as by a lucrative potential for commercial agriculture, the company sought buyers of stock in the Netherlands and England. To execute its plans, including the development of a gold mine and establishment of a new town colony of Dutch and English immigrant farmers, U.S. Freehold would have to settle all claims on the land and water resources along the Río San Luis de la Culebra and the Río de Costilla and subsequently employ the native hispanos as the only pool of available local labor. A survey commissioned by English capitalist William Blackmore sought to lure investors by describing the advantages of the Sangre de Cristo Grant: "Its fertile soil, its extensive pasturage, its abundant water-power, and inexhaustible mineral resources, its wonderful vegetable production, its industrious and quiet Mexican-American people, rendering labour cheap, make it the most inviting district west of the Missouri."[44]

Starting with a meeting in 1871, the investment company attempted to placate the hispano settlers of the Río de Costilla valley with a number of compromises in order to diminish opposition against its plans for development in the New Mexico portion of the Costilla Estate. In its first offer, U.S. Freehold agreed to confirm land titles to a smaller group of these citizens who could demonstrate they were original settlers on the land grant to Charles Beaubien, but at the same time the company proposed to end their customary rights of access to the common lands with grazing, timber, and water resources. The company's offer negated all claims by the settlers to their traditional long lots that extended beyond their dwellings and irrigated fields. The Costilla land settlers repudiated this alternative as well as subsequent overtures made in 1873 and later.[45]

When the corporate owners met continuous resistance, they sued the Costilla Valley and Río Culebra settlers for trespass in a series of lawsuits and threatened to evict them. U.S. Freehold did not manage to dislodge the original residents from their lands, but in a settlement embodied in the Hallett Decree of 1900 the company diminished the acequia water claims by successfully acquiring a water right junior to that of the twenty-three acequias already in existence. U.S. Freehold began to develop irrigation canals and large reservoirs to make use of its new waters rights, but two years later it withdrew its development plans and sold its interest to a successor corporation, the Costilla Land and Investment Company. By 1902, U.S. Freehold had abandoned its plans to develop a new colony of immigrants and instead sought to exploit the land grant's mining and timber resources under the new company and to lease thousands of acres as a sheep range within the traditional grazing commons in the upper watershed of the Río de Costilla in the Taos County portion of the Sangre de Cristo Grant.[46]

The Costilla Land and Investment Company also intended to build more dams, reservoirs, and canals in order to generate electric power, to sell off parcels of irrigated farmland, and ultimately to establish planned communities. This alternative was potentially feasible because the corporate successors to U.S. Freehold had acquired and retained water rights formerly held by the acequias for the purpose of transferring those rights for new development. The Costilla Valley settlers again stalled the company's efforts and mobilized a united front, this time by way of a counterorganization they incorporated as La Asociación Defensiva de los Pobladores de los Terrenos del Río de Costilla.[47] In the association's Constitution of 1902, the Costilla settlers expressed alarm over claims by foreign investment companies they believed would deprive them of their "primitivos derechos y previlegios" to the lands within "La Merced de la Sangre de Cristo":

> The object of this Association will be the united defense and mutual
> protection of its associates in their homes, property rights and domain
> that the settlers herein associated have acquired in the lands of the
> Río of Costilla . . . a quiet and peaceful possession of more than thirty
> years residing with their families and cultivating the lands, construct-
> ing dams and ditches for irrigating, building houses, raising livestock
> of the various domestic classes, in this way occupying said land with its
> forests, pastures, with its water springs for their common benefit. That
> when these lands actually claimed by strange companies to us, pretend-
> ing and claiming to be the owners of the land under a pretended grant
> given in 1843 to Luis Lee and Narciso Beaubien and commonly named
> the "Sangre de Cristo Grant," have come to perturb our rights, our

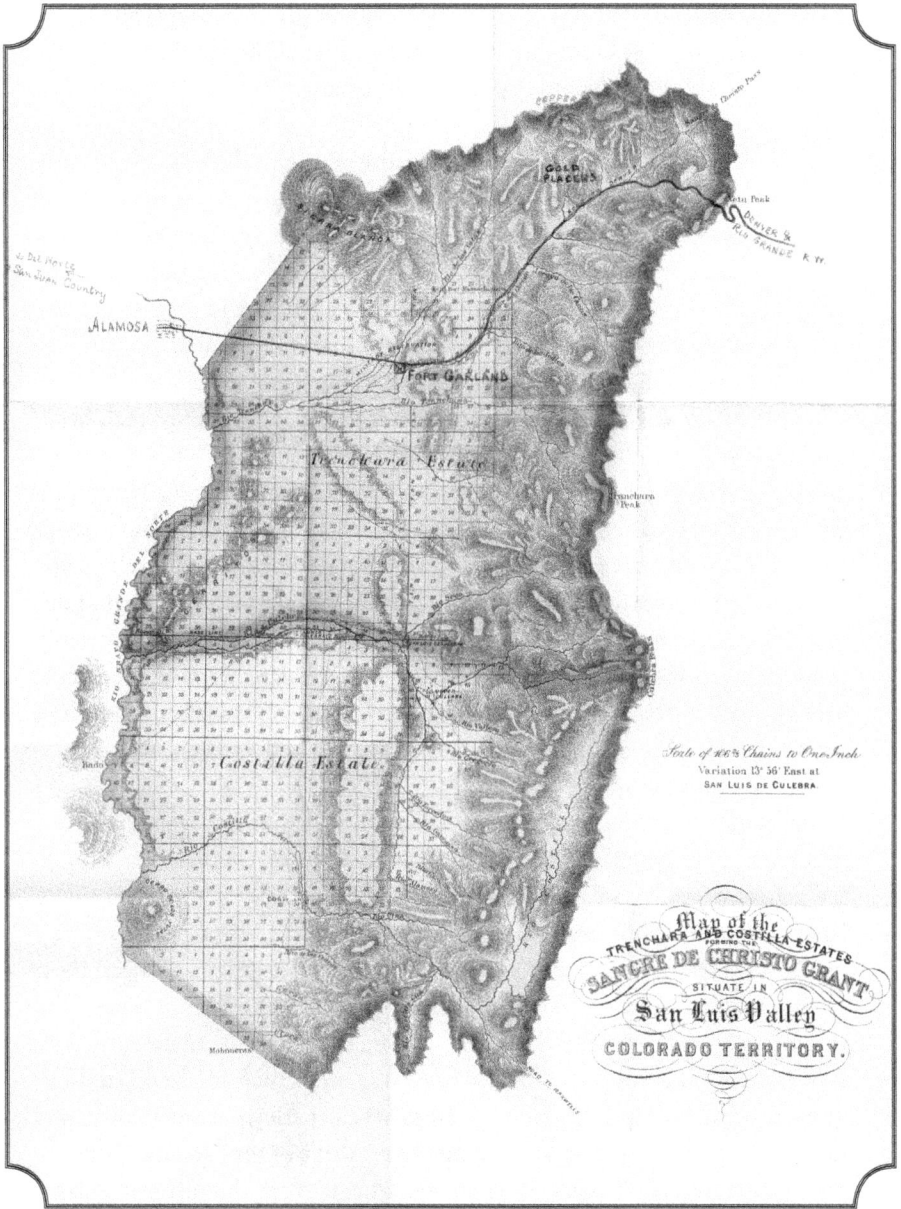

FIGURE 22. Map of the Trinchera and Costilla estates, Sangre de Cristo Grant, 1869. English capitalist William Blackmore commissioned a survey of the Sangre de Cristo Land Grant, calling it "San Luis Park," with the intent of developing a wide range of manufacturing plants and luring European emigrants, but ignoring the dozens of hispano farming villages already established on both sides of the Colorado–New Mexico border. From Blackmore, Colorado, 5.

possession, and wanting . . . to deprive us of our primitive rights and privileges, we have organized under the laws of New Mexico in a political body and incorporated to protect us mutually.[48]

From 1905 to 1921, Costilla Land and Investment and its other affiliated companies continued to challenge the hispanos' acequia water rights and claims of access to grazing and wood resources in the uplands.[49] The landholding companies made offers of settlement after winning each of the lawsuits, but they never effectively pacified the Costilla Valley residents, who insisted on free and open access to the surrounding lands and natural resources, which they viewed as perpetual commons rights dating to the Beaubien grant.[50] The subsistence farmers and sheep ranchers of Costilla eventually retained their original house lots and adjacent fields, and they reestablished part of their historic grazing commons by way of purchase with a federal loan from the New Deal's Farm Security Administration, but in the process they lost their long lot strips and some of their water rights. The development projects of U.S. Freehold and its successors were stifled and did not materialize as planned in large part due to the decades of resistance by the Costilla Valley settlers. In the end, however, water rights formerly held by acequia users were reduced when U.S. Freehold kept its share of water rights and those rights were later transferred to others for the development of lands to the west of Costilla and San Luis, well outside of the traditional acequia communities.[51]

Immigration to the San Luis Valley continued into the 1920s, resulting in a population boom and a transformation of the agricultural economy to the benefit of railroad commerce and related industries. Settlers from Iowa, Japanese horticulturalists from California, and farmers from eastern Colorado's dust bowl greatly intensified the valley's agricultural production. These groups established commercial farms from 1910 until after World Wars I and II, especially in the vegetable industry. The increased production required an expansion of the labor pool for the shipment of crops such as lettuce, cabbage, spinach, peas, cauliflower, carrots, radishes, wheat, barley, oats, hay, beans, and thousands of carloads of potatoes to markets outside of the San Luis Valley.[52]

The commercial farmers hired seasonal labor from the hispano villages in Conejos and Costilla counties of Colorado, from the adjacent counties of north-central New Mexico, and later from Mexico to thin, weed, and harvest the labor-intensive crops. Mechanization of farm equipment and the continued use of lower-paid immigrant workers eventually depressed wages and resulted in cycles of unemployment, however.[53] This period of labor competition and mechanization in both the agricultural and railroad industries coincided with

FIGURE 23. Monte Vista potato shipment, c. 1910–20. Agricultural production increased dramatically in the San Luis Valley following the introduction of railroad transportation linking the area to eastern markets. In this street scene in Monte Vista, Colorado, more than twenty horse-drawn wagons are loaded up with sacks of local potatoes ready for rail shipment. Courtesy of the Colorado Historical Society, Denver and Rio Grande Collection, Scan no. 200005380.

the rapid expansion of local SPMDTU councils into dozens of communities throughout the San Luis Valley and adjacent northern New Mexico during the 1920s and 1930s.

The Culture of Mutual Help

Two early forms of reciprocal cooperation predated the founding of La Sociedad and other mutualistas and served as models of solidarity: the water-management associations (acequias) dating from Spanish colonial settlements of the seventeenth and eighteenth centuries and the religious penitential brotherhoods (*cofradías de penitentes*) that flourished during the late eighteenth and nineteenth centuries in the Hispanic rural villages. This section explains the significance of these precursors and how they set the stage for the development of other adaptations to change following the introduction of the railroad into the agrarian economy of the upper Río Grande. Absent governmental intervention, social and economic survival depended on the mobilization of resources from within the agrarian villages based in large part on the traditions of self-reliance embedded in *la cultura de ayuda mutua*.

In common with the acequia associations and the penitente cofradías, the mutual aid societies of the late nineteenth century valued the forms of sharing that had survived among the people for centuries on a frontier isolated from the larger cities and distant government centers. For many generations, neighbors had banded together and time and again had replicated traditional forms of cooperation familiar to them in order to solve problems and mobilize resources for the common welfare. When necessary, the village people created new organizations of mutual help, adopted rules for self-government, elected their own leaders, and pooled their resources to finance local aid to families in need. During the period of rapid social and political change, from 1880 to 1930, membership within the acequias, penitente cofradías, and mutualistas often overlapped because the participants were of the same village and culture confronting the realities of survival as a people.

The community-based acequias in New Mexico are the oldest water-management institutions of European origin in the United States. These irrigation systems date to the time of settlement by *españoles mexicanos* in the northern borderlands of New Spain during the late sixteenth century with the first Juan de Oñate colony in 1598 and expanded after the Diego de Vargas reconquest of 1692. At the time, the northern frontier provinces encompassed a vast semiarid territory rich in natural and mineral resources but short on water supply. Due to conditions of aridity, Spanish colonization policies dictated that officials of the Crown and *pobladores* (settlers) must locate their communities in the vicinity of water resources essential for permanent occupation. The irrigation technology employed by the waves of settlers was gravity flow of surface water from rivers and streams diverted to headgates through a system of earthen canals, or acequias. The settlers constructed acequias in all of the present southwestern United States: Texas, New Mexico, Colorado, Arizona, and California. However, it was in La Provincia del Nuevo México along the upper Río Grande that Spanish colonization policies were the most effective, particularly with regard to the establishment of civilian towns and agricultural colonies.

The water resources were owned and managed locally, and the acequia de común, the local society of irrigators, served as the foundation for later forms of village participation and cooperation.[54] The construction, maintenance, and operations of local irrigation systems were beyond the capabilities of individual property owners. Thus, when the Spanish Crown issued a grant of land, settlers who petitioned for the land were required to build an irrigation system by mobilizing community labor, as in the 1794 decree establishing the San Miguel del Bado Land Grant. Here the fifty-two settlers were instructed by the alcalde of Santa Fe: "That the construction of their plaza, as well as the opening of the ditches, and all other work that may be deemed proper for the common welfare shall be performed by the community with that union which in their government they must preserve."[55]

Loose and informal, the acequias de común laid the foundation for the evolution of the community ditch associations recognized and empowered later in the territorial laws of New Mexico as corporate bodies during the 1890s. Today, the hundreds of local acequias in New Mexico and the San Luis Valley of Colorado continue to honor their bonds of mutual help, especially during the ritual of ditch cleaning, or "*la limpia*," at the start of the irrigation season in the spring. On that day, the Acequia Madre de la Joya in Socorro County, for example, still follows its "reglas y regulaciones para el gobierno y manejo de la acequia de comunidad." These "rules and regulations for the governance and management of the community ditch" include the assignment of *días de fatigas*, or labor days, to which all members are obligated for the cleaning of the acequia, but a special provision in the ditch rules exempts disabled persons and widows ("las personas que estén incapacitadas o mujeres solas viudas") from any labor requirements in accordance with local custom and traditions.[56]

In the northern part of the state, the acequias in the Taos Valley continue to share water during drought cycles, following their customary rules for the *repartimiento* (dividing) of waters, and by mutual agreement they offer *auxilio* (emergency water) to individual farmers during times of special need. To the irrigators, water also has a spiritual value. On the feast day of San Isidro, one of the Taos acequias celebrates this patron saint of farming by holding a novena and evening mass followed by a procession carrying a wooden statue of San Isidro along the parish roads and into the irrigated fields. As documented by anthropologist Sylvia Rodríguez, this route symbolically encircles both the lower Río Grande del Rancho watershed and the boundaries of the Catholic parish of San Francisco, underscoring the centrality of water to community as a place and the relationships of people to one another in affirmation of their common heritage and identity.[57]

For many generations and to the present, the acequias have coexisted with the penitential brotherhoods that also flourished in the hispano villages of the upper Río Grande. These early mutual aid societies were confraternities such as La Fraternidad Piadosa de Nuestro Padre Jesús Nazareno. Due in part to the shortage of priests in the northern frontier, the penitents associated for religious purposes through prayer and bodily penance and, importantly, for mutual help and Christian acts of charity. The penitential brotherhoods were first organized in the upper Río Grande during the late 1790s to commemorate the passion and death of Christ outside of the supervision of the Catholic Church hierarchy headquartered in the Archdiocese of Durango hundreds of miles from Santa Fe, the capital city of New Mexico. The members were rural Catholic men who conducted penitent rituals, including self-flagellation and simulated crucifixions during Holy Week as well as other religious practices throughout the year. Additional local brotherhoods of this society were established in the Province of New Mexico throughout the nineteenth century as regional adaptations of the cofradías brought by the Spaniards into Mexico in earlier times.[58]

The penitential brotherhoods in the villages of the upper Río Grande were unique in the autonomous manner with which they conducted their religious practices and observances outside of the Catholic Church hierarchy. From inception in 1598, Nuevo México was isolated from Spanish authorities in the realm of both politics and religion, and these frontier conditions were perpetuated after Mexican independence in 1821, when the Franciscans and other missionaries were expelled. For many decades, the dispersed settlements in the borderlands of the North were neglected in terms of spiritual administration, conditions that prompted the development of confraternities as mechanisms for solidarity and community identity. The penitential brotherhoods undertook religious practices of their own native design and established local constitutional rules for self-government.[59] They also built their own private chapels, where they organized prayers and performed their Christian rituals in secret, absent any priests. These ceremonial spaces were called *moradas* and doubled as meeting halls where the members conducted their business affairs and stored their crosses and other penitential instruments. The construction materials for building the moradas were mostly local: adobe bricks and stones for the foundations and walls; mud flooring; vigas, or wood beams, from nearby forests for the ceilings and roof supports; and rough lumber for the small window frames and the entrance doors.[60]

For governance and autonomy, the members elected the officials who directed the rituals of the local penitente chapter. In addition to the *hermano mayor*, who held the highest authority, other officers included a *secretario*, the clerk custodian of the confraternity records and book of rules; a *mandatorio*, the treasurer and collector of dues; a *celador*, who acted as a sergeant-at-arms; an *enfermero* who cared for the sick and performed charitable works; a *rezador*, who read prayers at important ceremonies; a *maestro de novicios*, who instructed and supervised the novices petitioning for admission; a *pitero*, who played a flute as musical accompaniment during services; and other officials who performed religious duties during penitential observances.[61]

By the late 1850s, the penitente chapters had extended into the villages of southern Colorado as hispano settlement patterns dispersed outward from the Taos basin. At the time, the San Luis Valley was still part of the Territory of New Mexico governed from Santa Fe. Various terms were used in the written constitutions of local brotherhoods with names such as La Sociedad Benévola del Condado de Taos, and their documents utilized a number of descriptors in Spanish: *cofradía, fraternidad piadosa, hermandad, hermanos penitentes*, and *sociedad*.[62] Throughout the phases of expansion within New Mexico and subsequently into the San Luis Valley of Colorado, the penitente cofradías' benevolence remained consistent village to village: ministering to the sick and elderly, providing food and emergency assistance, arranging funeral and burial ceremonies, assisting widows and orphaned children, helping each other with agricultural labor, punishing members who violated village norms, and occasionally settling village disputes.[63]

To care for the sick, the members appointed an enfermero. This official was charged with visiting the ill, reporting back on specific family needs, and mobilizing both spiritual and material assistance to be provided by the local brotherhood. If cash were needed for medical bills or other expenses, the enfermero requested the hermano mayor to draw from the common fund of the society or to solicit donations from the members.[64] If certain hermanos were not able to contribute cash, they often provided in-kind help or other goods and services such as firewood for home use, a team of horses and a wagon to help with farm chores, or staple foods such as wheat, potatoes, beans, peas, flour, or bread.[65]

In the event of death, the brothers prepared the deceased, conducted a *velorio*, organized rosaries, sang alabados, purchased the casket, dug the grave, led a procession to the *camposanto* after the funeral mass, performed the burial ceremonies, and at times paid for the Holy Mass expenses and meals. Should the surviving widow need cash, the members organized a collection or made a donation from a special fund. Families would also sometimes instead be provided with direct food assistance and clothing taken from the morada storehouse of grain, flour, potatoes, shoes, and other articles of clothing.[66] As the cash economy and better communications came to the villages, some chapters of the brotherhood formalized the burial assistance by way of a modest insurance policy administered by a finance committee, a bonded treasurer, a system of lump-sum benefit payments, and the ability take out loans and issue promissory notes. The chapters eventually affiliated across county boundaries into a three-tier hierarchy: the morada as the primary chapter for local members; districts composed of several chapters within a geographic area; and a regional body with a supreme council as the central governing authority ultimately recognized in 1947 by the Catholic Archdiocese of Santa Fe, New Mexico.[67]

Most of the other forms of mutual aid societies in the upper Río Grande were established a century or more after the inception of the first penitential cofradías, but they adopted similar rituals, organized local councils under the authority of a supreme body, and maintained charitable works. They recited Catholic prayers to open and close meetings; conducted funeral and burial services for deceased members; performed acts of charity in the village; and promulgated rules for ayuda mutua. Like the penitentes, the members built their own meeting halls, salas, utilizing familiar designs and construction materials obtained locally, much like the moradas. As these newer forms of mutual help proliferated into virtually every community, it was common to find penitentes who were members of the local cofradía in one or more mutualistas, where they also addressed each other as "hermano." Spanish-language newspapers in the region often noted the dual memberships in mutualista societies and penitent brotherhoods when they printed obituaries and resolutions of condolence in memory of deceased members. For example, when Onofre Lobato of Lumberton, New Mexico, passed away in the late 1920s, *El Nuevo Mexicano* noted that Mr. Lobato had been a member of the Cofradía de Nuestro Padre Jesús, the Liga Protectora Latina, and SPMDTU's Concilio No. 23. It further indicated that all three of these Lumberton societies had participated in the funeral wake for the deceased hermano: "el velorio fue asistido por tres sociedades."[68]

CHAPTER TWO

The Rise and Expansion
of La Sociedad

THE SPMDTU WAS FOUNDED IN 1900 at a time when the San Luis Valley of Colorado was in the throes of change, transforming from an agrarian culture to a capitalist industrial economy. In the decades prior to the turn of the century, this largely hispano valley had experienced land speculation, economic development, legal-political changes, and the early phases of modernization. The major factor of change was the introduction of the railroad during the late 1870s and early 1880s. Seeking economic opportunities in the Hispanic frontier, Anglo-Americans and other immigrant groups began to arrive from Texas, Oklahoma, Missouri, and other states in numbers significantly larger than previously. These newcomers acquired land, established homesteads, and invested in a myriad of economic development enterprises: the extraction of mineral, timber, and other natural resources; the establishment of land and cattle companies, often with eastern and foreign investment capital; and the building of hotels and mercantile businesses in the towns and trade centers.

The agropastoral hispanos who had lived off the land in the San Luis Valley since the mid–nineteenth century and since Spanish colonial times two hundred years earlier in adjacent north-central New Mexico found themselves transformed into wage workers as the means of production changed from subsistence agriculture to employment in railroad construction, mining, timber harvesting, commercialized agriculture, and livestock ranching. Most of the natives spoke only Spanish, the vernacular language of the villages. As a counterforce to the changes occurring in the region, La Sociedad became a support group for its members, a means to defend themselves against the racial and economic discrimination of the period and to help them protect their cultural identity not only in the first local councils within the San Luis Valley, but in

45

other more distant communities throughout the upper Río Grande. The rest of this chapter details the early steps taken by Celedonio Mondragón to establish the society, formulate the principles of ayuda mutua, and lay the foundation for the growth of the SPMDTU into a system of local councils that eventually expanded into the tristate area of Colorado, New Mexico, and Utah.

The Founders and Early Constitutions

The first meeting of La Sociedad was held on November 26, 1900, attended by a core group of residents from Antonito, Colorado. The meeting was held at the home of the principal founder, Celedonio Mondragón. Mondragón was born in Cenicero near Antonito in 1863 and had returned to the San Luis Valley after many years as a *platero* (jewelry maker) during the late 1880s and early 1890s in Santa Fe, New Mexico.[1] While residing in New Mexico, don Celedonio had joined La Orden de Caballeros de Protección Mutua por la Ley y Orden (Order of Knights for Mutual Protection in Law and Order), and he was also acquainted with the rituals, regulations, and charitable works practiced by the Catholic penitent brotherhood La Fraternidad Piadosa de Nuestro Padre Jesús Nazareno. Following his leadership, the men who gathered at the Mondragón residence established a fraternal society of their own and concluded the initial meeting by choosing seven officers to serve as its board of directors.[2]

Celedonio Mondragón had witnessed the turmoil of the late 1880s and early 1890s in northeastern New Mexico when Las Vegas in San Miguel County was the center of land struggles following the arrival of Anglo-Americans from West Texas and other eastern newcomers. In 1890, San Miguel was the most populous county in the Territory of New Mexico, some twenty-two years before statehood was granted by the U.S. Congress. Despite assurances in the 1848 Treaty of Guadalupe Hidalgo that former Mexican citizens' property rights would be protected, *hispano americanos* in San Miguel, Mora, Colfax, and other adjacent counties found that Anglo investors were gradually purchasing, partitioning, or illegally taking the hispanos' community land grants in order to establish large cattle and sheep companies in the vast plains of northeastern New Mexico.

Disputes over land titles, property boundaries, water rights, and fencing arose within several of New Mexico's land grants in the northeastern counties, pitting hispanos with small landholdings against Anglos who controlled extensive stock ranges and a few elite hispano families who collaborated with the newcomers as part of the land-development syndicates. Tensions escalated when these companies began to fence the countryside on the land grant commons. The more radical hispano groups in the Las Vegas area, such as the Gorras Blancas, turned to vigilantism and armed resistance in 1889–90. The Gorras Blancas were subsistence farmers and ranchers in San Miguel County who rode on horseback at night covered with white sheets and destroyed fences and crops, burned haystacks, killed livestock, and tore out railroad tracks on sections of range they claimed were part of the common lands belonging to the people.[3]

LAS VEGAS GRANT

The first major clash between the Anglo and Hispanic culture of the Las Vegas Land Grant occurred when the railroad reached Las Vegas in 1879. The railroad brought with it many technological innovations and economic institutions which radically altered the livestock raising and farming society of the Las Vegas Land Grant. The continual pressures of Americanization which followed during the 1880s had varying cultural, socio-economic and political effects on the Hispano. (Arellano and Vigil, Las Vegas Grandes on the Gallinas, 1835–1985, 42–43)

Don Celedonio Mondragón and his brothers fabricated Mexican filigree jewelry in Santa Fe, and from this base he traveled often to adjacent San Miguel County in furtherance of the business.[4] Although Mondragón sympathized with the Gorras Blancas' efforts to defend their land and property rights, he was a pacifist and advocated the principles of brotherhood, harmony, and service to the community rather than armed resistance. While living in Santa Fe, he had joined La Orden de Caballeros de Protección Mutua, a mutual protection society that served as a nonviolent alternative to the more radical Gorras Blancas.[5] This society was established and headquartered in Las Vegas, the San Miguel County seat, in December 1890, and by July 1891 it had organized a local council in Santa Fe, where Celedonio joined as a member.[6]

Around 1895, Celedonio returned to his roots in Conejos County. When he left Santa Fe, he intended to organize a mutual protection society like the one he had joined in New Mexico but was unable to do so because of his immediate and consuming occupation as a rancher and also as the postmaster of Cenicero, Colorado. After a few years of delay, he moved to the town of Antonito to resume his trade and business as an accomplished jewelry maker.

From this base, he consulted with two companions, Rafael Lucero and Juan Antonio Márquez, and together they began to recruit members in order to organize a mutual protective society of united workers in the San Luis Valley.[7]

To formulate the society's basic principles, Celedonio used copies of the rules of the Order of Saint Francis of Assisi along with the book of regulations and the Constitution for La Orden de Caballeros de Protección Mutua of Las Vegas. Parts of these two documents formed the SPMDTU's ideological basis and its initial set of rules for mutual aid that later shaped its General Constitution of 1909 and the preamble of the Constitution of 1911.[8] When the founders held the organizational meeting on November 26, 1900, they took an oath affirming their belief in brotherly aid, harmony, and fraternal union. Seven officers were chosen to serve on the board of directors for the society: Celedonio Mondragón as *presidente*; Rafael Lucero, *secretario*; José Ramón Quintana, *tesorero*; Andrés Trujillo, *consejero*; Juan Antonio Márquez, *calificador*; Teodoro Trujillo, *mariscal*; and Juan Filomeno Trujillo as the *guardia*. Subsequent meetings were held at the Mondragón residence and later rotated among the homes of the officers until they purchased a residence from Fidela Márquez at the north end of Antonito and remodeled the building for use as the first meeting hall for the SPMDTU.[9]

CELEDONIO MONDRAGÓN

La SPMDTU, para mí, es una organización que se comenzó en los mil novecientos . . . para organizar a la raza, para poder protegerlos en contra de las malas, y brutas pesadas que estaban pasando a la raza en esos tiempos. Era en tiempo de los territorios. Y se tuvieron que organizar, por el esfuerzo de Celedonio Mondragón, quien fue el que trujo esta organización a vida. [To me, the SPMDTU is an organization that originated in the 1900s . . . to organize the people of our race, to protect them against misfortunes and the brutal changes that were happening to the people in those times. This was during the territorial period. And so they had to organize, through the efforts of Celedonio Mondragón, the person who gave life to this organization.] (Rudy Maestas, Council No. 15, Placitas, New Mexico)

The society's basic principles inspired the board of directors to organize local councils not limited to Conejos County, but including the upper Río Grande region as a whole. Without government protection, hispano wage laborers and subsistence farmers had to fend for themselves in a changing and at

FIGURE 24. Mogote Concilio No. 3, 1933. This group photo of local council members from Mogote was taken in front of School District No. 4 at nearby Las Mesitas, Colorado. Courtesy of the Concilio Superior, SPMDTU.

times a hostile environment. The founders believed that they could help protect members and their families from poverty, unemployment, and economic hardships if they worked collaboratively and pooled their resources in a mutual union. At the core was a belief that help should come from the people in the community, "de nuestro pueblo," as they often would say, all for the good of the society and advancement of the common welfare. They limited their membership to U.S. citizens of Mexican American descent in order to counter the discrimination and inequities that had been developing for decades prior to 1900 in the schools and health-care facilities and in the wage economy of the San Luis Valley.[10] Their primary motive was to speak with a united voice, protect their mutual interests, and resist discrimination increasingly evident in the modern industries and centers of wage employment.

As an organization of *trabajadores unidos*, the fledgling SPMDTU turned its attention to services not available from employers or government: cash-subsidy benefits to members when they were unable to work due to illness or injuries; short-term grants and loans in times of family crises or medical emergencies; and funeral benefits paid to widows, orphans, and survivors at the time of a member's death. To formalize their actions, the board of directors adopted a set of *reglas mutuas* in Antonito, and over the next few years, from

1900 to 1905, they organized additional lodges at San Luis, Capulín, Mogote, Ignacio, Alamosa, and Ortiz, Colorado. The business of writing a general constitution was left for a later time, and they gave priority instead to the recruitment of members throughout the San Luis Valley to assure an organizational base strong enough to confront the injustices of the times and provide material relief to families in need.

Mirroring lay Franciscans and the penitential brothers, new members initiated into the society were obliged to follow the simple rules adopted by the founders: show personal humility, compassion, and mercy; help fellow members during times of illness or other misfortunes; and promote the community's general welfare.[11] At its peak during the late 1940s and early 1950s, the society included about two thousand members and approximately sixty-five local councils organized into seven districts across Colorado, New Mexico, and Utah. For a time, the SPMDTU geographically covered a vast territory, from Fort Collins in northern Colorado to Ogden, Utah, on the west, and as far south as Las Cruces, New Mexico.[12]

THE SUPERIOR COUNCIL

I have talked to older members, and one member told me that he used to go about ten miles . . . horseback riding, to a member's house just to stay with him during the time that he was very ill. And so, that is very interesting to me because the love or the amor of the hermanos was there. And they took their promises very seriously. They didn't take any kind of excuse for backing out of having to be with one of the brothers. The society grew in numbers throughout different localities in the San Luis Valley, and then they decided that it was necessary to have somebody in charge of everything, to kind of manage the local councils. And that's when they formed the Concilio Superior. (Tomás Romero, Council No. 19, Alamosa, Colorado)

In 1902, the founders and initial members established the Concilio Superior (Superior Council) as the supreme body to help coordinate the society's affairs and plan for its expansion into additional communities. Communication among the local councils was a priority during the formative years in order to unify the members under a common philosophy of brotherhood. In 1909, the Superior Council convened all of the local councils at an inaugural convention and consolidated the initial Reglas Mutuas and other articles and regulations that had evolved since the founding of the society. At this time, the members adopted a general constitution and a set of by-laws that stipulated the requirements for membership, initiation rituals, decorum and moral standards, criteria for suspension or expulsion, mutual aid obligations, rules for the conduct of meetings, and other internal procedures. Some articles and rules were carried over from the early years, and many newer ones were drafted and incorporated with the Superior Council's approval and certification.[13]

In the General Constitution of 1909, the society's name was initially given as "La Orden de Protección Mutua de Trabajadores Unidos por la Ley y Orden" (Order of Mutual Protection of United Workers in Law and Order), but it was changed a year later to "La Sociedad de Protección Mutua de Trabajadores Unidos" when the society filed legal articles of incorporation. The broad purpose stated in the preamble of the 1909 General Constitution was to associate for the welfare of "nuestro pueblo" and to establish a foundation of governance that would advance the order's social, moral, intellectual, and financial health into future years on a par with other stable and strong organizations. Article I of the Constitution designated the Superior Council as the supreme tribunal with the jurisdiction to govern the society and to adopt general rules, laws, and regulations fundamental to the society.[14] The Constitution stipulated that membership would be open only to persons (men) who were between the ages of eighteen and fifty-five (amended later to sixteen and sixty) and were free of chronic illnesses. Excluded from membership were persons who were of a disorderly or unlawful character and did not adhere to the society's principles as well as persons who were heads of political parties. All members were required to be sane and believe in the existence of a supreme creator of the universe.[15]

With the basic rules and regulations in place, the Superior Council took steps to organize new local councils in accordance with the authorization provided in Articles I and V of the 1909 General Constitution. Growth would be planned in an orderly fashion. Local councils were to be commissioned with a number in the sequence of their incorporation into the society relative to exiting councils and named according the place where established, as in "Concilio No. 6 de La Orden de Protección Mutua de la Plaza de La Isla." During the next decade, the Superior Council recruited members from a broad base of occupations in the San Luis Valley of Colorado and north-central New Mexico: mine workers, subsistence farmers, wage laborers in railroad construction, sheep ranchers, and others. For the initiation rites, new members took an oath of loyalty to the flag of the United States and made a promise to keep secret the society's rituals and transactions by signing their names on a *certificado de juramento*. The members stayed in constant communication by attending meetings and other events sponsored by La Mutua. For identification, the members used passwords and countersigns to gain entrance to local council meetings, and each member displayed the society devisa pinned on his clothing, embossed with the official SPMDTU logo showing clasped hands as a symbol of brotherhood. Attendance records were kept routinely, and *multas* (fines of twenty-five cents) were levied summarily against members who missed meetings or other society functions without a satisfactory excuse.

The rules obligated all members, regardless of class or occupation, to attend meetings faithfully; exhibit high moral standards; display courteous behavior; respect one another at all times regardless of diverse social opinions, politics or religious beliefs; and help one another in times of need, especially in cases of poverty or illness that led to unemployment and indigence. These mutual assistance duties were called *deberes mutuos* and were binding on the society and on each of the members. For each day of illness and lost wages, the 1909 General Constitution authorized a benefit of twenty-five cents to be paid from the society's treasury and the possibility of supplemental contributions by local councils through special dues levied on each member. To monitor the sick member's health condition and assess any continuing needs, the local *regidor* (director/president) ordered the local council's enfermero (nurse officer) to visit the member and determine eligibility for any further subsidies. If the member—or any others in the society—requested help in finding a job, the executive officers named a *comisión sobre trabajadores* charged with contacting businesses, corporations, or individuals to locate suitable employment. If a member found himself the target of a civil suit or criminal action, the society and membership were required to lend a hand in any legal way possible, including legal counseling or the use of other avenues of influence in order to obtain justice according to the law.[16]

To expand the range of benefits for the growing membership, the Superior Council filed articles of incorporation as a mutual benefit society with the secretary of state in Colorado on September 26, 1910, under the name "La Sociedad de Protección Mutua de Trabajadores Unidos" (the first "de" was dropped in later documents). In these articles, the officers and members stated their broad purposes for associating: "to promote social intercourse among ourselves and associates . . . to secure pecuniary aid to the widows, orphans, heirs and devisees of deceased members of said society who may be in need or want, to aid one another in distress, [and] to hold and convey such real estate and other property as may be necessary to conduct the affairs of the association."[17] Officers designated to conduct the association's affairs included *regidor superior, vice regidor superior, secretario superior, consejero superior, tesorero superior, calificador superior, mariscal superior,* and a *guardia superior.* These were the same officer positions described in the 1909 General Constitution along with a detailed set of their powers, duties, and responsibilities. Only the regidor superior could appoint and legally commission organizers to establish new local councils. The positions of regidor superior and vice regidor superior remained in effect until 1917, when the titles were changed to the more standard *presidente* and *vice presidente.*

The General Constitution was revised in 1911 with seventeen articles espousing the fundamental laws of the society, and the articles were published for wide dissemination a decade later in a printed booklet alongside the General Regulations approved in 1922. The revised General Constitution emulated the U.S. Constitution and formalized the governance of the society into three branches. The executive power was entrusted to the Superior Council, and other powers were delegated to the Cuerpo Legislativo Superior (Legislative Body) and the Cuerpo Judicial Superior (Judicial Body). From this point forward, amendments to the Constitution could be adopted only at the general convention, with local councils entitled to send voting delegates. The Cuerpo Legislativo Superior was authorized to meet at the conventions and take action on any proposed by-laws or constitutional amendments before presenting them to the delegates for a vote. Judicial powers were placed in the Cuerpo Judicial Superior, including the powers to hear appeals brought forth by the members, settle internal controversies, and impose classes of fines and penalties for infractions of society laws.[18]

The preamble to the 1911 revised Constitution reiterated the SPMDTU founders' intentions and elaborated on the principles of brotherhood and protection of their mutual interests and property against the forces of injustice:

> Para la protección de cada uno de los miembros que la forman, ayudando a sus miembros desvalidos y necesitados, a sus viudas y huérfanos . . . ; para protegerse contra las injusticias de los tiranos y de los déspotas, de los usurpadores de la ley y de la justicia, de los ladrones de vidas, honras y propiedades; para que [la sociedad] sea la salvaguardia de nuestras familias y de nuestros intereses; para estrecharnos la mano de hermanos en medio de nuestras alegrías, de nuestras dichas, de nuestras desgracias y nuestros martirios.[19]

> [For the protection of each of the members who compose it, aiding members who are destitute and in need, their widows and orphans . . . ; to protect each other against the injustices of tyrants and despots, the

usurpers of law and justice, and those who steal our lives, honor and property; so that (the society) may safeguard our families and our interests; to extend our hand of brotherhood in times of our joys, our fortunes and misfortunes, and our torment.]

Articles VI and VII of the Constitution compiled in 1922 designated Colorado and New Mexico as the society's *patria* (homeland) and Antonito, Colorado, as its capital city, and it stipulated that membership was available only to persons "de descendencia hispano-americana" (of Hispanic American heritage). This requirement changed an earlier description of eligible members as "compatriotas mexicanos" (Mexican countrymen), clarifying the intention that the SPMDTU was for hispano americanos born in the United States or citizens of the United States and not for Mexicans residing in the nation of Mexico. To underscore patriotism and loyalty to the United States, the rules for eligibility required that members must adhere to all pertinent constitutions: those of the SPMDTU, the state, and the United States.

Article XLII empowered the Superior Council to establish subordinate councils along with some advance work undertaken by the regidor superior and organizers that he commissioned. As each new council was formed, the Superior Council issued the initial members a "Certificate of Honor" recognizing the lodge as duly constituted and authorized to recruit additional members, as in the case of the Alamosa Council during its second commissioning in 1919:

Sepan todos por estas presentes que el Concilio Superior concede este Certificado de Honor a los miembros del Concilio Número 19 de Alamosa y a sus sucesores, legalmente calificados y que constituyen el antedicho Concilio Número 19 de Alamosa para los fines y propósitos de Mutua Protección de cada uno de los miembros que constituyen esta Gran Logia, compuesta de aquellos que hablan el Bello y Dulce Idioma de Cervantes. Este Concilio, estando debidamente organizado bajo los auspicios del Concilio Superior de la Sociedad Protección Mutua de Trabajadores Unidos, queda autorizado para recibir e iniciar miembros de todas aquellas personas que puedan ser admitidos, bajo las condiciones y en acuerdo con las leyes que gobiernan esta Sociedad y para que despache sus propios negocios al mayor interés del Concilio y de la Sociedad en general, y para el entero goce de todos los privilegios concedidos a sus miembros, por la Sociedad.[20]

[Summary translation: The Superior Council herewith issues this Certificate of Honor to the membership of Council No. 19 of Alamosa as a legally constituted council for the purpose of mutual protection of each of the members of this supreme lodge who are speakers of the beautiful and sweet language of Cervantes. This council, duly organized under the auspices of the Superior Council of the SPMDTU, is authorized to recruit and initiate eligible new members under the rules that govern the Society and to conduct the business of the Council and Society and enjoy all the privileges granted to its members by the Society.]

To disseminate information to the widely dispersed local councils, the Superior Council contracted with Spanish-language newspapers published in the San Luis Valley and New Mexico as the society's official ledgers, switching from one official newspaper to another from time to time: *La Aurora* of Antonito (1914–23), *El Heraldo del Valle* of San Luis Valley (1924–25), *La Victoria* of Raton, New Mexico (1926), *El Heraldo del Valle* of San Luis again in 1927 and into the 1930s, and *La Opinión de Río Arriba* of Tierra Amarilla (1940s to 1954). The 1922 General Regulations stipulated that these newspapers had to be circulated in places where councils existed, and the role of the newspapers was to publicize announcements of meetings, resolutions, and miscellaneous news pertinent to the society as a whole or activities of the local councils. The newspapers were also contracted to print the anniversary pamphlets of the Superior Council, the ballots for the election of officers, and the official booklets of La Sociedad such as the revised Constitución y Reglamentos of 1922 and the Código Ritualístico that was approved in February 1922 and revised in 1926. Other forms of communication included the attendance of local council meetings, to which members from other councils were invited to share information and present reports on their activities. In addition, the Superior Council periodically issued letters to the local councils to update members on the functions and business of the executive body and of La Sociedad in general.[21]

Mutual Aid Benefits and Acts of Charity

BROTHERLY AID AND PROTECTION

The acts of charity and mercy: When a man became a brother in the Society, his whole family was included in the benefits of the fraternal order. If a brother was out of work, the Brotherhood made it possible for the family to have enough food and other needs to live. When a brother

*died, the Brotherhood aided the family in many ways, such as opening
and closing the grave; it aided the family during the wake and the burial ceremony and the meal that followed the funeral rites; the brothers of
the Society stood as a guard of honor at the wake and the procession into
thechurch for the funeral Mass, and it stood guard at the grave of the
brother. (Frederick Sánchez, "The Acts of Charity and Mercy," La Sierra,
February 14, 2003)*

After a few years of operating as a mutual benefit society under the laws of
Colorado, La Sociedad expanded its network of local councils to New Mexico
starting in 1914 with Council No. 9 at La Madera. With more members contributing semiannual dues, the society's treasury increased proportionately. By
1915, the SPMDTU Superior Council had generated enough financial reserves
to pay a $175 *beneficio de muerte* (death benefit) to survivors, and a few years
later the policy amount was increased to $225. La Mutua also offered unem-
ployment and illness benefits that could be approved as emergency relief assistance at local council meetings. In 1917, the illness benefits paid out by the local
councils of Antonito, Capulín, Mogote, La Madera, San Miguel, Del Norte,
and El Rito ranged from $3 to $15 depending on the number of days with a confirmed illness, usually at fifty cents per day.[22]

With these concrete benefits in hand, the Superior Council officers continued with the initial plan to expand the society's work into new communities where the need was evident and in response to petitions initiated by local
people, as was the case in Centro and La Garita, Colorado, as well as in Ranchos de Taos, New Mexico, during 1916–17. By 1920, only twenty years after its
founding, the society had grown to thirty-two councils in the states of Colorado and New Mexico.[23] Each successive superior president appointed and paid
organizers to establish new councils and recruit members. Demetrio Trujillo
of Vallecitos, for example, helped to found many councils in New Mexico and,
later, Utah. When members from the San Luis Valley moved away to work at
distant locations such as Denver and Salt Lake City, they took copies of the
SPMDTU Constitution with them and petitioned for the establishment and
certification of local councils in their new surroundings.[24]

In each community, La Sociedad's primary motive was to unite workers
for their mutual protection by the pooling of resources. The material benefits
of cash assistance and in-kind services in times of social and economic hardships were critical during the early phases of mobilization. For their model
of solidarity, the founders valued the traditions already existing among the

hispano communities, exemplified in the customs of sharing water in the acequia irrigation systems and the charitable practices of the religious brotherhoods. As a parallel, Celedonio Mondragón and the other leaders reasoned that the trials of life were to be shared, so to implement this principle they instituted rules of ayuda mutua that all the hermanos were obliged to follow in order to ensure that families in need would be cared for and the sick visited—mutual aid services they described as *obras de caridad*. If a member became ill, injured, or disabled for a period of time, the hermanos were instructed to take over his daily chores, such as chopping wood so that the household would not be without fuel for cooking on the wood stove or for home heating during the winter months. In addition, emergency relief funds were available as subsidy payments for a period of weeks and sometimes a few months to members who were ill and certified as unable to work by special commissions that visited and consoled the members at their residences. Local councils raised these funds from regular assessments and supplemented the benefits by soliciting *ayuda voluntaria* (voluntary contributions) from among the members. Some councils had enough cash balances to pay the costs of hospitalization or burials that involved a member's family, whether a child, a spouse, or a parent.

The larger councils, such as Capulín Council No. 2, with more than fifty members in the early years from 1913 to 1919, were also able to provide loans for emergency purposes, and the treasurer's ledger documented the transactions and payments to ensure a continuous fund available to help other members as the initial loans were repaid.[25] This "revolving loan fund" at Capulín was, for its time, a significant innovation in how to respond to special financial needs in the community by way of pooling resources, similar to a credit union. A decade later, in 1929, the *reglas locales* (local rules) for Capulín taxed all members $1.50 annually to finance a local *beneficio de enfermedad*, or illness benefit, that would be available to eligible members at the rate of $1.00 per day for up to forty days of illness, and fifty cents a day for another 120 days if help was still necessary.[26]

Additional benefits were available from the society headquarters' office in Antonito. In the event of a member's death, the Superior Council provided the surviving widow with a coffin to ensure the proper Christian burial of the deceased brother. Death benefits were also provided in accordance with policies in the general regulations initially by way of internal money orders (*giros*) payable to the widow. These payments were delivered in person by a commission selected at a meeting of the local council and was charged with visiting the family to express condolences on behalf of the SPMDTU and its members.

A second commission would be named to prepare written resolutions of condolence to be published in area newspapers.

Local councils were free to provide supplemental benefits or donations to the survivors of the deceased and thus augment the benefits authorized by the Superior Council. As early as 1915, for example, Council No. 2 at Capulín provided its members an extra $25 death benefit from a local fund and extended this benefit to members' spouses in the event of their deaths. By decree of the local legislative assembly at Capulín, the occasion of a wife's death required the brothers to provide attention to the remains of the deceased woman in the same manner as if she were a member, such as taking charge of the body until burial time and organizing a commission to express condolences to surviving family members. By 1928, the council's treasury had sufficient funds to increase the local death benefit to $50, equaling the amount paid by Council No. 1 in Antonito from its own Fondo Especial de Funerales (Special Burial Fund) approved a few years earlier in 1923.[27]

TAKING CARE OF OUR OWN

And the SPM seemed to take over the cultural things, in terms of community needs. I remember my grandpa and grandma making food for people. I remember a lot of people taking stuff out to other people who were hurt or unemployed. We didn't need a social services system. I remember when a farmer was hurt for planting season. They would help prepare the land for him; and if it was irrigation time, they would irrigate for him. It was just a good system. We didn't need welfare, and we didn't need nursing homes. We took care of our own in-house. (Michael Atencio, Council No. 19, Alamosa, Colorado)

In the rural towns and villages where La Sociedad organized local councils, charity had to come from within because government aid or private philanthropy did not exist at the time except for temporary relief administered by county welfare offices mostly to elderly and blind recipients.[28] To formalize and extend charitable works across all of the local councils, the SPMDTU Superior Council created the Fondo de Indigencias (Indigence Fund), aimed at helping members who were sick or disabled or found themselves destitute. By 1925, this fund had a balance of $2,218, permitting the Superior Council to approve claims submitted by local councils when members were ill and confined to their homes, unable to work. Extended periods of critical care in hospitals were covered as a *beneficio de indigencia*, with payments issued for more than a month in some cases. By requirement in the regulations, medical claims were accompanied by doctor's certificates, and when necessary, this documentation was first reviewed and approved by the local Cuerpo Judicial prior to submission to the Superior Council for payment.[29] In addition to illness benefits, a burial fund was established so that all members would be provided an honorable burial. Upon the death of a member, the local council's brothers were instructed to pay their final respects and convey the last rites according to the society's rituals.[30]

La Sociedad's size and dispersed geography required that local councils in each community take charge of delivering services and aid to their brothers in need. Regular meetings were held at each locality, and a portion of the agenda was dedicated to the hearing of reports from special commissions and to review any claims for emergency assistance. Temporary commissions were appointed to visit a member who was ill, evaluate his need, and report at the subsequent meeting whether the brother was eligible to receive financial benefits. The commission would have to determine that the member was disabled, incapacitated, or otherwise not able to perform normal work activities for a minimum of five consecutive days. Once the member was determined to be eligible for benefits, the commission would provide the council president with updated reports on the member's health status until he fully recovered.[31]

The commissions' recommendations were most often approved by way of formal motions and voting at convened meetings of the local councils, especially in the case of any financial payments or other benefits. Financial assistance was made possible by a system of dues and assessments levied on the members according to local rules and regulations. These funds were collected at the local council level, and a pro rata share was forwarded by the treasurer to the Superior Council in Antonito. Income received into the Superior Council treasury in turn was allocated to a variety of special funds to invest in the society and to return benefits to the membership. In 1922, these central funds included *pólizas de vida* (life insurance certificates worth $500), *beneficios para enfermos* (illness and disability benefits at fifty cents per day), *beneficios de funeral* (burial fund initially at $25), and a special Fondo de Edificio (Building Construction Fund). Funds available for these and other society activities were limited in the early years, but in 1924 the organization's superior treasurer reported a balance of $13,538, a sign of financial stability for the times.[32]

During the 1920s and into the 1930s, much of the society's work was conducted by way of commissions tasked with implementing decisions made at meetings. In the event of a member's death, for example, the brothers convened

FIGURE 25 *(above left).* Grave monument for Hermano Perfecto Bueno (1890–1932) at La Garita cemetery in Colorado. Courtesy of Daniel Salazar, 1993.

FIGURE 26 *(above right).* Headstone of J. V. Archuleta (1865–1924) at San Miguel cemetery in New Mexico. San Miguel is located directly across the Colorado– New Mexico border and was home to Concilio No. 10. It was organized in 1914, a few months after La Madera Concilio No. 9, the first council commissioned in New Mexico. Courtesy of Ruben Archuleta, 2005.

a special meeting to prepare themselves for the arrival of the deceased at the home of the bereaved family; the local council president would then order the attendance by all members at the velorio and the burial of the member at the local cemetery. The local council president would appoint one or more commissions to dig the grave and to make the preliminary funeral arrangements. After the funeral, the president would appoint a special commission to draft formal resolutions of condolence for delivery to the deceased member's family and for publication in a community newspaper.

Other commissions were appointed to help members who presented grievances against members of the local council or against neighbors who were not members. If the dispute involved hermanos of the same council, the local president would appoint members from within as arbitrators to mediate and find a resolution, or in more complex cases he would refer the issue to the Cuerpo Judicial Superior for final disposition. Many of these petitions involved disputes outside of the society's internal matters but were of importance within each community's local economy, such as disagreements over the operations of the local gristmill, disputes over property boundaries, the failure to irrigate crops properly, or the settlement of debts. Commissions were also utilized to handle relations with other societies such as the penitente cofradías. In 1923, for example, a member of the Capulín Council No. 2 was owed money by a member of the local Sociedad de la Cofradía de Nuestro Padre Jesús (Society of the Brotherhood of Our Father Jesus). A special commission was appointed to help settle the dispute; within two weeks, the commission reported a successful outcome wherein the cofradía hermano had agreed to pay the SPMDTU member.[33]

In terms of legal aid, La Sociedad records document only a few cases of intervention, mostly during 1915–16 when a few members were involved in court cases as defendants. The society's duty was to support the accused member by whatever means were legal and feasible, such as counseling the hermano or contributing to his legal defense fund, and, it was hoped, to vindicate the member. In 1916, when a member was accused of homicide, the Superior Council approved a special tax on the membership to help pay for a defense lawyer after concluding that the brother was justified in protecting his honor and home when the homicide occurred.[34] The more common intervention was to help members settle personal disputes among themselves through a *paso de reconciliación* (process of reconciliation) to be mediated by a commission of appointed referees called *árbitros o mediadores en la causa*, as happened in 1917 when one member allegedly blemished another member's honor and character. Through the process of reconciliation, the parties resolved the issue in a manner that was mutually satisfactory.[35]

Superior Hall, Local Council Halls

In 1920, the Superior Council established a building fund to construct a permanent meeting hall large enough to accommodate events sponsored by the society. The SPMDTU officers had previously been renting the Antonito Opera House to host major social functions. With an initial tax of seventy-five cents assessed on all members, the society moved forward with plans to buy vacant property for the construction of an office and a general meeting hall.[36] The Superior Council appointed a commission to conduct a search for a building lot and convened a session of the Cuerpo Legislativo Superior so that laws could be enacted to authorize the construction. The legislature approved the project and decreed that all members would be taxed an additional $5 to $10 for the purchase of the land and to increase the construction fund. The law stated that the tax amounts would be refunded to the designated beneficiary at the time of each member's death. To document the contributions, the Superior Council issued certificates as members paid into the building fund. The initial assessment did not generate sufficient revenues, though, so the Superior Council again increased the tax, this time to $15, enabling the society to purchase a building lot for $850 in 1921, with $500 as a down payment and $350 in a promissory note.[37]

It took the Superior Council many years to raise enough funds for the construction of the Sala Superior, mostly by way of *cuotas especiales* (special assessments) levied on the membership annually. Treasurers' ledgers at the local councils noted in meticulous detail each time these taxes were collected and remitted to the superior treasurer in Antonito. The payments arrived by the hundreds of dollars in phases until $14,500 were raised to begin construction of the building. Meanwhile, the officers were not aware that the superior treasurer who was receiving and depositing the SPMDTU collections in several bank accounts had not balanced the financial records properly since 1923, when his tenure in office had begun. After a certified audit was completed, the president and Superior Council learned that most of their cash balances were missing from various accounts, resulting in a financial condition of near bankruptcy. The society eventually settled for $10,000 with the bonding agents and forced the former superior treasurer to make restitution for the rest of the embezzled funds in the amount of an additional $2,000, a debt he did not finish paying until years later when he signed over his residence as full payment for the balance.[38]

The officers at the time ensured that the design of the Superior Council headquarters would serve the needs of the growing membership in the San Luis Valley and north-central New Mexico; it would also serve additional councils planned for other areas of Colorado, New Mexico, and Utah. A large meeting hall would be essential to host the SPMDTU general conventions, the yearly anniversaries, public dances, and other major activities. The interior design reflected the multiple functions planned for use of the building: Superior Council meetings, conventions, banquets, cultural performances, showing of movies, youth boxing, and, during the 1940s, roller skating. The structure was built on a rectangular foundation with twenty-foot-high adobe walls and double-hung windows. The main floor contained an open-space interior with a wooden floor, a raised stage, rafters at the high ceiling section of the room, handcrafted wooden bleachers along the north and south ends, and a loft on a portion of the upper floor. The front wall of the building was

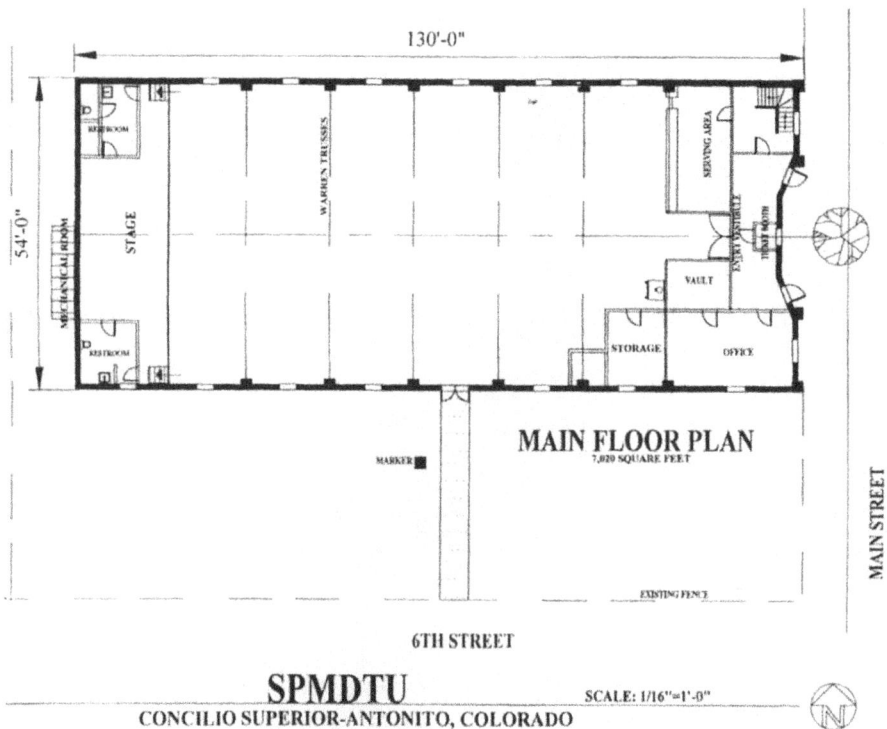

FIGURE 27. Concilio Superior meeting hall main-floor plan as depicted by Arnold Valdez in the nomination report for placement of this building on the National Register of Historic Places, U.S. National Park Service, certified by the State Historic Preservation Office of Colorado, March 2001. Note the details of the meeting hall, such as a ticket booth at the entrance, the office and vault to store SPMDTU records, and the raised stage at the rear of the main floor. The second floor contains a loft and balcony area (not shown) overlooking the main floor.

recessed, with double entry doors flanking a ticket booth; at the top of the facade, the initials "S.P.M.D.T.U." and the founding date "1900" were painted in red. The building was completed in 1925, some three years after the ground-breaking, and this date, too, was painted on the front wall below the right loft window. The east facade of the building was constructed of four concrete pilasters projecting slightly from the wall, one at each corner and two framing the entryway, and it immediately became a prominent feature in the Main Street business district of Antonito at the corner of Main and Sixth streets facing U.S. Highway 285.[39]

Local councils also constructed salas in their own communities to conduct their monthly meetings, host social events, and serve a multiple of other functions; they also rented these facilities to other organizations. The smaller meeting halls were retrofitted from residential buildings with minor remodeling of the interior spaces suitable for local council activities as in the example of the SPMDTU hall in Chama, Colorado, that for a time also doubled as the polling facility for the local precinct during voter elections. Other salas were constructed as new buildings, with labor contributed by the members, and, like the penitente moradas, the halls were built of local materials in the vernacular traditional style, utilizing rectangular or linear floor plans with flat or pitched roofs. The facades were located either at the gable or parapet ends or at the middle of the side elevations, often with double-entry doors and square or rectangular windows. A sign in the front gave the initials "SPMDTU" and the society's logo; in some communities, such as Ojo Caliente, New Mexico, the sign was also lettered with the local council's name and number.[40]

Some of the meeting halls were built soon after the founding of the local council. Council No. 42 at Arroyo Seco, for example, was organized in July 1927, and later that same year the members constructed a building with their own resources, calling it their *casa de reuniones*. For materials, they utilized adobes, vigas, rocks, cement, and tar, hauling the materials to the site with teams of horses. To pay for the costs of the materials, the local council assessed each member a special tax, and the council treasurer documented the names of the members and the days each one contributed as the construction progressed. For repairs and maintenance in later years, similar records were kept. To account for operating expenses, the treasurer maintained a ledger of all council expenditures in minute detail, down to the last penny: entries can be seen for the costs of oil lamps, paper supplies, money orders, locks for the door, lumber to build coffins, and other miscellaneous items.[41]

In most places, the local council halls were the only buildings large enough to accommodate social, cultural, and entertainment activities for communities in the surrounding area: fiestas, weddings, family movies, puppet theater shows, sports events, and roller skating for the youth and children.

FIGURES 28A AND 28B (*opposite and following page*). Treasurer's ledger 1931–32, Arroyo Seco Concilio No. 42. Similar to acequia associations, local La Sociedad councils kept meticulous records of annual and semiannual dues paid by each member, as shown in the left column of this particular ledger for the council at Arroyo Seco, New Mexico. The entries in the right column document balances owed by members whose dues were outstanding and by others who had borrowed money for emergency uses. When loans were repaid, the funds would be available to lend to other members. From SPMDTU Records, Box 5, MSS 696 BC, courtesy of the Center for Southwest Research, University Libraries, University of New Mexico.

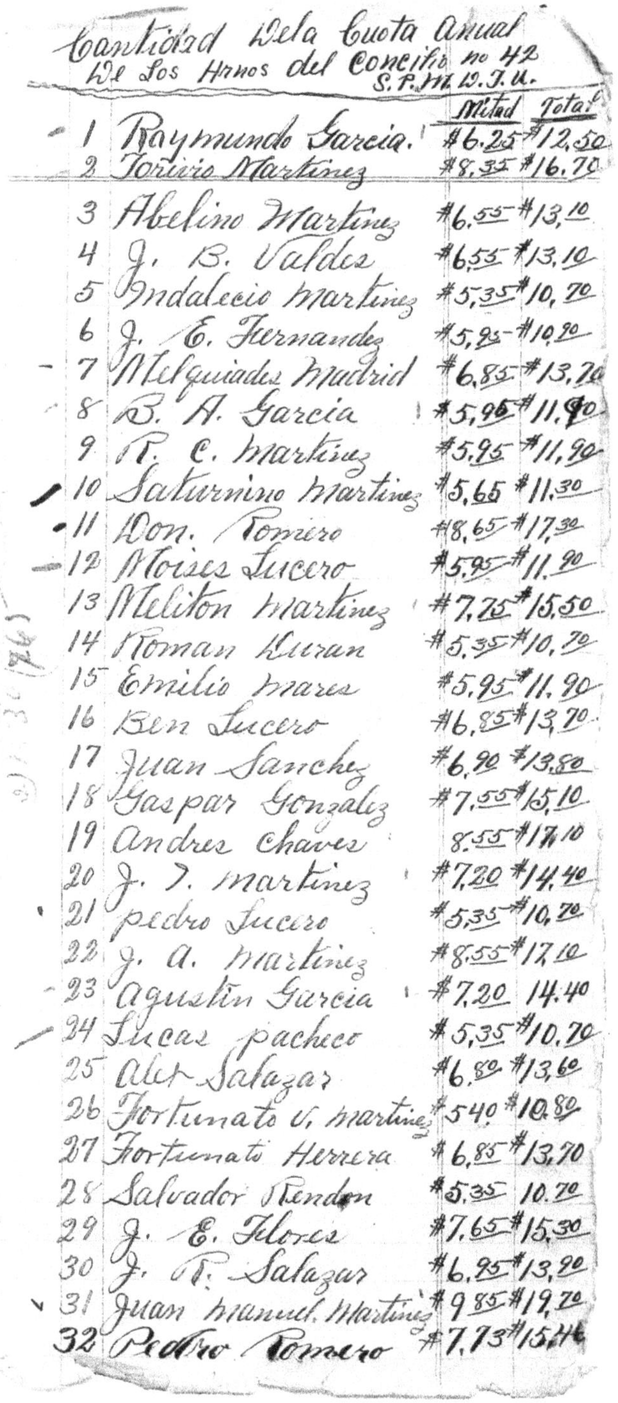

Cantidad de la Cuota Anual
De Los Hrnos del Concilio no 42
S. P. M. D. J. U.

		Mitad	Total
1	Raymundo Garcia	$6.25	$12.50
2	Toribio Martinez	$8.35	$16.70
3	Abelino Martinez	$6.55	$13.10
4	J. B. Valdes	$6.55	$13.10
5	Indalecio Martinez	$5.35	$10.70
6	J. E. Fernandez	$5.95	$10.90
7	Melquiades Madrid	$6.85	$13.70
8	B. A. Garcia	$5.95	$11.90
9	R. C. Martinez	$5.95	$11.90
10	Saturnino Martinez	$5.65	$11.30
11	Don. Romero	$8.65	$17.30
12	Moises Lucero	$5.95	$11.90
13	Meliton Martinez	$7.75	$15.50
14	Roman Duran	$5.35	$10.70
15	Emilio Mares	$5.95	$11.90
16	Ben Lucero	$6.85	$13.70
17	Juan Sanchez	$6.90	$13.80
18	Gaspar Gonzalez	$7.55	$15.10
19	Andres Chaves	8.55	$17.10
20	J. T. Martinez	$7.20	$14.40
21	Pedro Lucero	$5.35	$10.70
22	J. A. Martinez	$8.55	$17.10
23	Agustin Garcia	$7.20	14.40
24	Lucas Pacheco	$5.35	$10.70
25	Alet Salazar	$6.80	$13.60
26	Fortunato V. Martinez	$5.40	$10.80
27	Fortunato Herrera	$6.85	$13.70
28	Salvador Rendon	$5.35	10.70
29	J. E. Flores	$7.65	$15.30
30	J. R. Salazar	$6.95	$13.90
31	Juan Manuel Martinez	$9.85	$19.70
32	Pedro Romero	$7.73	$15.44

FIGURE 28A

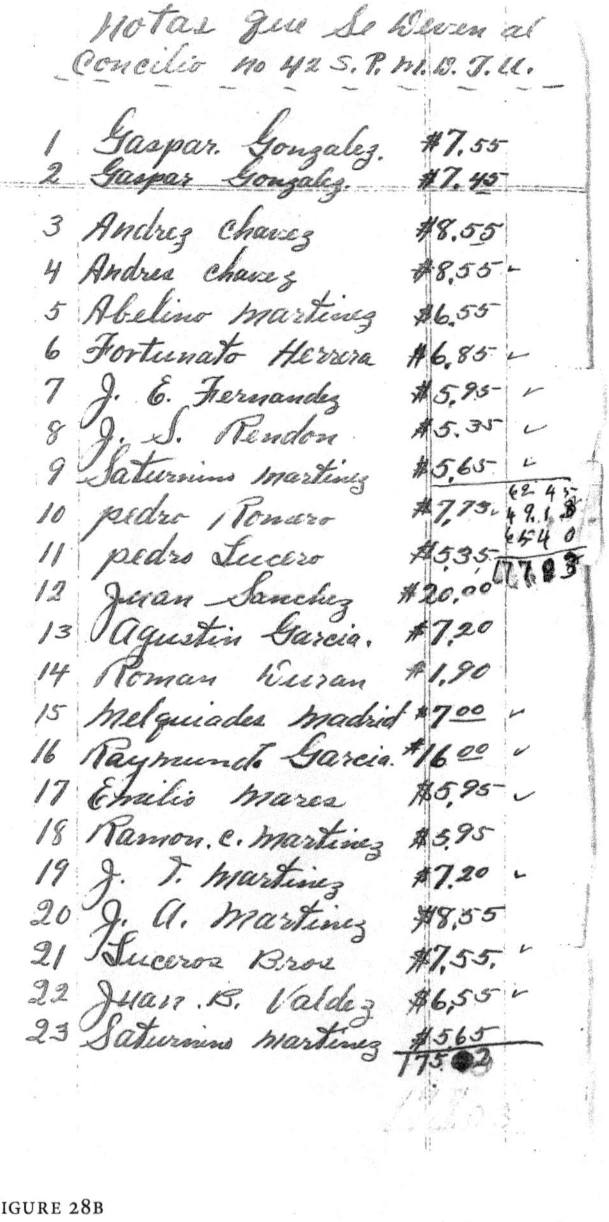

Notas que Se lleven al
Concilio no 42 S. P. M. D. T. U.

1	Gaspar. Gonzalez.	#7.55
2	Gaspar Gonzalez.	#7.45
3	Andres chavez	#8.55
4	Andres chavez	#8.55
5	Abelino martinez	#6.55
6	Fortunato Herrera	#6.85
7	J. E. Fernandez	#5.95
8	J. S. Rendon	#5.35
9	Saturnino martinez	#5.65
10	pedro Romero	#7.73
11	pedro Lucero	#5.35
12	Juan Sanchez	#20.00
13	Agustin Garcia.	#7.20
14	Roman Luran	#1.90
15	Melquiades madrid	#7.00
16	Raymundo Garcia.	#16.00
17	Emilio mares	#5.95
18	Ramon. c. martinez	#5.95
19	J. F. martinez	#7.20
20	J. A. martinez	#8.55
21	Luceros Bros	#7.55
22	Juan. B. Valdez	#6.55
23	Saturnino martinez	#565

62.45
49.1.8
654.0
7783

175.02

FIGURE 28B

66

The buildings also created fund-raising opportunities for the councils by the sponsorship of bingo games, raffles, public dances, or leasing of the space to private groups or other community organizations. In virtually all communities, the local SPMDTU meeting hall was the center of social life, recreation, and camaraderie, as exemplified in the larger salas at San Luis, Garita, Ojo Caliente, El Rito, Nambé, and other towns. During the 1950s, the Ojo Caliente meeting hall served as a special-events facility for dances, roller skating, and the showing of movies. At one event, Dick Bills, host of *K-Circle-B Time* of KOB-TV Channel 4 in Albuquerque, played country music at the sala for the general public from La Madera, Vallecitos, Las Tusas, and other communities in the Ojo Caliente area.

The meeting halls were utilized mostly for the purpose of conducting local council business meetings on a monthly schedule and to host the annual anniversary programs. Here the members could deliberate matters important to them and their community in an open and democratic environment. In the course of a year, members heard scores of reports from permanent and special commissions as well as from the council president, treasurer, and other officials. They voted on special assessments and on proposed changes to local rules and the benefits, disbursed emergency financial aid to members in need, and elected their local council officers and committee leadership.

Rules, policies, and regulations were applied uniformly to all members, regardless of position, rank, or other factors. The proceedings were open for review and comment at the meetings, such as the treasurer's report on financial data of expenses and income or the tallies of ballots during the elections of officers. To carry out decisions made at the meetings and in the absence of paid staff, the members themselves provided the labor. The most common practice was to name commissions that would follow through with the local council's mandates, from a special commission charged with planning the local anniversary program to a commission appointed to dig the grave in preparation for the funeral services for a deceased member. For accountability, the local council president called for reports from these commissions at the subsequent meeting or whenever the tasks were completed. Members who did not perform their duties or failed to attend commission functions would be fined summarily, with the infraction duly noted in the minutes of the council meeting when the action was taken.

For enlightenment at the monthly meetings, local councils organized debates around topics of interest to the members in the context of the times. During the 1930s, for example, the members of Council No. 42 in Arroyo Seco,

New Mexico, addressed questions regarding their livelihoods as farmers and ranchers:

"¿Cúal animal da más producto, las vacas o las ovejas?"
[Which animal produces more, cows or sheep?]
"¿Cómo le daría a un hombre su terreno más, sembrandolo de puro trigo o aveno, o de puro maíz?"
[What would yield more on a man's farmland, planting all of it in wheat or oats or all in corn?]
"¿Cómo hará un hombre su trabajo en su rancho mejor, con un tiro de caballos o con un tractor?"
[How can a man work his ranch better, with a team of horses or with a tractor?]

Other debates focused on domestic and social issues:

"¿Cúales viven mas felices, los casados o los solteros?"
[Who lives more happily, married men or bachelors?]
"¿Porqué deben o no deben tener las mujeres iguales derechos que los hombres?"
[Why should women have or not have rights equal to those of men?]

The debates were typically proposed extemporaneously by members at one meeting for placement on the next monthly meeting's agenda. The council president would then assign three to five members to serve on one team, an equal number on the opposite team, and one or two impartial judges to facilitate the event. After listening to the opposing teams, the members at the meeting voted for the team that presented the more compelling argument. The minutes of these meetings reported the outcome in the votes, and some noted that the debate was spirited, animated, and eloquent.[42]

Hardships of the Great Depression

By 1933, the SPMDTU held an account balance of $31,755 in the Bank of Del Norte, but the society nearly lost these assets when the bank closed in the wake of the Great Depression.[43] The membership responded by filing a claim against the bank and finally received payment in 1937. Meanwhile, some four hundred members, themselves strapped financially due to long periods of unemployment and the devastated economy, were unable to continue with their payment of dues, causing hardships on the remaining members, who had to support the ongoing insurance and benefits for those who could not afford the premiums. In a gesture of mercy to the brothers in arrears, the Superior Council passed an emergency resolution in November 1933 to provide moral, financial, and social support to members who were delinquent in the payment of their semiannual dues to the society. The resolution extended the deadlines to those who agreed to continue with minimal payments of one dollar per month until they became current, and thus those who did so were able to preserve their benefit rights. Some members left the organization, but most were eventually able to pay their delinquencies, enabling the SPMDTU to enter the 1940s in better financial health.[44]

The era of the Great Depression may have actually stimulated the growth and expansion of La Mutua. During the early and mid-1930s, the Superior Legislative Body met annually to hear updated reports on the two most significant benefits and financial aid offered by the society: the Fondo de Indigencias for use as emergency financial relief and the Fondo de Pólizas (Insurance Policy Fund) to provide death and funeral benefits.[45] The widespread dependence on these resources very likely spurred the formation of more local councils. In 1937, for example, the society listed fifty-four commissioned councils in dispersed locations: thirty-one in Colorado and twenty-three in New Mexico, for a total membership of 1,332. To the north, these concilios included Council No. 32 in Fort Collins, Colorado, near the Wyoming border, and to the south, Council No. 33 in Las Cruces, New Mexico, near El Paso, Texas.[46]

As documented in the SPMDTU records, La Mutua dutifully responded to members and families in times of need or misfortunes. Beginning in 1915 and continuously into the Depression years of the 1930s, the minutes of meetings document hundreds of cases yearly when the Superior Council and the local councils received claims for financial aid or requests for emergency loans from the Indigence Fund to cover lost wages while recovering from illnesses, hospitalization expenses, and other catastrophes such as fires that destroyed members' homes and household furnishings. A local concilio often corresponded with other councils in a *carta circular*, a special letter of appeal, to augment whatever sum could be mobilized locally, either from the council's own Indigence Fund or from *otros auxilios* (other sources of help), to help when members were in hospital care or rehabilitating from major illnesses. A dozen or more councils would usually respond with supplemental aid. These benefits became widely known because it took the vote of the officers and members themselves to approve payments from the local council's emergency funds and for the solicitation of voluntary donations. In the majority of cases, aid would be approved and communicated to the concerned parties, with the news shared across the system of councils.

To attract new members during the late 1930s, La Sociedad issued life insurance certificates at affordable premiums that could be paid in a one-dollar monthly installment. In 1938, the death benefits for natural or accidental causes ranged from $300 up to $800 depending on the member's age at the time of joining the "Sociedad de Vida Mutua," as one of the program descriptors noted in the certificates issued at the time.[47] As people in the community and surrounding areas heard of the life insurance and other financial aid benefits, the pool of prospective members likely increased and facilitated the organizing of new councils. The SPMDTU thus made good on the promise by the founders that the members could collectively provide more help to the largest number of people in the community by pooling their resources. By the mid-1940s and into the 1950s, the Concilio Superior held reserves sufficient to pay benefits for hundreds of *defunciones* (deaths) throughout more than sixty local councils in the tristate area of Colorado, Utah, and New Mexico, and at the end of the fiscal year 1957 it reported a cash balance of $156,862.[48]

Women's Auxiliaries

Although women were not eligible to join La Sociedad until 1978, they had organized auxiliaries since at least the 1930s with their own constitutions, rules, banners, ribbons, pins, meeting halls, and general conventions. One of the women's auxiliaries, the Auxiliarias Mutuas Beneficiarias, was established in 1937 and convened its members at a meeting hall adjacent to the SPMDTU Superior Council building in Antonito. The Auxiliarias Mutuas Beneficiarias was also known by its initials, La Sociedad AMB, and was constituted to provide mutual protection and strengthen family values in the community:

> Preámbulo: Esta sociedad es constituída originalmente para la protección y ayuda de todas las miembras que la forman en establecer la paz y armonía entre las mismas, cooperando siempre para promover los buenos ideales de moralidad, el respecto y buena crianza entre nuestra prole, considerando que es un deber absoluto de toda madre de familia, y que es el más precioso heredaje que una madre puede dejar al fruto de su vientre.[49]

> [Preamble: This society is constituted originally for the protection and help of all the members who compose it to establish peace and harmony

among themselves, cooperating always to promote the good ideals
of morality, the respect for and proper raising of our children, considering that it is an absolute duty of every mother of the family, and that
it is the most precious heritage that a mother can leave to the fruits of
her womb.]

Like the SPMDTU, La Sociedad AMB chose Antonito as its headquarters for
its own Concilio Superior. The executive officers governed the business and
activities of the local auxiliaries in the San Luis Valley, an urban affiliate in
Denver, and another lodge authorized in 1938 by the SPMDTU Council No. 40
of Velarde, New Mexico.[50] To be eligible for membership, a woman had to be
between eighteen and fifty-five years of age and of Hispanic American descent,
as stipulated in the society's General Constitution. The women elected the
same type of officers found in the SPMDTU, and the AMB's organizational
structure likewise provided for a Concilio Superior, a Cuerpo Legislativo Superior, a Cuerpo Judicial Superior, and a system of concilios locales. The local
councils were named for the respective town or plaza community where they
were established and assigned a number in sequence according to the founding date of each auxiliary with respect to the founding of the Concilio Superior
in Antonito. Twelve councils were authorized in the AMB Constitution, with
a requirement of a minimum of ten members in each locality. The AMB convened a general convention of delegates from each of the local auxiliaries in
June every year in Antonito and elected nine officers for the Superior Council
as the AMB's highest tribunal.[51]

In the event of death of a La Sociedad AMB member, women from the
respective local council were obligated to pay their final respects and to conduct the funeral rituals prescribed by the society. To aid the surviving spouse
or beneficiary, the AMB's Superior Council paid a death benefit from the
cuotas de defunción, a system of assessments collected at the local council and
remitted to the tesorera superior in Antonito. The amount of the death benefit
was left open depending on the amount of funds available from the treasury at
the Superior Council combined with supplemental local aid from the respective local council in the form of assessments. For funerals, processions, and
official ceremonies, the women wore special pins, devisas, and distinctive uniforms stipulated in the society's General Regulations. The uniforms consisted
of caps and blue dresses with white collars and cuffs, and the devisas were
pinned on the dresses as prescribed: "los concilios locales pueden usar vestidos
y cachuchas y devisas. . . . Los vestidos serán azueles siendo túnico con el cuello
y los puños blancos." During these and other special events, the members also

FIGURES 29–31. Devisas and membership pins, SPMDTU and women's auxiliaries. In addition to the devisa for SPMDTU Concilio No. 1 in Antonito, pins for the three women's auxiliaries are included in this collection owned and worn by María Filomena Trujillo-Archuleta (1890–1982): La Sociedad AMB, La Sociedad Protectora Cooperativa, and La Sociedad Femenil de Protección. Courtesy of Ruben Archuleta.

displayed the society's official flag, colored red, white, and green, with the initials "AMB" at the center.[52]

Antonito was also home to two other women's societies: La Sociedad Femenil de Protección and La Sociedad Protectora Cooperativa. The wives of the SPMDTU hermanos often joined one or more of these societies, especially those who resided in Antonito or in one of the nearby communities. At times, the SPMDTU officers assisted with the drafting of the auxiliaries' rules and regulations when requested by groups of women from the area. The common procedure was to appoint a commission of SPMDTU advisors in response to a petition for assistance from local communities, as happened on February 17, 1936, when the Concilio Superior considered a request from a delegation of women who wanted to organize an auxiliary at Ortiz, Colorado:

> Se presentaron unas señoras de Ortiz, Colorado, pidiendo ayuda de nuestra Sociedad, para que se les ayudara a formular su reglamento, a modo de que fuera en armonía, y [de] acuerdo con nuestra Sociedad . . . para caminar adelante con la organización que ellas han organizado. Despues de largas consideraciones y debates se determinó de que la silla nombre una comisión de cinco miembros para que tomen este negosio en consideración, [y] que formen un Preámbulo y Reglamento.[53]

> [A group of women from Ortiz, Colorado, presented themselves requesting assistance from our society to help them formulate regulations in harmony and agreement with our society to move forward with the organization they are forming. After a lengthy consideration and debate, it was determined that the president will appoint a commission of five members to take this business item into consideration (and) develop a Preamble and Regulations.]

Once established, the ladies auxiliaries were separate and autonomous organizations, but each one required that its members adhere to the shared principles of unity, protection, and the honor of their respective society, as expressed in one organization's *himno oficial*:

¡Gracias a Dios ya llegó	[Thanks to God it has arrived
La Protección Femenil!	The Feminine Protection!
Bajo el seno de la Unión	Under the breast of the Union
Que proteja el porvenir	May it protect the future
De nuestra vida al morir	Of our lives upon our death

Hará un recuerdo de amor	It will leave a memory of love
Y nos llevará al panteón	And will carry us to the cemetery,
La Sociedad Femenil.	The Feminine Society.
Compañeras, compañeras	Companions, companions
¡Levantamos el pendón	Let us raise the pendant
De Nuestra gran Sociedad	Of our great Society of
Femenil de Protección!	Feminine Protection!
Todas estamos resueltas	We are all resolved
En mantener el honor	To maintain the honor
De esta nuestra Sociedad	Of this our Society
Que es de importancia y valor.[54]	Which is of importance and worth.]

The Antonito auxiliaries prepared the meals for the SPMDTU Superior Council's major functions: conventions, anniversaries, banquets, and other community activities. The participation of women provided a family atmosphere and helped to bond the Antonito community. The one event that required total participation from both SPMDTU and auxiliary members was the yearly anniversary in which everyone celebrated the establishment of La Sociedad. The anniversary program was meant not only for the members and delegations from all the local councils, but also for the general public. Planning commenced a year in advance by way of an appointed commission charged with organizing a program suitable to a large gathering of people from the surrounding communities: a parade, lectures, songs, games, skits, lunches, prizes, and a dance in the evening with contracted musicians.

Members of one SPMDTU council often invited members of another council to a particular anniversary and hosted their stay. Members of the Ranchos de Taos Council No. 18, for example, looked forward to these functions, which often began with a procession where they walked the length of the community, stopping at homes for brief visits and then going on to a communal meal and the celebration:

Yo tenía una tía aquí en los Ranchos de Taos, que me platicaba que toda la gente de Ranchos siempre miraban pa'delante para el aniversario que tenían los hermanos de la Sociedad. Y todas las familias limpiaban las casas una semana antes. Y todos los hermanos venían de Colorado, de Antonito, y de todas otras partes; no había tal cosa como moteles y restaurantes. Todos los hermanos se los llevaban para sus casas, a dormir y a comer con ellos. Y la celebración no duraba un día, sino dos o tres.

FIGURE 32. María Filomena Trujillo-Archuleta was a member of the La Sociedad AMB, La Sociedad Femenil de Protección, and La Sociedad Protectora Cooperativa at the same time that her husband, Francisco Antonio Archuleta, was a member of SPMDTU Council No. 1, Antonito. She joined the auxiliaries in the late 1930s or early 1940s, shortly after they were founded, and remained a lifelong member. Courtesy of Ruben Archuleta from original photo taken around 1980.

[I had an aunt here at Ranchos de Taos who told me that all of the people of Ranchos always looked forward to the anniversary held by the hermanos of the society. All the families used to clean their houses a week earlier. And the brothers came from Colorado, from Antonito, and other places; there were no such things as motels and restaurants. The local members took them into their homes overnight, to eat and sleep there. And the celebration did not last just one day, but two or three.] (Juan de Vargas, Council No. 18, Ranchos de Taos, New Mexico)

For the society as a whole, the Superior Council in Antonito sponsored Founder's Day on November 26, the SPMDTU's anniversary date. As required by the Constitution, the celebration was held at the capital city of Antonito in a manner determined by the Superior Council: "La celebración del aniversario es esta Sociedad será tenida en la capital de la Sociedad (Antonito, Colorado) el día 26 de Noviembre de cada año y el Concilio Superior determinará la forma y manera de dicha celebración."[55] By tradition, the anniversaries started in the morning with a parade along Main Street led by a delegation carrying the U.S., Colorado, New Mexico, and Utah flags and the SPMDTU banner, followed by a marching band, the officers of the Superior Council, and delegations of members from the local councils, each one carrying his local council's banner. The afternoon programs were held inside the Sala Superior and featured entertainment organized by the nearby councils and the women's auxiliaries. In 1938, for example, the program started with a welcome from the superior president and went immediately to a variety show sponsored by the Alamosa Council: *canciones* (songs) by señoritas and a special *juego*, or satirical skit, titled *El bigote rubio*. The councils of Aguilar, Capulín, Center, Monte Vista, and Ortiz followed, each with its own presentations of more canciones and juegos: *El destino, Zapatos apretados, El muchacho-mujer, Joven América, El trabajo*, and a slapstick comedy titled *El diablo travieso*.[56] In addition to daytime events, the Superior Council hosted a *gran baile* (grand ball) featuring the dances of the times: "They used to have dances in the big SPM that were for the public. And we all used to dance. That is where I learned to dance the *vals de la escoba*, square dance, waltz, and all that, because I used to love to dance with don Fructoso de Herrera. November 26 was always a big celebration for the SPM. Everybody used to look forward to it. The town was booming with people from all over. They used to have dance contests, singing contests, all kinds of contests," remembered Ruth Salazar of Antonito, Colorado.

The anniversaries often served as recruitment opportunities to attract new members from among eligible adults who had not yet joined. Program brochures were handed out at the door describing the life insurance benefits available to members, such as the $650 to $800 benficio de muerte advertised in the 1938 brochure. Cash and raffle prizes were offered in order to boost attendance; games, music, and songs were performed by schoolchildren; and there was a banquet. To raise funds for the prizes and other costs of the anniversary celebration, contests for selecting a *reina del aniversario* (anniversary queen) sometimes were held, where local councils sponsored daughters from their own communities to compete against those from other locations, with each contestant selling raffle tickets as a means of winning votes and prizes. The reina led the parade on the morning of the anniversary and was crowned during the program ceremonies at the meeting hall later in the day.

The SPMDTU *aniversario* of 1976 included $1,000 in prizes, folkloric dancers, and an evening banquet prepared and served by one of Antonito women's auxiliaries. Two years later, in 1978, women were eligible to join the SPMDTU, but some of the women's auxiliary societies continued to function well into the 1980s.[57] Meanwhile, efforts to recruit women into the SPMDTU as regular members alongside the men progressed slowly and faced opposition in some of the local councils. During the early 1980s, the officers of Council No. 18 at Ranchos de Taos enrolled a few women who were close family mem-

FIGURE 33. Former superior president Esequiel Salazar at Nambé Council No. 57 with (from left to right) Kathy Rivera, Celina Ortiz, Florinda Luján, and Angela Archuleta. Women were eligible to join the SPMDTU beginning in 1978, but it took many years before local councils actively recruited women. Courtesy of Daniel Salazar, 1993.

bers, but to recruit additional members from a wider pool, nine of the spouses took initiative, and with the support of the hermanos then serving as officers, they organized a new SPMDTU council specifically for women. On April 28, 1984, the president of the Superior Council, O. G. Andy Vigil, convened a special meeting at the sala of Ranchos de Taos Council No. 18 and initiated thirteen women from the community into Concilio No. 20, the only women's council ever commissioned by the SPMDTU outside of the independent auxiliaries. The women held an election and voted Carmen Velarde as president and Feloniz Trujillo as vice president. The new council subsequently adopted rules patterned after those of Council No. 18 in accordance with the SPMDTU Constitution and the Code of Rituals. The women convened their own monthly meetings at the Ranchos de Taos sala, sponsored charitable works, aided their sisters who were ill or in the hospital, and, like the men, named commissions to visit and take care of the elderly in the community. The meetings of Council No. 20 provided the hermanas of the Ranchos de Taos area with space to express ideas, raise funds for emergency aid to needy families, and an opportunity to acquire leadership skills while directing a council of the SPMDTU on their own.[58]

In his report to the October 1984 biannual convention in Ogden, Utah, Superior President O. G. Andy Vigil reported to the general membership that Concilio No. 20 had been established at Ranchos de Taos and by then had grown to twenty-one women. The credentials commission certified Concilio No. 20 on the roster of councils, with two delegates authorized to participate and vote at the convention along with the other delegates from New Mexico, Colorado, and Utah. The superior vice president, Jerry Romero, informed the convention that his own council at Nambé had enrolled twelve women as members during the past year, increasing the total membership of Council No. 57 to 137. The subsequent biannual convention in 1986 was hosted jointly by Council No. 18 and Council No. 20 at Ranchos de Taos, and both councils were recognized and acknowledged with fourteen hermanos and four hermanas as delegates, proportionate to the respective membership enrollment.[59] A year later the women petitioned to merge with Council No. 18 in order to bolster attendance at the monthly meetings as a single council of men and women for Ranchos de Taos, a consolidation approved by the Concilio Superior on August 1, 1987.[60] With Ranchos de Taos and Nambé as examples for other local councils to follow, the Superior Council took a firm stand in 1989 and passed a motion that concilios should not make any distinction between applications by men and applications by women for membership. At the meeting, Superior President Esequiel Salazar emphasized that councils with women as members were having positive results, so all of the local councils gradually recruited and welcomed women.[61]

Life Insurance Programs

The pólizas de vida (life insurance policies) were initiated early in the society's history and in 1911 provided a basic $25 benefit to survivors. This amount was later increased in accordance with the reserves in La Sociedad's treasury, as was the case in 1919 when the value was increased to $500 and in 1933 when it was increased to $600.[62] Benefits were paid from the Superior Council's Mortuary Fund (Fondo de Pólizas, Fondo de Defunción) in the name of the survivors of deceased members based on a register of eligibility maintained by the Superior Treasurer. By 1936, the Mortuary Fund was capitalized at $26,406 with

1,342 certificates that amounted to $872,300 of insurance protection. Members were issued certificates that guaranteed the established value of the policy in force any given year and were documented in annual statements to the Colorado Commissioner of Insurance.[63] In 1938, the Mortuary Fund was converted to a mutual benefit life association with the issuance of certificates to members under the corporate name "SPMDTU Mutual Life Association" with an internal board of directors administering the death benefits formerly paid from the Superior Council's Mortuary Fund.

In May 1942, the legal status of the life insurance program changed once again when La Sociedad qualified as a fraternal benefit society under Colorado's insurance code. The Superior Council transferred and merged the benefit certificates for Mutual Life Association members into the SPMDTU fraternal benefit society with the assumption of all financial liabilities. The need for a separate board of directors was thus eliminated. Between 1941 and 1956, the SPMDTU paid out $236,006 in emergency funds to active members and death benefits to survivors, and in June 1957 it reported a balance of $152,478.[64] In 1954, the society established the Unión Cooperativa Mutual (Cooperative Mutual Union, CMU) as a separate reserve fund to ensure that elder members' policy certificates would pay the same benefit level afforded newer members by updating the death benefits to $1,000 for everyone. The prior system of declining policies was eliminated. To finance these benefits, dues of $1.35 per month were instituted and assessed to both old and new members who opted to participate. Those who enrolled were eligible to receive supplemental life insurance benefits from a special emergency fund. The board of directors appointed to govern CMU activities was made up of the same officers who served on the Superior Council as superior president, secretary-treasurer, and president of the Cuerpo Legislativo Superior. By 1965, the SPMDTU treasury amounted to $226,919 in payable insurance funds to older and newer members combined.[65]

The success of the benefit programs and La Sociedad's apparent financial stability helped to recruit additional members during the 1950s and 1960s. These practical benefits helped to offset the decline trend in membership due to the passing away of the elders who had joined during the 1920s and 1930s. In the 1970s, the society applied for and received a charter from the Colorado state insurance office and was able to increase the value of its life insurance certificates by offering optional straight life insurance or a twenty-year payment life policy of $1,000 to $5,000. Annual premiums for these policies were affordable to members, ranging from $20 to $75, depending on the age of the member at entry into the society. At the time, the society's assets included $450,000 in investment funds, and the amount increased to $750,000 by the

1980s. Meanwhile, at the general convention of 1982 members voted to dissolve the CMU as a subdivision program of life insurance, and its assets and policy certificates were transferred to the SPMDTU's Mortuary Fund for a guarantee of payment in the amount of $1,000 per CMU policyholder.[66]

The program of life insurance administered directly by La Sociedad ended in the 1990s. By this time, members were able to purchase life insurance from commercial companies or through benefits arranged by their employers at group rates. During 1993–94, the executive officers of the Superior Council seriously explored and then proposed the feasibility of a merger with the Woodmen of the World, one of the largest fraternal benefit societies in the United States with some two thousand local lodges and more than eighty thousand members. At the general convention of September 1994, the Cuerpo Legislativo Superior, however, staunchly opposed affiliation with the Woodmen of the World and submitted a written report to the delegates that the Superior Council should devote a few months of additional study to consider three basic alternatives: consolidate with the Woodmen of the World; merge with a different life insurance company; or liquidate the SPMDTU life insurance program. With the help of a legal opinion requested from the Law Clinic at the University of New Mexico's School of Law, the officers ultimately determined that consolidation with the Woodmen would diminish the autonomy of the Superior Council as a separate entity; SPMDTU would lose control of its assets and be relegated to the position of a local chapter within the Woodmen of the World national structure. A year later La Sociedad examined other alternatives and this time decided to merge its insurance policies with those of Western Slavonic Association (WSA) Fraternal Life. The Certificate of Assumption filed jointly with WSA Fraternal Life allowed the SPMDTU's governance structure and assets to remain intact; only the insurance policies and the payment of benefits were transferred to WSA.[67]

WSA Fraternal Life had originated in Denver in 1908 as the Zapadna Slovanska Zveza (Western Slavonic Association) for the purpose of helping eastern European immigrants of Slavic descent with affordable life insurance and to render aid to the sick and injured. Like SPMDTU's original members, the early members of WSA were laborers in the mining, railroad, packing, and other low-paid wage industries of Colorado, where they often confronted ethnic discrimination and exploitation. In 1958, the association decided to bolster its membership by offering its services to all potential members and subsequently changed its name to WSA Fraternal Life in 1991 to reflect accessibility regardless of ethnic heritage.[68] In May 1995, La Sociedad and WSA filed a Certificate of Assumption with the state insurance departments in Colorado and

New Mexico and began a process of transferring the SPMDTU insurance certificates to WSA.

La Sociedad's decision to end its internal program of life insurance was controversial within the membership, but after debating the advantages and disadvantages, the majority of the members voted in favor of the change. They determined that it was more cost effective to transfer this activity to WSA rather than continue with the regulatory burdens of financial reporting to the Colorado state superintendent for insurance, especially under a requirement that all records had to be stored on magnetic disks starting in 1990–91 and the continuing requirement from 1954 to translate the Concilio Superior minutes and other proceedings from Spanish into English. When the transfer of certificates was completed in April 1997, the SPMDTU insurance fund contained enough reserves to allow doubling the value of the members' policies taken over by WSA Fraternal Life. Under a special status, the WSA continues to administer the SPMDTU insurance certificates and issues payments and benefits as originally intended, and both organizations respect and follow the provisions in the 1995 Certificate of Assumption. Since 1998, WSA has contributed financial support for the expenses of the SPMDTU biannual conventions and donates funds for the scholarship program and the annual golf tournament sponsored by Council No. 7 in Denver.[69]

Meanwhile, the passing away of elders and outmigration from the upper Río Grande hispano villages, trends dating to the end of World War II, had decreased the SPMDTU membership and forced the decommissioning of many local councils. The economically depressed rural counties where La Sociedad had organized the majority of its concilios were not able to employ the new generations of hispanos. Young adults and entire families moved away and obtained employment in the defense and construction job markets of Pueblo, Colorado Springs, Denver, and Albuquerque.[70] The impact on the SPMDTU membership was severe. The peak enrollment of about 2,000 members around 1950 had dropped to 1,600 by 1958, 1,000 by the early 1980s, 600 in the early 1990s, and about half that number by the centennial year 2000.

MY LIFE FOR THE SOCIETY

Yo soy Clodoveo Valerio. Yo nací y fui criado en Talpa. Soy veterano de la Guerra Número Dos. . . . Mi padre tenía ganadito de borregas, y tenía terrenos. Y él nos tenía ocupados. Yo cuidaba las borregas con los demás de mis hermanos, hasta 1943, cuando entré en el servicio. Estuve en el Pacífico, [y] peleé con los japoneses; peleé por nuestra bandera para que fuera libre. Después de tres años regresé a mi nativo país con mucho orgullo. Mi padre, Andrés Valerio, me indució a que entrara a esta Sociedad. . . . La SPMDTU para mí es como una madre que ama a sus hijos. La Sociedad Protección Mutua De Trabajadores Unidos es una organización que llevaré al cabo y a pecho hasta que el infinito de más allá se acuerde de mí. Entré a la Sociedad en 1952 y, por la gracia de Dios, he servido y atiendo mis juntas. Y mientras Dios me conceda mi salud, la defenderé, y estaré listo para poner a pecho, en nombre de La Sociedad, Sociedad Protección Mutua De Trabajadores Unidos.

[My name is Clodoveo Valerio. I was born and raised in Talpa (New Mexico). I am a veteran of World War II. . . . My father was a sheep rancher with his own land, and he kept us busy. I tended to the sheep along with my brothers, until 1943, when I entered the service. I served in the Pacific, fighting the Japanese; I fought for our flag so it could be free. After three years, I returned to my native land with a lot of pride. My father, Andrés Valerio, induced me to join this Society. . . . To me, the SPMDTU is like a mother who loves her children. The society is an organization that in the end I will take to heart until infinity calls for me. I joined the society in 1952, and by the grace of God I have served and attend my meetings. As long as God will grant me health, I shall defend the society and will be ready to give my life, in the name of the Society, Society of Mutual Protection of United Workers.] (Clodoveo Valerio, Council No. 18, Ranchos de Taos, New Mexico)*

*Hermano Clodoveo served La Sociedad for fifty-six years, to his last day, as he had wished. He held the office of guardia superior as an elected member of the Concilio Superior when he passed away on August 10, 2008. He had previously served as the president of the Ranchos de Taos Council No. 18 for eighteen years.

CHAPTER THREE

Challenges in the New Century

L A Sociedad no longer offers an internal program of life insurance, but the organization has not lost sight of its original mission as a mutual union ready to lend a hand in times of need. Informal and supportive services continue to be provided at the community level: home visitations during times of illness; cash donations raised to help pay for medical costs incurred by members or their relatives; supplemental death benefits paid to survivors from local council funds; food baskets and clothing to poor families at Christmas; road cleanup projects; fund-raising events for local charities; and other community-service functions. Some local activities have become annual events, such as the Hispanic Arts Festival organized by Nambé Council No. 57, at which artisans from Nambé, Española, and Taos exhibit their work as a means of promoting sales just before the Christmas holidays. In Denver, Council No. 7 sponsors a golf tournament and uses the profits to disburse college scholarships to students in need of financial aid, a yearly program also supported by the WSA. Some of the larger councils continue the traditional anniversary programs commemorating the founding date of their respective concilios with community events such as parades along the main street, an entrance march into the meeting hall singing the official hymn, a program with orators and invited speakers, cultural presentations by local school children, potluck dinners of traditional foods, and raffle drawings.[1]

Despite a new set of circumstances and a reduced capacity to offer material incentives, the core principles of the SPMDTU motto have remain unchanged for a century and a decade: "Fraternidad, Ilustración y Progreso" (Fraternity, Enlightenment, and Progress). La Mutua leadership is cautiously optimistic about the future and notes that the society continues to honor its constitution, the principles of mutual help, the use of the regional Spanish language, and, most important, the preservation of the Hispanic culture that is unique to southern Colorado and New Mexico. For governance, the SPMDTU General Constitution (revised 1980) and the Código Ritualístico de Régimen Interior (revised 1980) remain in effect, as does the Superior Council's executive authority. And, much as before, officers of the local councils conduct the meetings in the prescribed order: "ceremonia de apertura, oración oficial, lectura de los procedimientos de la previa reunión, comunicaciones y reclamos, reportes de comisiones, ceremonia de admisión de nuevos miembros, negocios sobre la mesa del Presidente, debates para el bien de la Sociedad, reporte de colectaciones, y de embolsos y delincuencias de miembros, ceremonia de clausura."[2]

Participation in burial services continues, as has been the tradition since the founding of the society, and is viewed as a ritual of profound honor, a link to the value of *respeto*, a cornerstone principle—respect for the struggles of the elders who sustained the organization over the generations. As in the past, the hermanos assist with arrangements for the rosary and funeral and accompany the deceased member to the local cemetery. At the gravesite, a designated member pays oratorical tribute in Spanish. The members wear their SPMDTU devisas with the black side showing to represent their sorrow and mourning. According to the rituals of La Mutua, the members pass the coffin one by one, place their hands on it, and pay tribute by saying, "Adiós, hermano mío, descanse en paz" (Farewell, my brother, rest in peace). They form a circle, and each one tosses a siempreviva leaf into the grave as the coffin is lowered. Some of the local councils continue to provide supplemental assistance for survivors, adding to the benefit to be paid by the WSA for those who still hold insurance certificates from earlier times. To finance the local supplement, members vote at a meeting on the assessment to be collected from each member as a cuota de defunción in addition to any regular membership dues. Once collected, the amount is forwarded to the deceased member's beneficiary.[3]

In structure, SPMDTU local councils continue to function under the authority of the Superior Council, whose officers in turn are elected by vote of the general membership at biannual conventions and which acts as the chief executive body until the next convention. The local councils select delegates to represent them by districts assigned to them on a geographic basis. Current officer positions include presidente superior, vice presidente, consejero, calificador, mariscal, and guardia.[4] The superior president appoints a secretario-tesorero and a portero. The Cuerpo Legislativo Superior continues to function as the legislative body to promulgate rules and regulations for the governance of the society as a whole; its members are elected at the general convention

FigURE 34. Concilio Superior meeting in action during the term of Superior President Rogelio Briones, shown here wearing a shirt made a few years earlier for the centennial anniversary in 2000. Courtesy of Daniel Salazar, 2004.

from among the delegates. The Cuerpo Legislativo Superior convenes the day prior to the official opening of the convention to consider resolutions or other legislative proposals that can be brought forward by any of the local councils. Proposals that meet with the Cuerpo Legislativo Superior's approval are then submitted to the delegates attending the general convention. The delegates hold the power to decide all matters for the good of the society and to receive and approve or disapprove any resolutions submitted by the Cuerpo Legislativo Superior.

Other important bodies include the Cuerpo Regulador and the Cuerpo Judicial Superior. The Cuerpo Judicial Superior is composed of three elected members not already serving on the Cuerpo Legislativo Superior or the Concilio Superior. The Cuerpo Regulador is appointed by the superior president to advise the Superior Council on financial and other business affairs and to ensure that resolutions adopted at the general conventions are implemented. This body is composed of the most recent former president of the Superior Council, an appointee of the current president, and the president of the Cuerpo Legislativo Superior. The local councils elect their own officers and conduct their internal affairs, but they are subject to the society's General Regulations.[5]

FIGURE 35. The Honorable Ben Luján, Speaker of the House, State Legislature of New Mexico. Ben Luján joined the Nambé Council No. 57 in 1969 and credits his knowledge of parliamentary procedures to his years in service as the SPMDTU consejero and to his participation in SPMDTU biannual conventions during the 1970s. Courtesy of the Center for Regional Studies, University of New Mexico, video interview 2003.

As stipulated in the Constitution, one of the Superior Council's primary responsibilities has been to convene the local councils in biannual conventions. The remaining sections of this chapter focus on the centennial anniversary held in the year 2000, followed by the milestone conventions of 2002 through 2008. Each convention signals a critical step forward in sustaining the SPMDTU in the new millennia as its officers and members confront a set of new obstacles, challenges, and opportunities. Following this chapter, the conclusion to the book addresses the key question as to the future: Will La Sociedad adapt and survive another generation?

LEADERSHIP IN THE HOUSE

Y me siento orgulloso de ser tal manera, pero la cosa que nunca olvidaré son mis principios y de donde vengo yo, y la razón que yo quise representar la gente de mi distrito. Y la cosa es que los principios de nuestra organización, la SPMDTU, son los principios que yo quiero de corazón llevar acabo aquí como "Speaker" de la Casa de Representantes. . . . Una de las cosas que aprendí de las juntas que teníamos como la Sociedad Protección Mutua de Trabajadores Unidos, fue el "parliamentary procedure," como llevar acabo las diferentes juntas, y eso me ha ayudado mucho de llevar acabo el negocio y dirigir la palabra aquí en la Casa de Representantes.

[And I feel proud to be this way, but among the things I shall never forget are my principles and where I am from, and why I wanted to represent the people in my district. The principles of our organization, the SPMDTU, are the principles that in my heart I want to implement here as Speaker of the House of Representatives. . . . One of the things that I learned at the meetings we had at the SPMDTU was parliamentary procedure, how to conduct meetings, and all of that has helped me take care of business and address the House of Representatives.] (Honorable Ben Luján, Council No. 57, Nambé, New Mexico)

Centennial Anniversary

On September 2, 2000, the Superior Council convened the local councils at the SPMDTU meeting hall in Antonito for the biannual convention and to commemorate the society's one hundredth anniversary. Society members and their families from Denver, the San Luis Valley, and New Mexico came to witness and participate in the event and to celebrate the organization's history. The centennial weekend included a Saturday morning parade on Main Street followed by a program at the Sala Superior, where speakers and former leaders of La Sociedad highlighted the society's significance and values. The founder and first superior president, the honorable Celedonio Mondragón, was recognized as the man who had perceived the needs of hispano workers a century earlier when they had faced employment discrimination and threats to their property in violation of the Treaty of Guadalupe Hidalgo. To honor his memory, the officers of the Concilio Superior had commissioned artist Emanuel Martínez of Denver to cast a life-size bronze sculpture of him. During the anniversary program, the sculpture was displayed on the front stage of the meeting hall, and his only surviving daughter, Celina Barela, was present to accept the statue on behalf of the Mondragón family. Later that evening the members, families, and guests attended a banquet and a dance, and on Sunday morning they went to a special mass at the historic Our Lady of Guadalupe Church in Conejos.[6]

To coincide with the anniversary, consultants to the Concilio Superior prepared a report nominating the SPMDTU meeting hall for listing on the

FIGURE 36. Group photo at the centennial anniversary during a break in the ceremonies, September 2, 2000. Note the stage and mural at the back end of the main floor of the Concilio Superior meeting hall. Courtesy of Daniel Salazar, 2000.

National Register of Historic Places. The nomination was certified by the State Historic Preservation Office of Colorado, and the hall was placed on the State Register of Historic Properties in March 2001. The report acknowledged the historic functions of the headquarters building as a fraternal lodge dating to 1925 and described its significance to Hispanic culture, the social history of Colorado, and the architectural features of the period, such as in the use of steel trusses and Main Street facades in Antonito.[7] A month later the Concilio Superior meeting hall was approved for listing in the National Register of Historic Places in the areas of Ethnic Heritage and Social History.[8] The bronze statue of Celedonio Mondragón stands along the south wall of the building exterior as a remembrance of his role in establishing the core principles that have endured for more than a century, and a plaque at the base reads: "Don Celedonio Mondragón, Gran Fundador, SPMDTU, 26 de Noviembre, 1900."[9]

The 2002 convention was held at the Lakewood Elks Lodge in the Denver area. The SPMDTU delegates considered a motion from the floor to open membership to spouses and others who are not of Hispanic American descent. The motion was particularly contentious because the Cuerpo Legislativo Superior had already debated the proposal and reported to the assembly that the

FIGURE 37.
Superior President-Elect
Rogelio Briones addresses
members at the centennial
anniversary. Courtesy
of Daniel Salazar, 2000.

FIGURE 38.
Presentation of the
Celedonio Mondragón
statue to his surviving
daughter, Celina Barela,
during the centennial
anniversary ceremonies
in 2000. Courtesy of
Daniel Salazar, 2000.

Figure 39. "Guardiantes de Cultura," centennial anniversary at the Concilio Superior meeting hall. Courtesy of Daniel Salazar, 2000.

Figure 40. Celedonio Mondragón walking, south wall of the Concilio Superior meeting hall. Courtesy of Daniel Salazar, 2004.

Superior Council should research some of the legal implications. This outcome would postpone any recommendations by the Superior Council until August 2003 after completion of a study, and effectively table a vote by the delegates until the 2004 biannual convention. Those in favor of the motion spoke passionately about the need for the SPMDTU to welcome U.S. citizens of any race into the society as a matter of principle and as a strategy to broaden the base of membership. They urged that a decision be made without further delay and that steps be taken to amend La Sociedad's Constitution. The question was debated at length. Secret ballots were distributed to all members, and the motion to broaden the criteria for membership eligibility ultimately passed by a majority vote.[10]

With declining membership, local councils were urged to intensify recruitment especially of spouses, younger family members, and workplace associates regardless of race or ethnicity. Earlier in the convention, Reverend Stan Perea, a grandson of founder Celedonio Mondragón, had called on members of La Sociedad to instruct the youth about the pressing needs in the Hispanic community during times of a changing society in America: the need to promote multiculturalism by passing on the Spanish language to the younger generations; the need to help the older hispanos with their problems; and the need to serve low-income and poor members of the community, which the founders had envisioned as SPMDTU's major role. The president of the society, Rogelio Briones, informed the convention about a Superior Council plan under way to restore the headquarters building in Antonito for use as a multipurpose community center and as a cultural museum that would display SPMDTU memorabilia and showcase the organization's history with videos and exhibits. Delegates at the convention pledged $29,000 to begin raising the matching funds required for the structural repairs to the exterior of the building, with additional support to be raised from private donors and Colorado foundations for renovation of the interior spaces.[11]

RIGHTS OF THE ELDERS

Yes, well, you saw it today at this convention. Los ancianos, como el hermano Valerio [the elders, like Brother Valerio], they stand up, and say "¡Hermanos!"—which is something that's not afforded them any place else in a Hispanic organization, where they can actually stand up and have input and participate. Y en todas las convenciones nunca falta que se levante un hermano [And at all the conventions there is always a brother who stands up] that you've never seen before, un viejito, un ancianito que venga y diga: "Espérence, ¿qué está pasando aquí?" [an elder who comes forward and says, "Wait a minute, what is happening here?"] "¿Dónde están mis derechos como miembro?" ["Where are my rights as a member?"] It is a very beautiful thing, es una cosa muy bonita, that the society provides an avenue or a forum for our elders, to feel important, to give ideas, and provide input. (Rogelio Briones, presidente superior at 2002 convention in Denver)

Restoration of the Superior Council Meeting Hall

To restore the Sala Superior, La Sociedad received a $10,000 grant from the Colorado Historical Society to prepare a historic structure assessment report and a preservation plan for submission to the State Historical Fund of the Colorado Historical Society. The report was completed in 2002 and included an assessment of the structural engineering and mechanical systems to be addressed during the phases of extensive repairs and renovations. The plan resulted in a second grant of $61,875 from the Colorado Historical Society for preliminary repairs to the building and was followed by a third award in the amount of $87,862 to include $25,000 in matching funds donated by an SPMDTU member. Additional donations and matching contributions pledged by local councils will be raised to finance the $322,656 in total estimated costs for restoration of the meeting hall. The restoration and preservation plan calls for a number of major improvements: parking and landscaping on the property exterior; drainage and foundation repairs; rebuilding of structural systems, exterior walls, and roof; interior finishing work on floors, walls, and ceiling; upgrading of mechanical and electrical systems; and accessibility compliance.[12]

The 2004 general convention was held in Antonito, but due to the repairs needed to bring the Sala Superior into accessibility compliance, the members met at a private club to conduct the opening ceremonies and business sessions as well as to host the evening banquet and dance. All six local councils were represented by delegates, for a total of fifty-four seated at the convention, a slight increase from the delegate count at the 2002 convention held in the Denver area. The major agenda item involved the substantial work and financial commitments required to restore the meeting hall for use as a site at future conventions and to host other La Sociedad functions. During the business meeting, the SPMDTU Legislative Body presented a resolution that would enable the officers of the Superior Council to contract with Antonito Council No. 1

for the management of the meeting hall and assume responsibilities for the restoration project. The officers of the Antonito Council planned to complete the repairs and utilize the facility as a multipurpose community center. The resolution generated debate for and against a motion to approve the Superior Legislative Body's report. The discussion among the delegates centered around the ownership of the building if a legal contract for management services was executed. The motion in support of the resolution passed with the stipulation that the Superior Council would formulate and execute the details of the legal arrangement to ensure that the Superior Council would retain ownership. The contract was approved in February 2005, but due to the lack of enough revenue to pay the costs of maintaining the building, the officers of Antonito Council No. 1 rescinded the management contract after a trial period of a year.[13]

The renovations of the Sala Superior commenced in 2005, with plans made to continue various phases of work in subsequent years, depending on the availability of funds. With a $5,000 grant from the Buell Foundation and $8,000 of SPMDTU funds, a few emergency repairs were scheduled and implemented first: shoring up one of the corners of the building that had collapsed as well as substantial work on the roof, the south-side rafters, and the perimeter walls to stabilize the exterior foundation. Lime stucco was then applied to preserve the building's finish, and the original lettering and building ornamentation were restored. After all exterior repairs are completed, a business plan will be developed to propose multiple uses of the building and how revenues may be generated to pay for operational costs. The final remodeling of the building will include refurbished interior spaces to accommodate a wide range of community and educational activities to be sponsored by local organizations such as theater groups, arts and crafts cooperatives, and the schools in the area. To generate rental income, the kitchen facilities will be remodeled in order to lease the building for graduation parties, showers, wedding dances, family reunions, and social events. Other spaces described in the preservation plan, such as the second-floor loft, potentially will house a cultural museum with an exhibit of SPMDTU memorabilia and a gift shop.[14]

General Conventions 2006 and 2008

The 2006 general convention was held at Ranchos de Taos and was dedicated in memory of Tomás Romero, the secretary-treasurer who had served La Mutua from 1969 to 2005. During the business meeting, the members were updated regarding the major projects under way since the last convention: continued

FIGURE 41. Clasping of hands in brotherly friendship in sync with the lyrics of the himno oficial as part of the entrance march at the Ranchos de Taos convention in 2006. Courtesy of Daniel Salazar, 2006.

FIGURE 42. Hermanos Aarón Romero and Amos Rivera reciting the hymnal from the convention booklet at the 2006 Ranchos de Taos convention. Courtesy of Daniel Salazar, 2006.

FIGURE 43. President-Elect Rudy Maestes taking the oath to liberty and union during the hymnal at the 2006 Ranchos de Taos convention. Courtesy of Daniel Salazar, 2006.

FIGURE 44. Ashley Martínez receiving an award for being the youngest member in attendance at the 2006 Ranchos de Taos convention. Courtesy of Daniel Salazar, 2006.

FIGURE 45. Michael Atencio wearing the devisa of Concilio No. 5, Ortiz, Colorado, at the 2006 Ranchos de Taos convention. He inherited the devisa from his grandfather, Fredrico Ortiz Jr. Hermano Fredrico was a sheepman and an officer of the SPMDTU for many years at the same time that his wife, Adelaida Ortiz, was a member and officer of the women's auxiliary in Antonito. Courtesy of Daniel Salazar, 2006.

renovation of the Superior Council meeting hall in Antonito and the establishment of a Web site aimed at modernizing the society's communication system and at helping to market the value of joining the society, especially to the younger generation. The executive officers seemed optimistic, noting that the renovated building will last another one hundred years and thus will continue as the symbol of SMPDTU unity across the generations. During the awards ceremony, businessman James Perea from Denver Council No. 7 was recognized with a plaque for the timely and critical matching funds he donated toward the restoration of the Concilio Superior meeting hall under way in Antonito. Ashley Martínez received the award for being the youngest member in attendance. She had been recruited by Nambé Council No. 57 through a new program that encourages members to sponsor students from the local community as their *padrinos* and *madrinas* (godfathers, godmothers), pays their dues for the first year or longer while they are in school, and passes on the SPMDTU's history and traditions.

Speakers who addressed the delegates observed that attendance at the biannual conventions had not declined, with fifty-four delegates present at the Ranchos de Taos 2006 convention, a number equal to the attendance at the

2004 general convention held in Antonito. In his report as superior president, David Ortiz recognized the WSA for contributing to the convention expenses and called for closer ties with WSA Fraternal Life to include the possibility of a joint life insurance program as a way of recruiting and enrolling new members into La Sociedad. Esequiel Salazar, a former superior president, eloquently stressed the need to continue the SPMDTU as a fraternal society, using the expression "equality through unity" in remembrance of the founder, the honorable Celedonio Mondragón, and his organizing of Hispanic American workers and small-scale farmers and ranchers of the San Luis Valley to counter the injustices of discrimination. At the mention of his name, all of the convention delegates spontaneously rose from their chairs in unison as a sign of respect and a way of honoring the memory of the founder, a custom during society proceedings whether biannual conventions or local council meetings.[15]

The 2008 biannual convention was held at the Lakewood Elks Lodge in the Denver area. Prior to the opening session in the morning, a special initiation ceremony was placed on the agenda to enroll more women into the society, ensuring their participation in the voting of resolutions and the election of officers later in the day. Welcome addresses were given by the president of Denver Council No. 7, LeeRoy Perea, and by Dr. Antonio Esquibel, an emeritus professor of Spanish at Metropolitan State College of Denver who had joined La Sociedad some forty-four years earlier, when he was twenty-two and then living in his hometown of Alamosa. In his remarks, Dr. Esquibel emphasized the importance of the SPMDTU in the preservation and retention of a Hispanic culture in the Americas that is unique to southern Colorado and New Mexico, especially the heritage Spanish language spoken in the region, the ancestors' many traditions and institutions that have enriched American society, and the self-identity as an Indo-Hispano people with roots in both indigenous and European cultures. The keynote speaker, Reverend Stan Perea, spoke about the social forces of multiculturalism that are transforming the nation, as featured in his book *The New America: The America of the Moo-Shoo Burrito*. For the delegates, he noted that the SPMDTU was founded on the basis of mutual protection of united workers, a new vision for its time in 1900. The future of La Sociedad, he advised, will rest in the passing on of the importance of family, tradition, and community to an increasingly diverse nation and a global economy based on creativity and change. The president of WSA Fraternal Life, Randy Fuss, also addressed the convention and reiterated the importance of the SPMDTU as a special category of affiliation, and he concurred with the delegates that a joint life insurance program should be explored as a way of attracting new members to La Sociedad in future years.[16]

I have mixed feelings about wearing my grandfather's devisa. Normally, when one of the members dies, they choose to have the devisa with them in their coffin. And when my grandpa passed away, he was wearing his at the funeral home. I went and got it because he told me I could have it; so I took it off of his chest, and my grandma said I could have it; so this is what I have here. I also kept his cross. He was a member of los penitentes. And I got to keep his rosary too; I guess because I was the eldest grandson. (Michael Atencio, oral history interview, February 6, 2004)

CHAPTER FOUR

Conclusions and the Future

L A Sociedad plans to continue as a fraternal organization, conserving its past and maintaining its autonomy and system of democratic governance. As the executive body, the Superior Council convenes in regular and special sessions at the Sala Superior in Antonito to implement the resolutions and decisions reached by the membership during the previous general convention. The SPMDTU originated as a people's institution, and it has withstood the test of time, still functioning under the rules of self-government. The officers and members take pride in the fact that La Sociedad may be one of the oldest Hispanic organizations in the country that convenes its local councils at a biannual convention where the delegates can gather to address current issues and make plans for continuance of the society. During the entrance march in the morning and later during the business session of every convention, the members wear their traditional regalia of devisas and pins, and throughout the convention they display the Concilio Superior banner with its official colors and SPMDTU seal alongside the U.S. flag at the front stage of the convention hall. The floor of the convention provides a space where the members can express themselves on matters that are important to them and their local councils. They hear reports from the presidente superior and the Cuerpo Legislativo Superior, debate and vote on resolutions and motions, elect the officers for the Superior Council by a democratic process, and conclude the day with an evening banquet and social dance as customary.

Most of the current membership originates from the rural villages and small towns of north-central New Mexico and the San Luis Valley of southern Colorado, but there is also an urban chapter in Denver. The SPMDTU is the one organization that they control and govern with a great sense of pride, ownership, and empowerment. The society continues to operate as a regional mutualista organization, with about 200 members in six councils: Antonito, Alamosa, and Denver, Colorado; Ranchos de Taos, Placitas in the El Rito Valley, and Nambé, New Mexico. Women were granted eligibility to be members in 1978, and some have served as executive officers in the local councils and as members of the Cuerpo Judicial Superior. In February 2009, the members of Concilio No. 7 in Denver elected Vickie Frésquez as the first woman president of their local council; she is a descendent of some of the early hermanos affiliated with Concilio No. 3 in Mogote, Colorado, in 1902 and Concilio No. 19 in Alamosa, Colorado, in 1938.[1] To boost membership, a campaign is under way to recruit additional members—women, men, and youths, who are eligible to join at age sixteen.

The conditions and social issues that gave rise to La Sociedad no longer apply in the postindustrial economy of contemporary society in light of the multitude of health and social welfare programs accessible to individuals and families in need. Encroachment on the community land grants, racial discrimination, and labor exploitation in the mines and agricultural fields are not the salient issues of the twenty-first century, and other civil rights and legal aid organizations have evolved to engage in these arenas. The SPMDTU has persisted for more than a century, but what are the contemporary benefits of La Mutua, and are they enough to bond the current members and future generations well into the new millennia? No local councils have been commissioned since the women's Council No. 20 at Ranchos de Taos in 1984 and prior to that the three concilios in Utah during the mid-1940s.

The program of SPMDTU life insurance ended in 1996, a decision made with reluctance and an issue that continues to be examined in hindsight by some of the members who recall the high enrollments in La Sociedad due in part to the affordable life insurance premiums offered during the 1940s and 1950s. After the transfer of the insurance certificates to WSA Fraternal Life for administration more than a decade ago, the Superior Council no longer provides direct material benefits to survivors except for supplements and voluntary contributions at the local council level. For health care, hospitalization, and workman's and unemployment compensation, most members obtain coverage or other financial assistance from private and government sources. In the area of employment, La Sociedad is not positioned to help the members secure jobs in the more complex economy and specialized labor markets.

The future role of La Sociedad remains a challenge for the leadership of the Concilio Superior and the half-dozen remaining local councils. The SPMDTU emerged and sustained the membership by addressing unmet needs at a time when services were not readily accessible in the outlying small towns and rural communities of southern Colorado and New Mexico. The society rendered aid according to local pathways consistent with the culture and traditional ways of helping; and, of major significance, the bonds of affiliation and mutuality fulfilled an underlying need for identity and community. These factors of development are consistent with the origins of many self-help groups as alternative delivery systems under conditions of alienation and the lack of professional services and institutions.[2] Research on the longevity of voluntary organizations indicates, however, that to survive beyond the mobilization stage these groups must offer and sustain three basic types of incentives: material benefits such as income or services with monetary value; solidarity benefits created by the act of association, such as camaraderie and other social rewards; and purposive or expressive rewards that derive from a particular cause or ideological orientation in the pursuit of collective goals.[3]

In the case of La Sociedad, the environment of the twenty-first century is vastly different to and more complex in practically all respects—economic, political, technological, and cultural—than the social conditions during the early phases of its history and development. Will the SPMDTU endure another one hundred years without the material and financial assistance benefits offered to past generations, or will its original mission transform to fit an alternative set of needs or gaps in services? Are the social rewards of fraternalism and cultural unity sufficient for La Mutua's viability? How are these values transmitted to new members and the younger generation? Has the SPMDTU's experience been any different than that of many other ethnic-based societies that long ago fulfilled their missions and then dissolved? This final chapter addresses questions of continuity and the lessons we can learn from the experiences of this unique mutual aid society.

Cultural Endurance

The SPMDTU leadership is anxious to adjust to the challenges of the times and maintain the society's values into the twenty-first century. Many present members boast of the multigeneration tradition of La Mutua, where in some instances they can trace membership back three or four generations in their families. Several of the hermanos and hermanas who are active members of Concilio No. 7 in Denver are descendents of the founder, don Celedonio Mondragón, including James Perea, the superior vice president of the SPMDTU elected at the 2008 convention, and his brother, Eppie C. Perea Jr., who also served as a Superior Council vice president and president in the late 1990s.[4] In New Mexico, Ben Ray Luján joined Nambé Council No. 57 in 2007, a year before he was elected to the U.S. Congress in 2008—following in the footsteps of his father, Ben Luján, the Speaker of the House of Representatives in the New Mexico State Legislature, who joined the SPMDTU in 1969, and of his uncle, Ismael Ernesto Luján, who had joined a few years earlier, in 1958. His grandfather (Ben and Ismael Luján's father), Celedón Luján, was a member in the 1940s, and his great-uncle, Seferino Luján, served as vice president of the Concilio Superior from 1954 to 1970. Don Seferino helped to organize Concilio No. 57 at Nambé in 1929 as the first mariscal. In 2005–2007, one of Don Seferino's grandsons, David Ortiz, served as the presidente superior of La Sociedad.

The officers in La Sociedad's local councils and the Concilio Superior recognize the need to pass on the torch to a new generation of young adults committed to the continuity of the distinctive land-based hispano culture in southern Colorado and New Mexico. To preserve the significance of the society, the officers years ago established an archive of journals, financial ledgers, annual reports, and other documents for use by scholars who wish to learn more about the history of La Sociedad and its legacy of accomplishments. The Concilio Superior donated the SPMDTU Records to the Center for Southwest Research, University Libraries, of the University of New Mexico for preservation and research, but also to make them accessible to the public and especially other organizations that wish to examine the SPMDTU as a case study to emulate.[5]

The challenges to La Sociedad's sustainability are many and will be left for future generations to witness if and how it once again adjusts to a changing environment. To succeed, the society must address the realities of more complex times in balance, understand the strengths that have made the organization unique, and link the past with the future. La Sociedad Protección Mutua de Trabajadores Unidos was founded in 1900 to provide for the welfare of hispano americanos at a time of economic hardships, land encroachments by newcomers to the region, sweeping legal-administrative changes, and many uncertainties about survival as a people and culture. Faced with these conditions, hispano villagers responded in the way they had solved problems traditionally: with a cooperative spirit, solidarity, and the principles of sharing embedded in a culture of mutual help. They repeatedly mobilized the human and social capital in *nuestro pueblo* to undertake a number of key innovations: the Fondo de Indigencias (a fund for emergency cash assistance), the beneficios para enfermos (a subsidy for lost wages during illness), the comisión sobre trabajadores (an internal employment referral service), the beneficios de muerte (death benefits), the pólizas de vida (affordable group life insurance), and in some of the councils a revolving loan fund to help with short-term financial emergencies. In brief, La Sociedad created its own welfare programs and strategies of social security at low cost and simultaneously affirmed the people's identity and solidarity.[6]

Unlike the mutual aid societies of immigrant groups in other regions of the United States, the SPMDTU did not dissolve or transform into a new institution. The convergence of industrialization and economic modernity in the upper Río Grande did not foster hispanos' assimilation into the dominant American society; to the contrary, the process of change facilitated collective action to safeguard a traditional way of life. Research studies in ethnic relations reveal that group boundaries are accentuated and intercultural conflicts may emerge during periods of modernization, political change, and economic development.[7] Under conditions of rapid social change, competition to acquire valued resources in the same market often intensifies, causing groups who experience uneven development to assert their ethnic identities and mobilize for self-preservation and the protection of their mutual interests.[8] In the case of the San Luis Valley of Colorado and north-central New Mexico, land-based hispanos found themselves cast as a conquered people in the wake of the Anglo-American invasion that followed after the war between the United States and Mexico from 1846 to 1848.[9] Formerly an agropastoral people with a premodern culture, the hispanos in this region faced a set of new legal and economic institutions that redefined the ownership and uses of community assets such as forests, grazing lands, and scarce water resources. When confronted with competition for resources in a capitalist political economy, which was fueled by the introduction of the railroad and its related industries, traditional hispanos in the agrarian sector resisted by organizing La Sociedad as a vehicle for cultural affirmation and economic security, a strategy described by one historian of the American Southwest as the "sacred right of self-preservation."[10]

La Sociedad originated and flourished as a mutual aid society for protection and cultural solidarity, factors that may help to answer questions about its future role in modern society and provide lessons to be shared. The SPMDTU's history offers a different explanation of voluntary association in comparison to the experiences of ethnic immigrant groups elsewhere in the United States when they, too, confronted economic and social change during periods of industrialization. One departure from the literature on assimilation theory is that hispanos of the American Southwest were not the newcomers, but instead were in a reverse historical position: they were land and property owners in their own homeland. The early waves of hispano colonization in La Provincia del Nuevo México (later New Mexico, southern Colorado, and parts of Arizona) occurred in the sixteenth and seventeenth centuries, some 250 years prior to the conquest and annexation of the territory by the United States in

1848. Most non-Hispanic settlers did not enter the region in large numbers until after the arrival of the railroad in the late 1870s and early 1880s: Texans, midwesterners, Mormons from Utah and a few southern states, and English capitalists attempting to establish colonies for immigrants from across the Atlantic. European immigrants arriving on the eastern shores of the United States in the nineteenth century, in contrast, came across the ocean prepared to assimilate into the American culture, as most ethnic groups of the era gradually accomplished with the efforts of their labor in the factories of the Industrial Revolution.[11] The immigrant enclaves during this time of transition, places where they organized mutual aid societies, were largely in urban centers, in contrast to the SPMDTU councils, which were set primarily in rural villages, agricultural trade centers, and mining boomtowns.

New Directions

The motive for native hispanos of the upper Río Grande to establish mutualista societies was not to mold themselves into an accepted form established by American society, but to endure at a time when competition for the resources of survival intensified. With regard to future directions, La Sociedad can serve as a model of self-determination and cultural retention, a people's institution that found solutions to problems of survival against the unrelenting forces of social, political, and economic modernization. This unique organization has adapted and survived into the twenty-first century, preserved its records for posterity, and taken action to restore its grand meeting hall for use by future generations. The building currently serves as a landmark promoting heritage tours of the San Luis Valley in remembrance of the struggles against racial intolerance and land losses by the early hispano settlers.[12]

The SPMDTU hopes to utilize the building, once the restorations are completed, as a cultural museum exhibiting the region's history and interpreting the work and significance of La Sociedad as a model organization of self-help that continues to express the important human values of family, tradition, and community. Steps in this direction took place at the 2008 general convention when the speakers urged the delegates to link the past with the future by preserving the legacy of La Sociedad while sharing the lessons of mutuality—a way of adding new benefits of membership and making the SPMDTU valuable to the larger multicultural America.[13] In the final business session, the delegates adopted a legislative proposal authorizing the executive officers to explore the feasibility of housing a proposed Conejos County Museum and Cultural Center at the SPMDTU meeting hall. The officers of the Superior Council were

Figure 46. Aarón Romero, mariscal superior, addresses delegates at the 2008 convention held at the Lakewood Elks Lodge in Lakewood, Colorado. The banners are from Concilio No. 7 of Denver and the Concilio Superior. Courtesy of Daniel Salazar, 2008.

FIGURE 47. Initiation of women members at the 2008 convention by the president of the Superior Legislative Body, Lucas Trujillo. Left to right: Dianna Rael Trujillo, Ranchos de Taos Council No. 18; Cynthia Mares, Denver Council No, 7; and Trini Baca Rivera, Nambé Council No. 57. Courtesy of Daniel Salazar, 2008.

FIGURE 48. Group photo at the office of the Concilio Superior after the semiannual meeting in February 2004, with representation from Antonito Council No. 1. Courtesy of Daniel Salazar, 2004.

directed to study how an Antonito building listed on the National Register of Historic Places can successfully attract tourists who travel on the Cumbres & Toltec Scenic Railroad that runs from Chama, New Mexico, to Antonito, Colorado, as well as other visitors along the Caminos Antiguos Scenic and Historic Trail.[14]

Shortly after the 2008 convention, Denver Concilio No. 7 responded to this opportunity and pledged the remainder of matching funds needed to complete the interior remodeling of the Concilio Superior.[15] In October 2008, the officers of the Concilio Superior submitted a proposal to a committee in charge of selecting a site for the Conejos County Museum and stressed the role of its meeting hall as a longtime center of social and cultural events in Antonito and Conejos County. The committee has not yet decided on a location. For residents of the greater San Luis Valley, a museum program, whether under county auspices or as an independent not-for-profit entity, might sponsor a series of recovery and preservation projects to document the history of human settlement and distinctive uses of the land by the competing cultures that have laid claim to the resources of the valley over the centuries: Amerindians,

FIGURE 49. Founder Celedonio Mondragón and his second wife, María Elena Casias, married 1899. The caption was superimposed later when don Celedonio was no longer the superior president and the members wished to recognize him officially as the founder of La Sociedad. From the José A. Rivera Pictorial Collection, PICT 000-587, courtesy of the Center for Southwest Research, University Libraries, University of New Mexico.

Spanish Mexican settlers, Anglo-Americans, Mormons, Japanese Americans, German Americans, Scandinavian Americans, and other immigrants of European ancestry. To sustain member interest and engagement, especially the youth, La Sociedad might make its archive records at the University of New Mexico available online to support genealogical research and oral history projects based on lists of members of the scores of local councils in Colorado, New Mexico, and Utah over the past one hundred years. Other sponsors or agencies from the upper Río Grande may want to utilize the Concilio Superior to organize workshops on the Spanish Mexican mercedes y acequias (land grants and commons ditches) or to exhibit the aboriginal occupation and use of the region and its resources by the Utes, Apaches, Navajos, Pueblos, and their ancestors.

In the end, these and other similar programs may help to revitalize La Sociedad in terms of a new mission to create a sense of fraternalism across cultures in the validation of diversity, mutual help, and the pooling of human resources to address the common problems of growth and development. Community building as a strategy for survival worked previously for La Mutua and may now offer to human settlements in other parts of the world lessons in the power of sharing in ways that are equitable, adaptable, and enduring, especially in the context of environmental stresses on the land, water, energy, and other resources vital to sustainability.[16]

The pressures of development exist in other multicultural regions and will increase in the era of globalization and socioeconomic restructuring, creating new situations of conflict where traditional and indigenous cultures are subordinated to dominant or more powerful elites who may attempt to monopolize and perhaps deplete resources essential to all human communities. Changes in the social order, accelerated technological advances, periods of economic recession, environmental crises, and other turbulence undoubtedly will continue into the twenty-first century. As a counterbalance, the trend toward a transnational human society across international boundaries will also continue, however, and create new opportunities for mutual cooperation and sharing.

Cultural diversity itself is a global resource, as are people's institutions that provide voluntary services under rules of self-government in accordance with local customs, beliefs, and values that are important to the collective good. A wise course of action for policymakers and governmental agencies to take would be to honor, strengthen, and incorporate the social capital of traditional cultures so that all people can share the common resources essential for survival on equitable terms. The principle of reciprocal cooperation, mutualismo, is as ancient as human culture itself and perhaps will remain valid as the determinant factor of social and cultural evolution for all time. As Peter Kropotkin put it in 1902, "In the practice of mutual aid, which we can retrace to the earliest beginnings of evolution, we thus find the positive and undoubted origin of our ethical conceptions; and we can affirm that in the ethical progress of man, mutual support—not mutual struggle—has had the leading part. In its wide extension, even at the present time, we also see the best guarantee of a still loftier evolution of our race."[17]

Selected Oral Histories

The documentary survey conducted for this book included digital video interviews of members in which they related personal memories and reflections of their participation in the SPMDTU. Selections from a few oral histories are included here for the unique information each one provides to readers. The members describe their connections to the society and the importance of the organization to them, their families, and their local communities. Limitations of space precluded the use of all the interviews. In addition, the narratives presented here are not entirely complete or verbatim and instead are excerpted from the video transcripts with minor editing, and some were translated from Spanish where needed. We acknowledge and thank Rosa López Gastón for transcribing the interviews from the original video and audio recordings.

Rogelio Briones and Daniel Salazar, Interviewers

Memories of the Founder: James Perea

James Perea is a grandson of don Celedonio Mondragón, the acknowledged founder of the SPMDTU. Hermano James is a member of Council No. 7 in Denver. Like many others of his generation, he left Antonito to seek opportunities in Denver right after high school graduation in 1964. He is very well respected within La Sociedad not only because of his pedigree, but because he is a successful businessman and a person who lives up to his commitments. He helps with various charitable projects in the Denver area sponsored by the local council, and he contributed financially to the renovation of the Superior Council meeting hall in Antonito. In his interview, Hermano James shares how his mother passed on the legacy of Celedonio Mondragón and why he and many other family members continue to participate in the society. (Date of interview: September 14, 2002.)

CELEDONIO MONDRAGÓN, my grandfather, started the SPMDTU in 1900 as a fraternal organization dedicated to helping Hispanics and to combat rampant discrimination that existed at that time. My mother, Eliria Mondragón Perea, was very young when her father died; however, she often related to us the memories she had of the good things my grandfather accomplished for the community. My grandfather was a jeweler by trade in Santa Fe, New Mexico, and later in Antonito, Colorado, and for a while he also was postmaster of the small town of Cenicero, Colorado, about two miles from Antonito and now called Lobatos. He was widely known and respected, and he left a legacy that all of our family is very proud of.

My grandfather was very committed to the SPMDTU. I recall my mother talking about all the meetings he attended and the trips he made to recruit new members at a time when traveling was very difficult and expensive. He sacrificed quite a bit to help the organization grow. He also spent countless hours, along with other members, establishing a life insurance program at a time when Hispanics could not get this coverage from traditional sources. He and other members also assisted their neighbors, friends, and relatives in harvesting their crops or with other needs they had in times of illness or injury. When an hermano passed away, the members would help cover the cost of the funeral, provide an honor guard, and assist with the burial services.

One of the memories I have when I was growing up in Antonito is of the SPMDTU anniversary celebration on November 26 each year at the Concilio Superior meeting hall. I remember how dedicated the members were and the pride they took in their organization. The program and ceremonies were conducted flawlessly, and the speakers were very articulate. The society also presented entertainment and a talent show, which was always something we looked forward to.

Currently, my brothers, Eppie Perea Jr. and Billy Perea, and I are members of the SPMDTU Council No. 7 in Denver, and our sister, Bernadette Armenta, is a member of the Antonito Council. At this time, our goal is to keep the organization that my grandfather founded going and continue to provide help and assistance to our people even though things have changed and needs are different today. I see the help we have given people here through the Denver local council. We've had a Christmas program for many years when we put together food baskets, and we purchase clothing and toys for families in need. The members deliver these goods themselves, and we get to see the looks of joy in these children, one of the most gratifying things that we do. We also organize golf tournaments to raise funds for a scholarship program. Each year we award six $1,000 scholarships to needy and deserving college students. It's very rewarding to help people.

Values of the Society: Esequiel Salazar

Esequiel Salazar is a member of Nambé Council No. 57. He joined the society in 1955 and served as president of the SPMDTU Superior Council from 1971 to 1983 and again from 1989 to 1993. During his terms as president, Hermano Esequiel was widely appreciated—along with Tomás Romero, Pancracio Romero, and Frank López Sr.—by the members for safeguarding the SPMDTU's insurance reserves. While serving as superior president, Esequiel "Zeke" Salazar was the authority, and his decisions on behalf of the society always commanded tremendous respect. He is one of the exemplary figures in the history of the SPMDTU, steering the organization during the critical times of his leadership and later as an advisor to seven presidents who followed in his footsteps. For guidance today and for the benefit of all members, he articulates in depth the principles of the society from the time of the first president, Celedonio Mondragón, to contemporary times. (Date of interview: July 11, 1997.)

I LIVE HERE IN POJOAQUE [New Mexico]. I have been a member of the SPMDTU since the early 1950s. I joined the society because I thought that this was one group that really had good goals and principles to guide our people to survival. It's now one of the oldest Hispanic organizations in the country. This organization was recognized in a proclamation by the Congress of the United States in 1938. We want to make sure that people who join the society have those thoughts—that we the Hispanic people have to keep our culture going and preserve our language. We have to get involved in all aspects of our culture. Our handicrafts are brought to the forefront, our silverwork, our weaving. All those things are important. That's our life, our culture.

There was a man with a special vision, and that was Celedonio Mondragón. There was a need for the protection of rights for Hispanic peoples. And this man had the right idea. The only way to protect our rights was through unity, illustration of faith, and the example of progress, and those are our mandates: "Progreso, Ilustración, y Amor Fraternal." We have principles that have helped guide the society, and I think that the only reason that we have survived through the years is because of these principles. They are so fundamental to the life of our people and necessary for all life. We believe that the fraternal life is what really sets us off from other people. We are interested in preserving our way of life, and the only way we can do it is through unity. And this is what this gentleman, Celedonio Mondragón, figured out we have to do. We have to unite, and we have to be able to fight. We are always bound by those sacred agreements that we took when we joined the society. You take an oath and you promise fidelity to your brothers, to the needs of your brothers, and the only way that could be done was to help them with the funeral expenses or help them harvest the crop if they were sick. Those are in-kind benefits that the society gave in those days. It wasn't monetary. It couldn't be, because people didn't have the money, but they certainly had the goodwill to bring you a load of wood if that's what you needed.

If somebody dies, we have a ritual that calls for our brothers to arrange the funeral, and before the service, at the wake, we gather around the casket in a tight circle. We make and adopt a motion that the deceased brother is entitled to all the benefits of the society as prescribed in our rule book. And then we go back to the hall and say, "What else shall we do?" According to our beliefs, we take our deceased brother to his last resting place. We have to be there as a group. We have to wear our badges. We once again make a circle, and we plant the siempreviva, the little leaf that symbolizes eternal life, and after we dispense with the eulogies and the priest says his prayers, then the members pass one by one, and they put their right hand on the casket, and they say, "Adiós, hermano mío." Using the same route, we all pass the casket giving our last respects at that time.

So the society has been the right avenue for me to walk through, and I have enjoyed it. In Nambé, we had beautiful dances with all the older members, old *cultios* and *cuatrillos*. There's something beautiful about the Hispanic culture. Not only is the language beautiful, but also the way the people treat life. In order to appreciate another person, you have to know them, and the only way to know them is you have to socialize. The society here offered me this opportunity. We had our own meeting hall; we had our activities; the society had picnics and campouts where the people could go and talk about the happenings of the day or the week. . . . Right now, we are in a period of transition. When you come down to it, and you look . . . all we had was the fraternal part; the insurance came much later. The fraternal part was what kept us going; and we still have those principles, those ideals and respect for each other.

The Women's Auxiliaries and Grandfather Ortiz: Michael Atencio

Little is known about the role of women in the SPMDTU prior to the time they became eligible for membership as hermanas in 1978. The recollection by Michael Atencio given here provides important details by a member who was a boy of six years old at the time when ladies auxiliaries were still very active in Antonito. His grandmother, Adelaida Ortiz, was a member of one of them and kept meticulous financial records during the time she served as the treasurer in the late 1950s. The women had their own meeting hall next to the SPMDTU building, and Michael Atencio attests: "Without the women, the men couldn't do what they needed to do." Hermano Michael also recalls his grandfather's life as a sheep rancher, bus driver, and officer of the SPMDTU. From his grandfather, Fredrico Ortiz Jr., he learned the values of the organization and how to treat people with kindness and to lead an exemplary life, or, as his grandfather would say to him, "como los hombres." Hermano Michael is a member of Alamosa Council No. 19 and served as the portero for the Superior Council from 2001 to 2005 and as vice presidente superior from 2005 to 2009. (Date of interview: February 6, 2004.)

MY EARLIEST MEMORIES of the SPMDTU were really through the ladies auxiliary of the SPMDTU in Antonito. I recall playing with other children and staying around the ladies, who would cook for funerals, meetings, and weddings in their building, which was attached to the SPMDTU meeting hall in Antonito. As a six-year-old boy, I was taking piano lessons from the nuns who taught at our local schools when my grandmother, Adelaida Ortiz, recruited me to play the piano accompaniment to the "SPMDTU Entrada" (entrance march). I recall attending the ladies auxiliary meetings for the first fifteen minutes or so until I played piano, and then I was asked to leave after that. Eventually, after about four years of doing this, I protested, and my grandmother had me show her how to play the *entrada*, and she played it for the auxiliary from then on. She also purchased a new piano and donated it to the auxiliary. About this time, she was elected to the position of treasurer; and not having one single bit of education nor experience with bookkeeping and reporting, she had me set up the ledgers and membership lists, and then she purchased a hand-cranked adding machine and kept the books for the organization until her death in 1989. And she was proud of saying, after balancing the books, "Hasta el real" (To the penny!).

I can't remember if the ladies auxiliary had badges, but I remember that in church the men would sit to the right of the altar, and the women to the left. The ladies would all wear flowers on their coats. The auxiliary served a vital and important function of the SPMTDU, not only by entire families' being involved in the organization, but by providing the needed food preparation, serving, and community bonding necessary to conduct funeral and other social activities in the community. We would hang around with the grandmas and mommas, and they would cook and serve the meals to the hundred-plus members of the SPMDTU, and every meeting had a meal afterwards. The men and the women could come together and have dinner with all of us there. The women were the ones that really introduced me to the SPM in the sense of [the] feeling of community that we had. I recall there were other auxiliaries that would share the facility next door to the meeting hall. I remember one auxiliary that wore blue capes, and they looked like nurses; the other auxiliary would just wear flowers.

My grandfather, Fredrico Ortiz Jr., was a person of status in the Antonito community, having been born into the Ortiz family of sheepmen and landowners. The town of Ortiz, Colorado, was named after the family. My grandfather owned two ranchos of about 450 acres in San Antonio, Colorado, and was a sheepman with more than 2,800 sheep, 4 sheepherders, 10 horses, and 7 sheep dogs in the 1950s to mid-1960s. He retired and sold his land and sheep in 1962 and became a bus driver for our local elementary school. He was secretary of the SPMDTU for many years and was known for his elegant and legible handwriting style. I remember begging to go to the meetings with him, but my grandfather would laugh and tell me: "Cuando es tiempo, puedes entrar" (When it is time, you may join). I remember the hermanos of that era. They were larger than life to me, in their long overcoats and hats, discussing important issues of the community in hushed tones, talking endlessly about procedure and proper etiquette late into the night. These men were my heroes and role models, and nothing made me tremble more than being initiated into the SPMDTU in 1966 or 1967. Learning all of the signs, countersigns, handshakes, and passwords associated with membership was exciting to me. I wanted to be like the men who were in there. To me, I would look at them, and I saw men who were trustworthy, who would not lie. I saw men who took care of their families, took care of each other. The exposure to positive and vital hermanos at this time in my life has laid my foundation of responsibility, maturity, and service to others that the SPMDTU personifies. To this day, my grandfather's legacy of kindness and compassion follows him. Many of the parents of elementary-age children remember him carrying their children from his school bus to their doorsteps if the snow was too deep. When I meet old friends from Antonito, this story always comes up. If I could be half the man my grandfather was, I would be grateful. As he always said, "¡Como los hombres!"

The Story of Manuel Jesús Trujillo: Ruth Salazar

Ruth Salazar was the mother of SPMDTU member Donald Salazar, a member of Council No. 19 in Alamosa, Colorado. When Hermano Donald was growing up, his mother often told him stories of when her father, Manuel Jesús Trujillo, was a member of La Sociedad and how fond he was of the organization. Don Manuel Jesús worked for the Denver and Rio Grande Railroad and lived with his wife and children in company housing at Big Horn, New Mexico, adjacent to the Colorado border. Big Horn was one of the water tank locations along the railroad tracks between Chama, New Mexico, and Antonito, Colorado, servicing steam locomotives that carried ore, lumber, livestock, and other freight along narrow gauge tracks. During the 1930s, Hermano Manuel Jesús was a member of the nearest SPMDTU council at San Miguel, New Mexico, and later the Antonito Council No. 1 after he moved his family there. Big Horn is now deserted, but the remains of the place are still visible. The tracks are used presently by the Cumbres & Toltec Scenic Railroad as a living history museum on the route from Chama to Antonito passing alongside Big Horn. At the time of this oral history, Ruth Salazar lived in Antonito. She passed away in the winter of 2006. (Date of interview: February 6, 2004.)

I REMEMBER WE USED TO LIVE in Big Horn. My dad used to work for the railroad. And he used to go on Saturdays once a month to his SPMDTU meetings in San Miguel held at *la escuela*, the schoolhouse there. And that was very important to him—to go to his meetings. He used to walk about three or four miles from Big Horn. There is a llano on Big Horn to go to San Miguel and then straight down a hill until you get to San Miguel. He used to walk that trail after he ate dinner, at six-thirty, to make sure he was there at seven for the meeting. And he used to come back home that same night, whenever the meeting ended, walking along the trail from San Miguel with his little flashlight. Even in the cold of winter, he never missed a meeting. My dad would be happy to know that Donald, my son, belongs to the SPM. Oh my God, he would be so happy and proud that Donald joined something that was so important to him.

I was not more than eight or ten years old, or even younger, because I remember my daddy very clearly, him going to the meetings when I was pretty young. And then we moved over here to Antonito, the same thing with his meetings every week or two weeks. The original building of the SPMDTU in Antonito was small, but long on the back, with a meeting room there; and the rest was just open, with a little stage and chairs along the side. The building only had one window, due to the cold. For the meetings, a member would build the fire for the night, just before the others arrived. . . . My dad made sure he had his fifty cents to pay his dues at the meetings because he loved the organization, and it was very important for him to go there. Even when there was no meeting, they used to get together without a quorum. He never missed a mass, and he never missed a meeting. He was very faithful to the SPM.

They used to have dances in the big SPM [sala] that were for the public. And we all used to dance. That is where I learned to dance the *vals de la escoba*, a square dance waltz, and all that because I used to love to dance with don Fructoso de Herrera. Sometimes it was somebody's birthday, and they used to have parties up there. November 26 was always a big celebration for the SPM. Everybody used to look forward to it. The town was booming with people from all over. They used to have dance contests, singing contests, all kind of contests. We all used to sit around in the back of the stage. And they used to bring the *matachines* from New Mexico in 1943, around there, '42, '43, '44. People were afraid of them. They used to dress funny with big dressings over their heads or hats, and some had feathers or something like that, with their faces painted. You know, they used to dance and make noises. We would go and see the contests and the matachines because my daddy belonged to the SPM.

Multigenerational SPMDTU Family: Juan de Vargas

Juan de Vargas was a member and president of Council No. 18, Rancho de Taos, New Mexico. Born in 1923, he served many years on the Superior Council and on his local council as president, secretary, treasurer, qualifier, and counselor. Hermano Juan passed away in 2005 and is remembered fondly by members of the society who knew him during his many years as an active member and officer. He was a musician and a storyteller with a vivacious personality and great sense of humor. The oral history given here was taken in 2002, when eight of his family were members of SPMDTU. Both his father and grandfather had been members during their lifetimes. One of his daughters, Elena de Vargas Williams, was one of the youngest women of the Taos area to join the society when women were first admitted as members. She also joined the women's Council

No. 20 in 1984 and continues as an active member of Council No. 18, where she plans to follow in her father's footsteps. (Date of interview: February 16, 2002.)

MY FATHER AND MOTHER CAME TO TAOS from Ojo Caliente and La Madera, around 1920. I am extremely proud that presently eight members of my family belong to the SPMDTU, and at one time there were actually eleven of us. I almost was the society here in Ranchos! Two of my sons have mature insurance policies and are on their own. My wife and I also have mature policies. I joined the society in 1953, 1954, or around there. But I remember the society well before then, still a boy at that time, when I was in the second grade, at about seven or eight years of age. . . . We were born in Taos, and then my father purchased land here in Ranchos de Taos, and we moved. During the winters, we stayed with my grandparents in Taos since the school was just across the road from them. My grandfather was president of the SPMDTU council in Taos. They had a large membership. From that time on, I observed the society, and my father always took me to attend funerals, other activities, and anniversaries, being that he was a musician, and I played the guitar with him. For the anniversaries, we were always asked to play music during the program between the speeches by the orators. So I have many years here, and only one time did I sit in the audience, while being initiated. At the following meeting, the president appointed me as the temporary secretary. After that, I served as president, secretary, treasurer, and qualifier. The only position I have not held is that of the portero. Today, I am the counselor of the Ranchos de Taos Council and also an officer of the Superior Council as the qualifier, for about six years or more so far.

I had an aunt here at Ranchos de Taos who told me that all of the people of Ranchos always looked forward to the anniversary held by the hermanos of the society. All the families used to clean their houses a week earlier. And the hermanos came from Colorado, from Antonito, and other places; there were no such things as motels and restaurants. The local hermanos took them into their homes overnight, to eat and sleep there. And the celebration did not last just one day, but two or three. They held a procession that went everywhere, with people from all over, followed by a church function on the day of the patron saint, San Francisco, and then to the homes of the hermanos to eat and celebrate.

When there was a funeral, there were no funeral homes in those days, and instead the funerals were held at the family homes, where all-night wakes would be held for the deceased. All the men would gather around a fire outside to warm themselves and make conversation. They prayed the rosary as a group, and then sang alabados. We would be summoned to eat, and a different group would pray the rosary, until dawn and the sun appeared. From the time we were notified of a member's death, we took charge of the funeral arrangements, processions, carrying the deceased to church for the mass, and then we buried him. With the use of shovels, we dug the grave, and we, the hermanos, covered the grave. Then we would say to the widow, "Everything is concluded." And if we had donations, we gave them to her. We almost always had a donation for the widow and the survivors. For several deceased, we paid the burial costs out of our own pockets. Mr. Manuel García was the casket builder in Taos. He helped us a lot, like when he gave us a casket to bury an elderly man here who did not have the means to be buried. So there have been many things that have been done, para alivianarnos unos a los otros, to aid and help one another.

From the Nambé Council to the State Legislature: Ben Luján

Ben Luján is a member of Council No. 57 in Nambé, New Mexico, and has served as the Speaker of the New Mexico House of Representatives from January 2000 to the present (2010). He joined the SPMDTU in 1969, following the tradition in his family. His uncle, Seferino Luján, became a member in 1929 and served as vice president of the Superior Council from 1954 to 1970, and his brother, Ismael Ernesto Luján, has served as an executive officer as well. At the local council in Nambé, Hermano Ben served in the past as the consejero, the official who interprets parliamentary rules and by-laws. He was selected as a delegate to the SPMDTU conventions during the early 1970s. After this, Hermano Ben was elected to the New Mexico House of Representatives in 1975 and served in key positions of legislative leadership from House Democratic Whip to Speaker of the House. In his oral history interview, he credits the SPMDTU for instilling basic values that he followed in his House leadership roles and that continue to guide him. His son, Ben Ray Luján, a representative for New Mexico in the U.S. Congress, joined Nambé Concilio No. 57 in 2007, ensuring family participation in the society for another generation. (Date of interview: November 14, 2003.)

I WAS BORN AND RAISED in the community of Nambé in the Pojoaque Valley. I attended elementary school there, and then graduated from high school in Pojoaque. I had an uncle who was very involved with the society,

Seferino Luján, as well as my father, Celedón Luján. My brother, Ernesto Luján, is presently a member of the organization. In our youth, we always looked forward to the anniversaries of the SPMDTU of Nambé on the fifteenth of November when we held the community parade on that day. At the time, we had about forty or forty-five members, and the membership grew after that to more than one hundred. The anniversaries were public fiestas, where the whole community and the schools would observe and participate, whether they belonged to the organization or not.

Within the local Nambé Council, I served as an officer in the role of consejero, more or less as an advisor; plus, I was a delegate of our council to the general conventions. I wish I would have participated more, but that is when I entered politics at the county level, elected as a county commissioner in 1970. I served two terms, the maximum allowed for those positions, and so I next ran for the state legislature. The voters elected me in 1974, and I took office as a state representative in 1975. I served as the Majority Whip for fifteen years and later as the floor leader for two terms when Ray Sanchez was the House Speaker. I learned a lot from Mr. Speaker, Ray Sanchez, and when he was not reelected to the House, my colleagues elected me as their Speaker, something I had not anticipated.

And I feel proud to be this way, but among the things I shall never forget are my principles and where I am from and why I wanted to represent the people in my district. The principles of our organization, the SPMDTU, are the principles that in my heart I want to implement here as Speaker of the House of Representatives. We should never forget we are here to represent our people and see how we can do better to improve services, such as education for our children. One of the things that I learned at the meetings we had at the SPMDTU was parliamentary procedure, how to conduct meetings, and all of that has helped me take care of business and address the House of Representatives.

Our organization has more than one hundred years of history and has helped many young people with scholarships as well as those who passed away. Finding ways of helping, such as [assisting] those members who are ill, is very important to our people. As Hispanics, we all have a lot of heart and the desire to extend our love to our fellow citizens, especially our neighbors and hermanos. We should not forget our roots and that we need to continue our culture as one where each person helps another with open arms and stretching out our helping hands as we say in the SPMDTU official hymn. I feel very proud to have held these principles of the SPMDTU. I know what "*trabajadores unidos*" means, in more ways than one. This is one of the organizations that reminds me of what I have to do here as a representative from my district, first of all, and also for all of the people of the state of New Mexico. I believe that our organization was founded to protect one another, to find employment for our workers, to support our families, and also to protect our culture, language, and widows and family survivors of deceased members. Those are principles I will never forget when I conduct myself as Speaker of the House of Representatives.

Records and Documents

Oración de Apertura (Opening Prayer)

The oración de apertura *is the official prayer of La Sociedad for reading during the opening ceremonies of local council meetings (from the Código Ritualistico de Régimen). The prayer is not recited until the guardia and the mariscal assure the president that only members are present, with no intruders in the meeting hall, and that all concilio officers are in attendance. Persons who are delinquent in paying their dues or who are otherwise not eligible to participate are expelled from the meeting hall. Those who remain must provide the* contraseña *(secret countersign) and whisper the* paso semianual *(semiannual password) when approached and quizzed by the mariscal. At this time, the president then directs the calificador to invoke the opening prayer:*

O, Dios Omnipotente, que sois todo amor, os damos las gracias por haber criado para nosotros la luz y por habernos proporcionado con ella tantos goces. No permitais, O, Dios Santo, que abusemos de ella para hacer el mal, iluminad nuestras almas con la luz de vuestra verdad, por lo cual, la que hiere nuestra vista no es más que una imperfecta imagen, mas proponemos, O Dios Santo, amarte y servirte sobre todo lo que sea bueno y finalmente, te pidimos, O Dios Santo, que des un buen suceso al cuerpo de esta Sociedad.

Todos en armonía responderán reverentemente:

Nuestro Dios sea para siempre alabado, para siempre ensalzado, para siempre bendecido, por los siglos de los siglos, Amén.

[Oh Omnipotent God, Thou art all love, we give Thee thanks for having created for us the light and for furnishing us with it so many joys. We beseech Thee, Oh Divine God, that we may not abuse and use it to do that which is wrong. Let the light of Thy truth so shine in our souls that we may see how

imperfect we are, yet we resolve, Oh Divine God, to love Thee and to serve
Thee above all for that which is good, and, finally, we beseech Thee, Oh
Divine Lord, that Thou grant success to the body of this Society.

All brothers in harmony shall respond reverently:

May our God be always praised, be always exalted, and be always blessed,
forever and ever, Amen.]

Oración de Clausura (Closing Prayer)

*After a motion is made to adjourn local council meetings, the president seeks
assurances from the guardia and the mariscal that peace, harmony, and security
have prevailed among the members, free of any intruders, and that the meeting
can now be concluded. After these two officers respond affirmatively, the president then instructs the calificador to invoke the help of God by reading of the
closing prayer:*

O Dios, Todo Poderoso, por vuestra infinita caridad, y como vos sois la
fuente de donde dimanan la ciencias y la sabiduría os suplicimos que mora-
lices en nuestra unión la más grande paz y concordia que a los fieles es dado
conocer, y que la Paz, amor y fraternidad haya reinado en nuestro Concilio entre nosotros un vivo deseo de hacer lo bueno ante tus ojos e impartir el
amor fraternal entre los miembros de esta Sociedad.

Todos en unión responderán:

Nuestro Dios sea para siempre alabado, para siempre ensalzado, y para
siempre bendecido, por los siglos de los siglos. Amén.

[Oh Almighty God, through your infinite charity and because Thou art the
fountain from which all science and wisdom flow, we beseech Thee to implant
in our union the greatest peace and harmony that to all the faithful has been
given to understand, and may Peace, love, and fraternity abide with us in our
Council and grant to us a burning desire to do that which is good before your
eyes, and may we impart fraternal love among the members of this Society.

All brothers in unison shall respond:

May our God be always praised, be always exalted, and be always blessed,
forever and ever, Amen.]

SPMDTU Preámbulo (Preamble) of 1911

*The preamble was written and approved with the General Constitution of 1911
and was printed in 1922 along with minor amendments to the articles and the*

general regulations adopted by the society. The preamble reveals in vivid and forceful language the motives that gave rise to the SPMDTU in the context of the times: to provide for the welfare of the members and their families, combat the injustices of tyrants, and protect land and other property against thieves and usurpers of the law. (Source: Constitución y Reglamento de la Sociedad de Protección Mutua de Trabajadores Unidos, revised and approved February 18, 1922, José A. Rivera Papers, Box 8, Folder 3, Center for Southwest Research, University Libraries, University of New Mexico, Albuquerque.)

Deseando los firmados al fin de este preámbulo formar una sociedad legalmente constituida y amparada bajo las leyes de los Estados Unidos de América y del estado de Colorado en particular, nos hemos reunido y de común acuerdo determinamos lo siguiente:

Formar una sociedad fraternal . . . que lleve por nombre SOCIEDAD PROTECCION MUTUA DE TRABAJADORES UNIDOS, con cabecera principal en la plaza de Antonito, condado de Conejos, estado de Colorado . . . y que dicha sociedad quede establecida para los fines que en seguida se exponen:

Considerando que todas las naciones civilizadas del mundo tienen formadas sociedades fraternales o agrupaciones idóneas para la protección, ilustración y progreso de los miembros que las forman, y deseando nosotros entrar en el camino de la prosperidad, del adelanto y de la luz, hacemos con la incorporación una reforma de gran importancia a la sociedad que llevó el mismo nombre que la que hoy incorporamos, y que fue fundada el 26 de Noviembre, A.D. 1900, por el Hon. Celedonio Mondragón, para proseguir en los mismos fines para lo que fué constituída originalmente, es decir, para la protección de cado uno de los miembros que la forman, ayudando a sus miembros desvalidos y necesitados, a sus viudas y huérfanos y a todas aquellas personas que por algún vínculo de consanguinidad estén unidas con alguna persona de esta sociedad; para mitigar los estragos y sinsabores de la vida; para protegerse contra las injusticias de los tiranos y de los déspotas, de los usurpadores de la ley y de la justicia, de los ladrones de vidas, honras y propiedades; para que sea la salvaguardia de nuestras familias y de nuestros intereses; para estrecharnos la mano de hermanos en medio de nuestras alegrías, de nuestras dichas, de nuestras desgracias y nuestros martirios, para caminar por el rudo camino de la vida con los ojos empapados con las lágrimas de la alegría, con la sonrisa verdadera en nuestros labios y con la frente levantada con el laurel del triunfo y de la humanidad, y así prosiguiendo en nuestra vida llevaremos grabada en nuestro corazón la fé segura de que hay una madre tierna y cariñosa que se llama Sociedad de Protección Mutua, que en nuestra última hora de existencia nos impartirá los auxilios bienhechores que toda madre prodiga al fruto de su vientre, y ya en nuestra última morada, regará nuestro sepulcro con las lágrimas del consuelo y plantará la siempre-viva fraternal.

Considerando que para que esta sociedad sea estable y duradera es requerido sujetarla a una constitución y reglamentos por las leyes de esta República, hemos tomado carta de incorporación y de autoridad en el estado de Colorado, así como también hemos hecho nuestra Constitución, Leyes y Regulaciones, las que en otro lugar de este libro estampamos y por las cuales seremos governados.

A. F. Márquez   Epifanio García   Eligio Ruybal

[Desiring all those who have undersigned this preamble to form a legally constituted society and protected under the laws of the United States of America and the State of Colorado in particular, we have met and in common agreement determine the following:

To form a fraternal society . . . to carry the name SOCIETY OF MUTUAL PROTECTION OF WORKERS UNITED, headquartered in the town of Antonito, Conejos County, State of Colorado . . . and that said society shall be established for the objectives explicated as follows:

Considering that all civilized nations in the world have organized fraternal societies or other groups suitable for the protection, enlightenment, and progress of its members, and ourselves desiring to enter the road to prosperity, progress, and enlightenment, with this incorporation we undertake a reform of major importance to the society by the same name, which we incorporate today, and that was founded on the 26th of November, 1900 A.D., by the Honorable Celedonio Mondragón, in order to carry on with the same objectives for which it was founded, to wit, for the protection of each of the members who compose it, assisting the members who are invalid and needy as well as their widows and orphans and all other persons who through some blood relation are united with a member of this society; to mitigate the ravages and sorrows of life; to protect each other against the injustices of tyrants and despots, the usurpers of law and justice, and those who steal our lives, honor, and property, so that it may serve as the guardian protector of our families and our interests; to stretch out our brotherly hand in the midst of our joys, fortunes, and misfortunes and our torment; to walk in the course highway of life with our eyes engulfed by tears of joy, with a truthful smile on our lips, and with our foreheads lifted by the laurel of triumph and of humanity, and in this manner proceeding in our life we carry engraved in our heart the certain faith that there is a kind and loving Mother known as the Society of Mutual Protection that in our final hour will impart to us beneficent assistance that every mother lavishes on the fruit of her womb, and in our final resting place our sepulcher will be washed with tears of consolation and will be planted with the evergreen leaf of fraternity.

Considering that in order to make this society stable and lasting, it is necessary to subject it to a constitution and regulations under the laws of this Republic, we have taken a certificate of incorporation under the authority of the State of Colorado as well as developed our Constitution, Laws and Regulations, that we have certified elsewhere in this book and under which we shall be governed.

A. F. Márquez   Epifanio García   Eligio Ruybal]

Beneficios de Funeral (Funeral Benefits and Services) 1922

The Constitution and General Regulations of 1922 included a detailed account of the benefits offered by the SPMDTU under a certificate of life insurance valued at $500 along with other special payments. Article XXXVIII stipulated that in addition to the certificate of insurance, the families of deceased members were entitled to receive a $25 cash supplement to help pay for a portion of the funeral expenses. Local council members in turn were required to guard the body of the deceased, attend the funeral services, and pay their last respects at the burial site. (Source: Constitución y Reglamento de la Sociedad de Protección Mutua, 1922, José A. Rivera Papers, Box 8, Folder 3.)

BENEFICIOS DE FUNERAL

Se llaman beneficios de funeral a aquellos otorgados por el Concilio Superior a la muerte de algún miembro activo de la Sociedad como un extra a su póliza de vida. Este beneficio será de $25.00 en efectivo los cuales se pagarán del fondo de pólizas. Esta suma será entregada a la familia del finado, tomando recibio de ella para que conste en el libro de registro del Tesorero.

[We call funeral benefits those authorized by the Concilio Superior upon the death of an active member of the Society as a supplement to the life insurance policy.

This benefit will be $25.00 in cash that will be paid from the Policy Fund. This amount will be turned over to the family of the deceased, with a receipt taken to enter into the Treasurer's Ledger.]

(a) En caso desgraciado de la muerte de un miembro de esta Sociedad, es obligación de los miembros del Concilio al cual pertenecía el finado, atender en el acto al lugar de la defunción para tomar información o pormenores del caso.

(b) En todo caso de defunción el Presidente local o el oficial más inmediato nombrará una commission de no menos de cuatro miembros para que atiendan al lugar del finado y tomen los primeros pasos para el arreglo del velorio, asistencia, funeral, etc.

(c) El Presidente o el oficial inmediato notificará en el acto y por cualquier medio possible a los demás miembros del concilio, la noticia de la defunción para que se presenten al lugar.

(d) El Presidente o el oficial inmediato notificará en el acto por cualquier medio possible a los demás Concilios para que atiendan por medio de representantes a las ceremonias que se tributarán al finado. Estas notificaciones serán de preferencia al Concilio Superior.

(e) Cuando un miembro sea notificado de tal defunción, está obligado a presentarse al lujar donde esté el cuerpo, a menos que tenga excusa legal.

(f) El Presidente o el oficial inmediato nombrará en el acto tantas comisiones cuantas crea propicias para el mejor arreglo de los negocios, ya sea de guardias al cuerpo, sepultura, velorio, acarreo del cuerpo, orden de formación, oradores, etc.

(g) Las guardias se harán de día y de noche por todos los miembros del Concilio, turnándose de dos en dos cada media hora. Dichas guardias estarán a la cabecera del cuerpo y permanecerán con todo respeto en ese puesto.

(h) Todos los miembros del Concilio cumplirán con la mayor obediencia y punctualidad la comisión que les sea designada, a menos de que tengan una exusa legal.

(i) En todo caso de defunción, el cuerpo social oficialmente no intervendrá en asuntos religiosos de ningún credo, según lo estipula el Artículo VIII de nuestra constitución. Por tal motivo no se tributarán ningunos servicios religiosos por parte de esta Sociedad.

(j) Es deber de cada uno de los miembros de cada Concilio, acompañar al cuerpo de un hermano finado desde la casa o lugar en que se encuentre tendido, al sitio religioso que su familia o parientes lo deseen llevar.

(k) Según la marca el Artículo XXVIII de nuestro Reglamento en las Sec. 1 letra (b) todo miembro de cada Concilio está en la obligación de presentarse al lugar designado con su devisa y en la procesión oficial portarán sus insignias según su categoría.

(l) Queda bien ententido que todos los miembros de cada Concilio se presentarán al ser notificados para asistir al funeral de un socio finado según lo marca el Artículo XXVIII del Reglamento, en la Sec. 1, letra (f) a menos que haya excusa legal.

(m) Después de terminada la última ceremonia, o sea después de haber depositado el cuerpo del socio finado en su última morada, todos los miembros presentes regresarán en orden de formación a la sala de sesiones del Concilio, donde se tendrá un junta especial para determiner sobre los últimos negocios relativos al socio finado.

[*(a)* In the unfortunate event of death of a Society member, the members of the corresponding local council are obligated to take action and visit the location of the death to obtain information about or the details of the case.

(b) In all cases of death, the local President of the officer nearest shall appoint a commission of not fewer than four members to visit the home of the deceased and take steps to make arrangements for the wake, assistance, the funeral, etc.

(c) The President or the nearest officer shall take action and notify through any means possible the rest of the council members, with notice of the death so they may present themselves there.

(d) The President or the nearest officer shall take action and notify immediately through any means possible the other councils so they may designate representatives to attend the ceremonies in tribute to the deceased. These notices should preferably be sent to the Superior Council.

(e) When a member is notified of a death, he is obligated to present himself at the place where the body of the deceased is located, unless he has a legal excuse.

(f) The President or nearest officer shall take action and immediately appoint as many commissions as he deems appropriate to arrange all business matters efficiently, such as for honor guards over the body, the grave, the wake, carrying of the body, the procession order, eulogy orators, etc.

(g) The honor guard duties shall take place all day and night on the part of all council members, taking turns every half-hour. These guards shall position themselves at the front of the casket and remain there with all respect in that position.

(h) All council members shall comply with obedience and punctuality in any commission they are assigned, unless they have a legal excuse.

(i) In the case of all deaths, the society shall not intervene in the religious affairs of any creed, in accordance with Article VIII of our constitution. For

this same reason, no payments for religious services shall be made on the part of this Society.

(j) It shall be the duty of each council member to accompany the body of the deceased member from his residence or where he has been attended and to the religious site that his family or relatives have selected.

(k) In accordance with Article XXVIII of our Regulations in section 1 (b), each member of the council is obligated to present himself at the designated location with his devisa and display his insignia during the official procession per his position.

(l) It shall be understood that all members of the council must present themselves upon notification to attend the funeral of a deceased member in according with Article XXVIII of the Regulations, section 1 (f), unless they have a legal excuse.

(m) After the funeral ceremony is completed or after the body of the deceased member is laid to rest, all the members present shall return in the order of the set formation to the council meeting hall, where they will convene a special meeting to determine the final business matters relative to the deceased member.]

Ceremonia de Difuntos
(Ceremony for the Deceased)

The hermanos and hermanas of the local concilio honor in many ways those members who pass away. One of the most moving events is a special ceremony conducted in the meeting hall after the transport of the deceased to that location as prescribed in the Código Ritualístico de Régimen Interior (Code of Rituals and Internal Regulations) adopted in 1922 and revised 1926. After the members arrive and assume their designated places inside the hall, the president calls the meeting to order and ensures that only eligible members are present by requesting that the semiannual password be taken. He then instructs the members to stand as he begins the Ceremonia de Cuerpo Presente in accordance with section 4 of the Ceremonia de Difuntos dentro de la Sala de Reuniones. (Source: SPMDTU Records, Box 1, Folder 1, Center for Southwest Research, University Libraries, University of New Mexico, Albuquerque.)

a. Se llamará la lista del Concilio a la que cada uno responderá.

b. El Presidente preguntará al miembro finado, por tres veces con intervalos, desde su puesto, lo siguiente: "Hermano . . . ¿por qué no responde Ud.? Su deber es responder: ¡Responda Ud. Hermano!"

c. En seguida pasará el Mariscal junto al cuerpo y poniendo su mano derecha sobre el cadáver, dirá al Presidente con voz fuerte: "Hermano Presidente, nuestro hermano muerto es . . . [nombre del hermano]." El Mariscal se estará en este lugar hasta terminar la procesión de vista.

d. Después de las palabras del Mariscal, el Presidente pasará seguido de los demás miembros presentes (según plano 4) dando vista al cuerpo y tomarán de nuevo sus puestos.

e. Cuando todos estén en sus puestos, el Presidente dirá al Concilio, "Oficiales y Hermanos, todos hemos visto que nuestro hermano es muerto. ¿Qué debemos de hacer?"

f. El Calificador tomará la palabra y dirá: "Hermano Presidente y hermanos, hago moción que la Sociedad cumpla en todas sus partes lo referente al Reglamento General a los hermanos difuntos."

g. El Mariscal secundará la moción y el Presidente la llamará en el orden regular.

h. En seguida el Calificador parasá a la cabecera del finado y poniendo la mano derecha sobre la cabeza del hermano difunto, dirá: "hermano, como Calificador de este Concilio lo declaró intitulado a los beneficios de esta Sociedad."

i. El Presidente dirá: "Que así sea."

j. En seguida pasará el Presidente a la cabecera del finado y con pocas palabras y a lo menos de su capacidad, dará la despedida al finado y poniendo como ejemplo a los miembros presentes los beneficios que la sociedad imparte a los miembros activos.

k. Al terminar de hablar, el Presidente, éste seguido de los miembros presentes, pasarán en el orden indicado en el plano 4, por la cabecera del finado y cada uno al llegar a este lugar con el mayor respecto dirá, "Adios Hermano mío."

l. Cuando el último de los presentes termine de hablar, el Concilio tomará o pasará a tomar orden de formación, según el plano 5 para conducir el cadáver al lugar religioso correspondiente a su credo.

[a. The membership list of the Council shall be read with responses from those present.

b. The President will ask the deceased member, three times with intervals, from his position, the following: "Brother . . . why do you not respond? It is your duty to respond. Respond, Brother!"

c. Then the Marshall will walk next to the corpse and place his right hand on the cadaver and will reply to the President in a loud voice: "Brother

President, our deceased brother is . . . (name of brother)." The Marshall will remain in this position until the end of the viewing procession.

d. After the words spoken by the Marshall, the President will pass and will be followed by the rest of the members (in accordance with plan 4) to view the corpse, after which they all resume their places.

e. When everyone is in their places, the President will address the Council: "Officers and Brothers, we all have seen that our brother is deceased. What shall we do?"

f. The Qualifier shall then address the members and respond: "Brother President and brothers, I move that the Society comply with all its obligations stated in the General Regulations regarding deceased brothers."

g. The Marshall will second the motion and the President will call (for a vote) in the normal order.

h. Next, the Qualifier will walk to the head of the deceased, and, placing his right hand on the forehead of the deceased brother, he will say: "Brother, as the Qualifier of this Council I declare that you are entitled to the benefits of this Society."

i. The President will confirm: "It shall be so."

j. Then the President will walk to the head of the deceased, and in a few words no less than his abilities he will express his farewell to the deceased and give examples of the benefits to the members who are present that the society provides to active members.

k. At the conclusion of his remarks, the President will be followed by the members present in the order indicated in plan 4 to the head of the deceased, and as each arrives at this location, he will express with the utmost respect, "Farewell, my brother."

l. When the last member says his farewell, the Council will assemble in formation, in accordance with plan 5, to transport the cadaver to the religious place in accordance to his creed.]

Minutes of Superior Council Special Meeting 1917

On September 15, 1917, the Superior Council convened to consider a request from Council No. 5 of Ortiz, Colorado, that the SPMDTU approve the life insurance and funeral benefits of their deceased brother Apolinario Durán. The local officers appeared before the Superior Council and attested to the fact that Hermano Apolinario had been an active member of the concilio local and that therefore his family was entitled to society benefits. In response, the Superior Council named a commission of three members to express condolences and deliver to the widow a money order payable to her for the life insurance and burial funds due to the family. In accordance with the society's customs and practice, a second commission was named to author resolutions of condolence for presentation to the family. Here are the minutes from this meeting. (Source: SPMDTU Records, Journal of Minutes, Concilio Superior, 1917, Box 18.)

Junta especial del Concilio Superior, por razón de la defunción del Hno. Apolinario Durán.

El Mariscal tomó el paso anual y reporta el concilio correcto, y en seguida se resó la oración de apertura.

Se llamó la lista por el secretario. . . . Por moción hecha y llevada la orden del día fue suspendida, para atender al asunto de la difunción de Hno. Difunto Apolinario Durán. En seguida se presentaron los oficiales locales del Concilio No. 5 de Ortiz, Colo., y testifican que el hermano Apolinario Durán, se hallaba activo y intitulado a los beneficios de nuestra sociedad. Por moción hecha y llevada la comisión siguiente fue nombrada por la silla, para que imparta los beneficios y dé el pésame a la familia del difunto, sigue: hnos. J. Santiago Valdez, Severo Salazar, y Rafael Valdez. Por moción hecha y llevada, los hnos. Bonifacio Gonzalez, Fructuoso Chávez, y Hermán Chávez, como comisión para redactor resoluciones de condolencia. Estando y hallándose el hno. difunto Apolinario Durán activo y correcto, por lo tanto se ordenó y se le giró un giro en favor de la señora Teresita R. Durán, pago lleno, por beneficios de funeral y póliza del hno. Apolinario Durán. Por moción hecha y llevada, la orden del día fue dispensada. Por mocián hecha y llevada la junta fue porrogada hasta su término regular o llamada del Regidor.

Fidel E. García   Atestiguó: Melitón Velásquez, Secretario Superior
Regidor Superior

Petition to Indigence Fund 1923: San Miguel Council No. 10

The letter given here was prepared in 1923 by the concilio local of San Miguel, New Mexico, and submitted to the Superior Council in Antonito. In summary, the officers petitioned that the SPMDTU provide financial assistance to one of their members, José Victor Archuleta, who had been incapacitated and was unable to work and support his wife and daughter due to a paralysis illness that had lasted some three years. At the time, the Superior Council administered a special Indigence Fund to provide emergency relief to members who were unemployed, ill, or disabled. The officers from San Miguel noted that the local council had already provided some financial assistance from its own fund, and in this letter they requested additional support from the SPMDTU Indigence Fund. (Source: SPMDTU Records, MSS 696 BC, Box 1, Folder 4.)

SPMDTU
Concilio Número 10
Oficinia del Secretario
San Miguel, N. Mex. 12/29, 1923

Nosotros los abajo firmados por medio de esta declaración jurada hemos jurado solemmemente bajo un Dios todo poderoso que lo que aquí declaramos es la verdad y nada mas que la verdad. El Hno. J. V. Archuleta es un miembro activo de este con. no. 10 de SMPdeTU, San Miguel, N. Mex., y por espacio de 3 años el dicho Hno. viene padeciendo una penosa enferme- dad de parálises y a la presente se haya encapacitado de trabajo para ganarse la vida, y es un Hno. avanzado en edad y hombre pobre que no posea ningu- nos bienes ni personales ni propiedad. Mas tiene a su esposa y una niña en su poder. Nosotros lo hemos llevado ayudándole de nuestros fondos y otros auxilios adicionales, y ahora por lo tanto pidemos del Con. Superior que este Hno. sea ayudado de los Fondos de Indigencia y así quedamos a vuestra orden, y para que coste la frimamos.

Daniel Gallegos, Presidente
Pat. Archuleta, Secretario
Doy fe, Frank Archuleta, Calificador

Treasurer's Ledger 1931: Arroyo Seco Council No. 42

The treasurer of each local council is required to maintain a ledger of income and expenses for reporting to the officers and the members on a regular basis. Here the incoming treasurer of the Arroyo Seco Council No. 42, Raymundo García, dutifully notes the amount of balance he received from the outgoing treasurer, Juan B. Valdez, and then details the transactions during his first two months in office, November 1931 to January 1932. Income received included the monthly and semiannual dues as well as the income from the sale of cigarettes that was left over from the local council's anniversary event. Expenses included the local council's various needs and the upkeep of the meeting hall, such as the purchase of ledgers, money orders to mail members' dues to the Superior Council in Antonito, stamps for correspondence, oil for lamps, a chimney for the wooden stove, matches, and a lock for the door. (Note: The original spelling of words has been retained even in cases of errors. See SPMDTU Records, Box 5, for the rest of the ledger and other related documents from Council No. 42.)

Nov. 25th, 1931

Reseví yó, Raymundo García, tesorero entrante, la suma de $32.63 dinero en mano, y $81.33 en notas, un total de $114.00 del tesorero sesante, Juan B. Valdez.

INGRESOS

11–25–31. Deposité 90 ct [centavos] que pagó el Hermano J. T. Martínez por sigarros quo compró del sobrante de nuestro aniverzario. .90 ct

A[de]más, este mesmo día deposité 10 ct que pagó el Hrno. J. B. Valdez por una caja de cigarros. .10 ct

Amás este mesmo día deposité 35 ct que devía yó Raymundo García por unos cigarros .35 ct

11–25–31. Deposité $1.50 que pagó el Hermano E. Mares por la cuota semianual del Concilio Local $1.50

12–2–31. Deposité $1.50 que pagó el hrno. Torivio Martínez y $1.50 que pagó el hrno. Melquiades Madrid por la cuota semianual del Concilio Local $3.00

Amás 25 ct que pagó el Hrno. Toribio M. por los mensuales por Sept. .25

12–17–31. Deposité $3.00 por la cuota semianual por los hrnos. J. B. Valdez y R. C. Martínez $1.50 cada uno. $3.00

12–17–31. Deposité $4.50 que pagaron los hermanos Verjilio A. García y Agustín García y Raymundo García por la cuota semianual del Concilio Local $4.50

12–26–31. Deposité $1.50 por el hermano Juan Sánchez por la cuota semianual del Concilio Local $1.50

12–28–31. Deposité por el hrno. Melitón Martínez $1.50 el seminanual local y $2.25 por los mensuales por 9 meses y 50 ct por el finado P. D. Martínez $4.25

1–7–32. Deposité 25 ct que pagó el Hrno. J. B. Valdez por el mensual de un mes .25

. . . .

1–22–32. Deposité $1.50 que pagó el Hrno. Román Durán por su semianual local y amás pagó $1.25 mensuales por 5 meses y $26.50 pago una nota que devía y réditos 52 ct   Total $29.77

11–30–31. Saqué $1.35 para comprar un livro para uso
de registros $1.35

12–17–31. Fueron sacados 20 ct para comprar aceite para uso
de la caza   .20

12–17–31. Fueron sacados $3.85 para mandar la cuota
semianual del Hrno. Lucas Pacheco, cuales fueron
prestados por el Concilio No. 42 $3.85

12–22–31. Fueron sacados 15 ct para pagar una money
order de $28.20 semianuales de seis hermanos   .15

12–28–31. Fueron sacados 10 ct para mandar el seminanual
del Hrno. J. Sánchez   .10

12–29–31. Fueron sacados 10 ct para pagar una money
order de $6.25 del Hrno. Melitón Martínez   .10

1–7–32. Saqué 50 ct para comprar un livro de notas   .50

1–17–32. Fueron sacados 10 ct para pagar al Hrno. Gaspar
Gonzales los cuales fueron incluídos en su semianual   .10

1–18–32. Saqué 25 ct para comprar estampas para uso de las
correspondencias   .25

. . .

2–1–32. Fueron sacados 15 ct para comprar un chiflón y 25 ct
para comprar un candado y 5 ct para comprar mechas   .45

Carta Circular (Circular Letter) 1970: Ogden Council No. 61

Under conditions of catastrophic illnesses, disabilities, or long-term care, local councils did not have sufficient reserves to extend benefits to members indefinitely. With the Superior Council's permission, concilios locales corresponded with other concilios in a carta circular to augment whatever could be mobilized locally, as in this appeal for "obra de caridad" from the officers of Council No. 61 in Ogden, Utah, to Council No. 42 in Arroyo Seco, New Mexico. The request for cash donations was made on behalf of an elderly member from Brigham City who had been released from the hospital but was unable to find steady employment due to the severity of his illness and diminished vision. The member remained in good standing with the SPMDTU during his illness thanks to his wife, who kept up with the payment of dues to the local council. The letter was signed by the officers of Council No. 61 and circulated to Arroyo Seco and other councils in the tristate area of Colorado, New Mexico, and Utah. (Source: Treasurer's Ledger, 1949–73, SPMDTU Records, Box 5.)

Concilio No. 61
Ogden, Utah
August 28, 1970
Al Presidente Concilio #42:

Salud: Hermano, hemos obtenido permizo de nuestro Presidente Superior Hno. Pancracio Romero, para circular cartas a los diferentes Concilios de nuestra Sociedad para una ayuda voluntaria, para ayudar a uno de nuestros hermanos que responde al nombre de Narciso Velásquez de Brigham City, Utah, miembro de este local. Este hermano a estado muy enfermo, en el hospital y ahora en la casa. Este hermano, ya viejito y haciendose ciego, no puede consiguir trabajos estables. Siempre, con la ayuda de Dios, y su amble esposa, se quadra en sus cuotas y está en buenas cuentas con su amable Orden "La Sociedad." Este hermano a suplicado ayuda de este Local; él no pidiera se no lo necesitaba.

Por lo tanto, pidemos de Vds que muestren una obra de caridad para este hermano, quien verdaderamente necesita vuestra ayuda en tan deplorable condición de salud. Por consiguiente suplicamos de Vds que manden sus contribuciones directamente al hermano Louis Payán, tesorero local de este Concilio: 5947 S. 2200 W, Roy, Utah, 84067

Ubaldo López, Pres.
Louis Payán, Treas.
Demetrio Trujillo, Consejero

Himno Oficial (Official Hymn) of the SPMDTU

SPMDTU general conventions begin with the singing of the official hymn after a procession into the meeting hall in double file. The SPMDTU flag is featured prominently during the hymn and remains displayed at the front stage for the rest of the convention proceedings. The colors of the flag are red, white, and blue in alternating bands, with the letters "SPMDTU" across the bands and the seal of the society in the middle, showing clasped hands within a circle. The members sing the hymn in unison to the accompaniment of a guitar, saluting the flag and clasping hands with members on the opposite row in sync with the lyrics. The lyrics were composed by J. R. Valdez to the tune of the American Civil War song *"The Battle Cry of Freedom,"* composed in 1862 by George F. Root. *(Source: The version given here is printed in the Código Ritualístico de Régimen Interior, revised 1980, SPMDTU Records, Box 1, Folder 1.)*

Hispano-Americanos	Hispanic Americans
Al son de la libertad,	To the sound of liberty
Estrechémosnos las manos,	Let us extend our hands
Estrechémosnos las manos	Let extend our hands
Con amor y caridad,	With love and charity
Estrechémosnos las manos.	Let us extend our hands.
CORO	CHORUS
¡Juremos ser LIBRES	Let us pledge to be FREE
Y viva la UNION!	And long live the UNION!
¡Que viva la LIGA	Long live our LEAGUE
DE MUTUA PROTECCION!	OF MUTUAL PROTECTION!
Defendemos su Bandera	We defend her Flag
Con nuestras Fuerzas y Unión	With all our Strength and Unity
Defendemos su Bandera.	We defend her Flag.
Defender nuestros derechos	We defend our rights
Nuestra patria y nuestro honor	Our country and our honor
Y sostener nuestros hechos	And sustain our deeds
Y sostener nuestros hechos	And sustain our deeds
Con firmeza y con valor	With firmness and valor
Y sostener nuestros hechos.	And sustain our deeds.
CORO	CHORUS
Lidiemos por la justicia	Let us fight for justice
La verdad y la razón	For truth and reason
Y que muera la malicia	And death to malice
Y que muera la malicia	And death to malice
Cobardía y la traición,	Cowardice and treason,
Y que muera la malicia.	And death to malice.
CORO	CHORUS
Estrechémosnos las manos	Let us extend our hands
Con sinceridad y amor	With sincerity and love

Como libres ciudadanos	As free citizens
Como libres ciudadanos	As free citizens
Amemos nuestra Nación,	Let us love our Nation
Como libres ciudadanos.	As free citizens.
CORO	CHORUS
Sigamos nuestra Bandera	Let us follow our Flag
Con fidelidad y honor	With loyalty and honor
Y firmeza verdadera	And truthful fimness
Y firmeza verdadera	And truthful firmness
Sin reproche y sin temor	Without fear and reproach
Y firmeza verdadera.	And truthful firmness.
CORO	CHORUS
Por fin, queridos hermanos,	And finally, dear brothers,
Hagamos nuestro deber	Let's perform our duties
Como fieles ciudadanos	As loyal citizens
Como fieles ciudadanos	As loyal citizens
Hasta morir o vencer	Until we die or prevail
Como fieles ciudadanos.	As loyal citizens.
CORO	CHORUS

Constitución y Reglamento (Constitution and Regulations) of La Sociedad AMB 1937, Revised 1964

Antonito, Colorado, was home to at least three women's auxiliaries whose memberships often overlapped with the membership of the SPMDTU made up of their husbands. The auxiliary with the most evident ties to the SMPDTU was called La Sociedad Auxiliarias Mutuas Beneficiarias, also known by its initials, La Sociedad AMB. The meeting hall for the AMB was in a building adjacent to the Superior Council headquarters on Main Street. Here the women conducted their own business meetings and often prepared food for SPMDTU social functions and anniversaries. Their devisa was designed with the fraternal symbol similar to the SPMDTU's, two hands outstretched and clasping in friendship at the top of the ribbon, followed by the society's name and near the bottom the initials "S.P.M.D.T.U." Despite the auxilary's close relationship to the SPMDTU, the women governed the AMB based on their own constitution and regulations from their founding in 1937 and into the 1960s, when they revised this document. Like the SPMDTU, La Sociedad AMB convened general conventions in Antonito every year, at which the delegates from the local auxiliaries elected officers to serve on the AMB's Superior Council. Included here are portions of the AMB General Constitution and Regulations from a booklet that belonged to María Filomena Trujillo-Archuleta (1890–1982), courtesy of one her grandsons, SPMDTU member Ruben Archuleta, Antonito Council No. 1.

Preámbulo

Nosotros las abajo firmadas beneficiarias legales, que nos amparamos bajo el Preámbulo, Constitución, y Reglamento de la sociedad que lleva por nombre, Auxiliarias Mutuas Beneficiarias, tenemos una sociedad fraternal que se compone de miembras del sexo femenino, y la Sociedad Auxiliaria Mutua Beneficiaria ampara a tales miembras hasta su muerte y sepultura.

Esta sociedad es constituida originalmente para la protección y ayuda de todas las miembras que la forman en establecer la paz y armonía entre las mismas, cooperando siempre para promover los buenos ideales de moralidad, el respecto y buena crianza entre nuestra prole, considerando que es un deber absoluto de toda madre de familia, y que es el más precioso heredaje que una madre puede dejar al fruto de su vientre.

Esta sociedad se extiende a doce cuidades del estado de Colorado. Esta sociedad fue organizada actualmente para señoras y madres de familia de buenas costumbres, morales, y sociales, que tengan el amor fraternal y desean unirse con el mismo propósito para el cual esta sociedad ha sido organizada. Para que de esta sociedad puédamos sacar beneficios que de ella se derivan hacemos un reglamento por el cual seremos gobernadas.

Constitución General de la Auxiliaria Mutua Beneficiaria

Artículo 1. Esta sociedad será conocida con el nombre de Auxiliarias Mutuas Beneficiarias.

Artículo 2. Es propósito de esta sociedad es protección mutua, paz y armonía.

Artículo 3. Esta sociedad será pública en su representación, pero secreta en su manejo interior.

Artículo 4. Esta sociedad se esmerará siempre en todo lo qe le sea posible por el adelanto y progreso de la A. M. B.

Artículo 5. Esta sociedad se entenderá solamente a cuidades en el estado de Colorado.

Artículo 6. Podrán ser admitidas en esta sociedad señoras de entre los 18 y 55 años de edad que cumplan según provisto en nuestro preámbulo.

Artículo 7. Todas las miembras de que se componga esta sociedad deberán ser de decendencia hispano-americana.

Artículo 8. La patria de esta sociedad estará dentro de los límites de Colorado, y la capital de ella será la plaza de Antonito, Condado de Conejos, Estado de Colorado.

Artículo 9. Los concilios o Auxiliares Locales serán libres en su manejo local, no desviándose del propósito para el cual estos Auxiliares han sido originalmente organizados.

[Artículos 10–19] . . .

Reglamento General

Artículo 1.

Sección 1. El tribunal más alto de esta sociedad será el Concilio Superior, el cual se compondrá de nueve miembras, las cuales serán electas según proveído por la constitución.

Sección 2. El concilio superior se reunirá cuatro veces cada año. . . .

Sección 3. . . .

Sección 4. El Concilio Superior suplirá sus propias insignias, tales como emblemas, devisas, sellos, y tendrá que designar los colores de uniforme y cachucha y cuándo serán usados.

[Secciones 5, 6, 7, 8] . . .

[Artículos 2–32] . . .

Artículo 33. Deberes y Obligaciones a las Miembras Finadas

Sección 1. En caso de la muerte de una miembra de la Sociedad, será el deber del Concilio Local al cual dicha miembra pertenese y las miembras de dicho concilio pagarán sus últimos respetos a la miembra finada, y conducirán los último ritos según proveídos por la sociedad.

Sección 2. Si miembra y beneficario mueren juntos se pagará el beneficio doble.

[Secciones 3–7] . . .

Artículo 34. Cuotas de Defunción

Sección 1. Se llamarán cuotas de defunción aquellas las ordenadas por el concilio superior con objeto de colectar fondos para cubrir a la defunción de alguna miembra que muera y tenga sus cuotas y devitas pagadas.

Sección 2. Estas cuotas serán colectadas por las tesoreras locales y remitidas a la Tersorera Superior para que sea cubierta la defunción, y entregado el dinero a la persona asignada por la finada.

Sección 3. Las cuotas de defunción deberán ser pagadas al recibir la noti-ficicación y de no hacerlo así, se le dará un plaza de 30 días con beneficio y 15 días sin beneficio. Si al finalizar el último día del segundo plazo no se paga la cuota, quedarán completamente separadas de la Sociedad las miembras delinquentes.

[Secciones 4–10] . . .

[Artículos 35–36] . . .

Artículo 37. Devisas y Emblemas

Sección 1. Solamente las miembras de esta Sociedad portarán el botón oficial de la misma.

Sección 2. Todas las devisas y emblemas serán uniformes menos las del Concilio de Denver, Colorado. El cambio que pidió Denver fue acceptado por el Concilio Superior.

Sección 3. Los botones y devisas que usen las miembras al ser inciadas serán prestadas a ellas solamente durante la ceremonia.

Sección 4. Se espera que cada miembra porte su botón en todas las juntas.

Artículo 38. Organización de Concilios Locales

Sección 1. La Presidenta Superior tendrá poder para nombrar no más que dos organizadoras para el fin de organizar concilios nuevos según espeficicado en la ley. Esto será si alguna vez tendrá que organizar otro concilio.

[Secciones 2–7] . . .

Sección 8. Tal organización de un nuevo concilio será conforme prescrito por las leyes, reglas y regulaciones del Concilio Superior.

Sección 9. El número de miembras requeridos para organizar un concilio nuevo será no menos de diez.

[Sección 10] . . .

[Artículos 39–46] . . .

Artículo 47. Bandera de la Sociedad

Sección 1. La bandera de la sociedad y sus colores serán rojo, blanco y verde y tendrán las iniciales A.M.B. en el centro de los tres colores.

Artículo 48. Vestidos y Estandartes

Sección 1. El concilio que desea tener estandarte podrá tenerlo.

Sección 2. Los vestidos serán azueles siendo túnico con el cuello y los puños blancos.

Sección 3. Todos los concilios locales pueden usar vestidos y cachuchas, y devisas cuando sean invitadas por alguna organización o atiendan un funeral de una miembra o de un beneficario.

Himno Oficial (Official Hymn) of La Sociedad AMB

This hymn was composed by J. R. Valdez to the Tune of "Home Sweet Home."
SPMDTU member Ruben Archuleta, Antonito Council No. 1, provided a copy
to José A. Rivera from the materials that his grandmother, María Filomena
Trujillo-Archuleta, collected. It is included in the AMB Constitution booklet.

Dedicado por J. R. Valdez.

Unión de las mujeres	Union of women
Unión bien protejida,	Well-protected Union,
En todos los quehaceres	In all of our tasks
Eres valor y vida.	You are valor and life.
CORO	CHORUS
¡Unión! ¡Unión	Union ! Union
De Mutua Protección !	Of Mutual Protection !
En ti está la esperanza,	In you is hope,
La fe del corazón.	The faith of the heart.
Mujeres Auxiliares	Auxilliary Women
De Mutua Protección,	Of Mutual Protection,
Defendemos los lares	We defend our hearths
En nuestro honor y unión.	In our honor and union.
Marchemos adelante,	Let us march forward,
Marchemos con valor,	Let us march with valor,
En paso muy constante	With very constant stride
Y crecido vigor.	And growing vigor.
Ese sacro estandarte	That sacred standard
Que siempre ha de flotar,	That will always float,
Nos levanta un baluarte,	Raises up a barricade,
Protección del hogar.	Protection for the hearth.
Publíquese ante el mundo	May it be published before the world
Los bienes de esta unión,	The benefits of this union,
Con un amor profundo	With a profound love
Con fe en el corazón.	With faith in the heart.

Llevemos la porfía	Let us carry our resistance
Con un valor sincero	With valor sincere
Por fin llegará el día	The day will finally arrive
De un triunfo verdadero.	Of a real triumph.

Caminemos unidas	May we walk united
Este bello camino.	This beautiful road.
Que corone las vidas	That crowns our lives
Un glorioso destino.	A glorious destiny.

¡Que viva la bandera	Long live the flag,
Levántese el pendón !	Raise up the pendant !
¡Viva la unión entera	Long live the whole union
De Mutua Protección!	Of Mutual Protection !

Himno Oficial (Official Hymn) of
La Sociedad Femenil de Protección

La Sociedad Femenil de Protección (SFDP) was another of the women's auxiliaries affiliated with the SPMDTU. Like the men's organization, the SFDP was founded on the principle of unity for mutual protection to include funeral services for deceased members, as alluded to in the society's official hymn. The himno oficial of the SFDP, along with the Constitution and Regulations of La Sociedad AMB, were provided to SPMDTU member Ruben Archuleta by his grandmother María Filomena Trujillo-Archuleta. Her husband, Francisco Antonio Archuleta (1883–1951), joined the Antonito Council No. 1 in 1915, was also a penitente at Los Pinos, New Mexico, and later served as the hermano mayor of the morada at San Antonio, Colorado, after the two cofradías merged. Ruben Archuleta recalls that his grandmother Filomena, born in 1890 in Las Mesitas, Colorado, belonged to three women's auxiliaries and faithfully paid her membership dues to each society: the SFDP, La Sociedad AMB, and La Sociedad Protectora Cooperativa. From her meager old-age pension, she also contributed to the Fondo de Defunción collected when other members passed away—not only those from Antonito, but also others who lived in the surrounding communities, such as La Jara and Manassa—and she kept meticuluous receipts along with songs, pins, devisas, constitutions, and other records. The SFDP and the Sociedad Protectora Cooperativa had their own adobe building as their meeting hall located by the railroad tracks in Antonito. Ruben Archuleta also recalls that the ladies wore uniforms consisting of caps and capes when attending funerals, processions, and other events and were also very businesslike and patriotic. (Source: Ruben Archuleta, copy e-mailed to José A. Rivera, November 12, 2003, May 29 and June 20, 2007.)

¡Gracias a Dios ya llegó	Thanks to God it has arrived
La Protección Femenil !	The Feminine Protection !
Bajo el seno de la Unión	Under the breast of the Union
Que proteja el porvenir	May it protect the future
De nuestra vida al morir.	Of our lives upon our death.
Hará un recuerdo de amor	It will leave a memory of love
Y nos llevará al panteón,	And will carry us to the cemetery,
La Sociedad Femenil.	The Feminine Society.

CORO	CHORUS
Hoy con gusto y con amor	Today with pleasure and love
Todas debemos decir,	We should all say,
¡Viva, viva nuestra Unión	Long live our Union
De Protección Femenil !	Of Feminine Protection !

Compañeras, compañeras,	Companions, companions,
¡Levantemos el pendón	Let us raise the pendant
De Nuestra gran Sociedad	Of our great Society of
Femenil de Protección!	Feminie Protection!
Todas estamos resueltas	We all are resolved
En mantener el honor	To maintain the honor
De esta nuestra Sociedad	Of this our Society
Que es de importancia y valor.	Which is of importance and worth.

CORO	CHORUS

Hoy se nos ha presentado	Today has been presented
El deber y obligación	The duty and obligation
De promover con agencia	Of promoting with agency
Esta causa y su misión.	This cause and its mission.
La Sociedad Femenil	May the Society of Feminine
De Protección nos proteja.	Protection protect us.
Les dan grandes garantías	It gives great guarantees
Con que la mujer se abriga.	With which a woman is guarded.

CORO	CHORUS

Nuestra Unión es liberal	Our Union is generous
Y de noble corazón.	And of noble heart.
Cultivar quiere el amor	It wants to cultivate love
De todas en general,	Of all in general,
Y darnos su protección,	And we give it protection,
Y cuidar de nuestro hogar,	And care of our home,
Y así desea elevar	And thus it wants to raise up
En nosotros el amor.	In us love.

CORO   CHORUS

Esta es una obra Cristiana	This is a Christian labor
Que no se puede invadir.	That cannot be invaded.
Es también la regla de oro	It is also the golden rule
Que mide nuestro vivir.	That measures our living.
Nos mantendremos unidas	We shall mantain ourselves united
Con el fin de proteger	With the goal of protecting
Nuestras votos y promesas	Our votes and promises
Para que puedan valer.	So they can be worth something.

CORO   CHORUS

La insignia de Unión	The insignia of Union
En el Sol resplandeciente,	In the Sun resplandant,
Sus rayos y resplandor	Its rays and splendor
Iluminan nuestra mente.	Illuminate our minds.
Sus iniciales al frente	Its initials in the front
Son de infinito valor,	Are of infinite worth,
Dan testimonio, evidente	They give evident testimony
De nuestra organización.	Of our organization.

CORO   CHORUS

¡Gloria a nuestra Sociedad	Glory be to our Society
Por su bondad y talento !	For its goodness and talent !
Nuestro hogar será su templo	Our home will be its temple
Donde triunfe la verdad,	Where truth may triumph,
Y sirva como un ejemplo	And serve as an example
De nuestra formalidad,	Of our formality,

Y proclame el firmamento,
Gloria a nuestra Sociedad.

CORO

And proclaim to the firmament,
Glory to our Society.

CHORUS

Cántico Nacional (National Song) of
La Sociedad Protectora Cooperativa

The Sociedad Protectora Cooperativa (SPC) was founded on May 1, 1933, as documented in the text of this cántico, the society's official song. The devisa for the Antonito SPC local council identifies the council as Concilio No. 6, thus documenting that there were several other affiliates. The SPC was headquartered in Capulín, Colorado, with local auxiliaries in Ojo Caliente and El Rito, New Mexico, as well as one in Antonito. For a photo image of the SPC members in Ojo Caliente, see José A. Rivera Papers, Box 8, Folder 2. The women in the photo are wearing dark capes with white, rounded collars on their blouses and devisas pinned to the capes. Ruben Archuleta copied the SPC song from documents provided by his grandmother, María Filomena Trujillo-Archuleta. He remembered:

I can still sing this song since my grandma Filomena sang it at home all the time along with other songs, including alabados. Her maiden name was "Trujillo." She belonged to all the SPMDTU auxiliaries. Sometimes after their meetings, they would gather at Grandma's house, and Grandma Mena would play polkas on her harmonica while her friends danced and had a great time. When I attended the juntas with Grandma Mena, I had to sit real still and not say a word while they held their meetings and sang their songs. I could sense that the other women did not approve of my being there. (e-mail to José A. Rivera, November 11, 2003).

DÍA PRIMERO DE MAYO
Mil novecientos trienta y tres
Se formó esta sociedad
Del valor de una mujer.

CORO
¡Viva la bandera
De la libertad,
Y viva la liga
De nuestra sociedad!

ON THE FIRST OF MAY
Nineteen thirty-three
This society was formed
From the valor of a woman.

CHORUS
Long live the flag
Of liberty,
And long live the league
Of our society!

Se juntan varias señoras	Various ladies get together
Con respeto y con amor,	With respect and with love,
Y prestan sus juramentos	And lend their oaths
Por su patria y por su honor	For their country and honor.

CORO   CHORUS

Amemos como hermanas,	Let us love one another like sisters,
Amenos con amor,	Let us love with love,
Como libres cuidadanas	As free citizens
Caminemos con valor	Let us walk with valor.

CORO   CHORUS

Sociedad Cooperativa	Cooperative Society
Estás en nuestro corazón	You are in our hearts
Porque eres la protectora	Because you are the protector
De la patria y la nación	Of the country and nation.

CORO   CHORUS

Madre unión cooperativa	Mother cooperative union
Saludo reverente,	Reverent salute,
Hoy todititas en unión	Today all of us in union
Entre millares de gente	Among thousands of people

CORO   CHORUS

Para poner este nombre	To put this name
Con tres letras escogidas,	With three chosen letters,
Es sociedad protectora	This protective society
Se firma cooperativa.	Signs itself cooperatively.

CORO   CHORUS

Nos tomaremos las manos	We will hold hands
Con orgullo y con valor.	With pride and with valor.
Viveremos como hermanas	We will live as sisters
Con ánimo y con honor.	With energy and with honor.

SPMDTU Superior Presidents

Thirty-one members have served in the position of regidor superior or presidente superior since the founding of the SPMDTU in 1900. Some of the presidents were elected to more than one term and thus appear twice. The list follows the chronological order of terms from 1900 to 2010.

Celedonio Mondragón (1900)
Jesús María Lobato
Luis Jaramillo
Manuel Chávez
Epimenio García
Jacobo Ortiz
Epifanio J. García
José L. García
Fidel E. García
Onécimo Suazo
Francisco A. Espinoza
Bonifacio Gonzales
Senón Maestas
Epimenio Valdez
Severo González
Librado Martínez
Antonio P. Sena

Juan M. Salazar
Librado Martínez
Eliseo DeHerrera
Luis R. Montoya
José Benito Vigil
Efrén Quintana
Juan I. Medina
Pancracio Romero
Esequiel Salazar
O. G. Andy Vigil
Jerry Romero
Esequiel Salazar
Jerry Romero
Eppie C. Perea Jr.
Dan Valdez
Rogelio Briones
David Ortiz
Rudy Maestes (2010)

Geography of Local Councils

At its peak, the SPMDTU consisted of about sixty-five councils, surpassing sixty as early as 1937 in Colorado and New Mexico, with three more commissioned in Utah during the 1940s. An exact count is difficult to determine because some councils went inactive for a period of years, were decommissioned, and reorganized later, resulting in the use of duplicate or omitted council numbers. Other councils were terminated altogether due to movements of people in search of employment in the defense and construction industries, leaving some villages depopulated for a time. The smaller councils or those with declining membership were often consolidated into a nearby council in order to sustain participation and continue life insurance coverage for members who opted to remain active in the society for its highly valued material benefits and popular social functions. In 1961, when total membership was already in a decline trend, sixty-four listed councils were organized into seven districts across the tristate area, but only forty-five were reported as active, with 1,212 insurance certificates in force. (*Source*: SPMDTU Records, Box 1, Folder 12, Center for Southwest Research, University Libraries, University of New Mexico, Albuquerque.)

Colorado

No. 1 Antonito	No. 7 Los Sauces/Salida	No. 12 Del Norte,
No. 2 Capulín	No. 7 Denver	Nos. 8, 30
No. 3 Mogote	No. 8 Del Norte	No. 15 Center, No. 41
No. 4 Saguache	No. 8 Los Valdezes	No. 16 La Garita
No. 5 Ortiz	No. 10 La Jara	No. 17 Lobatos
No. 6 La Isla	No. 11 Fort Garland	No. 18 La Jara

No. 19 Alamosa

No. 20 Oak View

No. 21 Ignacio

No. 22 Conejos

No. 24 Pagosa Junction

No. 27 Monte Vista

No. 28 San Pablo

No. 29 Los Pinos/Valle

No. 30 Del Norte

No. 31 Chama

No. 32 Fort Collins

No. 34 Pagosa Springs

No. 35 Durango

No. 36 Montrose

No. 41 Center

No. 45 McPhee

No. 48 Aguilar

No. 49 San Luis

No. 50 Cañon

No. 52 Leadville

No. 54 García

No. 60 Brighton

No. 62 Walsenburg

New Mexico

No. 4 Rodarte

No. 9 La Madera/
Vallecitos

No. 10 San Miguel

No. 11 Las Tusas

No. 12 Costilla

No. 13 Ojo Caliente

No. 14 El Rito

No. 15 Placitas

No. 18 Ranchos de Taos

No. 20 Ranchos de Taos

No. 21 Española Valley
(Española, Alcalde,
Velarde, Lyden)

No. 23 Lumberton

No. 24 No Agua/
Tres Piedras

No. 25 Chama

No. 26 Española

No. 29 Los Pinos

No. 30 Chamita, No. 34

No. 30 Raton and
Dawson

No. 32 Arroyo Hondo

No. 33 Las Cruces

No. 34 Chamita

No. 37 Rosa

No. 38 Tierra Amarilla

No. 39 Alcalde

No. 40 Velarde

No. 42 Arroyo Seco

No. 43 Cerro

No. 44 Questa

No. 45 Dulce

No. 46 Embudo/Dixon

No. 53 Taos

No. 57 Nambé

No. 58 Peñasco

No. 63 Amalia

No. 64 Lyden

Utah

No. 59 Clearfield

No. 61 Ogden

No. 63 Salt Lake City

NOTES

Foreword

1. See the glossary at the end of the book for terms, phrases, and names related to La Sociedad; translations of Spanish words are also provided within the text.

Introduction

1. See Hernández, *Mutual Aid for Survival*; Gutiérrez, *Walls and Mirrors*; and Krainz, *Delivering Aid*.

2. See Peter Kropotkin's classic work *Mutual Aid: A Factor of Evolution*, especially his discussion in chapters 3 and 4 about the tribal origins of human society and how the evolution of the village community necessitated the development of new forms of organization. In chapter 5 (171–74), he describes the 1785 statutes of a Danish guild as typical features of brotherhoods among various professions and trades in medieval cities that often lasted for centuries. Kropotkin was one of the founders of modern anarchism, but as a social theorist he influenced trade union movements across the world by his advocacy of solidarity, reflected in one of the organizing principles of the SPMDTU, the mobilization of *trabajadores unidos* (united workers).

3. Foster, "Cofradía and Compadrazgo," 11–16.

4. Wirth, *Ghetto*, 138, 148, 160.

5. Gist, *Secret Societies*, 39–40; Gist "Fraternal Societies," 172–73, 180–81. For a history and the current activities of the major fraternal benefit societies in the United States and Canada, see the National Fraternal Congress of American Web site at http://www.nfcanet.org. These nonprofit fraternals adhere to the principles of mutual aid by providing welfare services and other charitable works, but they also operate under a system of local lodges and offer various forms of insurance to their members and families.

6. Katz and Bender, "Self-Help Groups in Western Society," 276.

7. Martin and Martin, *Helping Tradition*, 39–42, 54; Pollard, *Study of Black Self-Help*, 49–90; Stuart, *An Economic Detour*, 7–9, 35.

8. See Hernández, *Mutual Aid for Survival*, and Rivera, "Self-Help as Mutual Protection." The largest mutualista society in the American Southwest was the Alianza Hispano-Americana, founded in Tucson, Arizona, in 1894. The Alianza

offered low-cost life insurance and other services until 1965, when it ceased issuing new certificates and then disbanded. At its peak in the late 1930s, it had approximately eighteen thousand members in eight states and northern Mexico, with the leadership centered mostly in Arizona and New Mexico. The Alianza's fundamental principles were prototypical of other late-nineteenth-century and turn-of-the-century Hispanic mutual aid societies, expressed in the motto "Protección, Moralidad, e Instrucción" (Protection, Morality, and Instruction). See Briegel, "Alianza Hispano-Americana," and Arrieta, "Alianza Hispano-Americana."

9. Deutsch, *No Separate Refuge*, 34–39; Forrest, *Preservation of the Village*, 110–11.

10. Arellano, *"La Querencia"*; Nostrand, *The Hispano Homeland*, 24–25; Rivera, *Acequia Culture*, 172–73. In his article, Arellano depicts the strong attachment of Nuevomexicanos to the upper Río Grande bioregion as the essence of *querencia*: "El que pierde su tierra, pierde su memoria" (He who loses his land, loses his memory). For hundreds of years prior to annexation into the United States in 1848, the region was a distant outpost on the northern frontiers of Spain and Mexico. Insularity from Mexico City and other centers of population made possible the development of a distinctive Hispanic culture in the Americas, as reflected in the regional Spanish dialect described by linguists as sixteenth-century "[t]raditional Spanish" (Bills and Vigil, *The Spanish Language of New Mexico and Southern Colorado*, 29–47). During the early period of expansion, the SPMDTU Superior Council described itself as a "Gran Logia compuesta de aquellos que hablan el Bello y Dulce Idioma de Cervantes" (Supreme Lodge composed of those who speak the beautiful and sweet language of Cervantes). See the Certificate of Honor presented by the Superior Council to the Alamosa Council. Sociedad de Protección Mutua de Trabajadores Unidos (SPMDTU) Records, Box 1, Folder 1, MSS 696 BC, Center for Southwest Research, University Libraries, University of New Mexico, Albuquerque (hereafter "SPMDTU Records").

11. Deutsch, *No Separate Refuge*, 26.

12. While still a territory in the 1880s and into 1912, New Mexico developed early forms of public social welfare, but these initiatives were limited to the care of institutionalized persons such as orphaned children, the mentally disabled, and the speech and hearing impaired. Finally, in 1915, just a few years after statehood, the New Mexico State Legislature passed a law that permitted counties and municipalities to provide minimal levels of assistance to families in poverty. Modern social welfare programs, however, did not commence until 1937, when the State of New Mexico passed the Public Welfare Act to administer the Social Security programs initiated by the federal government in response to the economic hardships of the Great Depression. See Engstrom, Korte, and McDonough, "Understaffed, Underfunded."

13. For a discussion of the transition into new forms of Mexican American voluntary associations during the 1930s and 1940s, see Hernández, *Mutual Aid for Survival*, chap. 8; Márquez, *LULAC*; and Ramos, *The American G.I. Forum*. Founded in 1929, LULAC includes some seven hundred local councils nationwide and promotes the educational and economic advancement, the political influence, and the health and civil rights of Hispanic groups in the United States (see the league's Web site at http://www.lulac.org). The American GI Forum was founded in 1948 to address the concerns of Mexican American veterans who were denied equal access to veteran's

medical services following World War II and later expanded its issues to include voting rights, jury selection, employment assistance, and the civil rights of Mexican Americans in health, mental health, and education (http://www.americangiforum.org). In her study of LULAC and the Mexican American civil rights movement, "The Origins of the League," Cynthia Orozco distinguishes between the working-class mutualistas and the largely middle-class emergent voluntary associations that adopted strategies of political action to eradicate racial oppression and discrimination.

14. David Ortiz, telephone communication with José A. Rivera, December 18, 2003.

Chapter One

1. Articles of Incorporation of the Association of Mutual Protection and Mutual Benefit of the Town of Cerro de Guadalupe, April 7, 1888, May 24, 1930, County of Taos, State of New Mexico, no. 0624, filed with the state Corporation Commission, File no. 918, Santa Fe.

2. Constitución de La Asociación Defensiva de los Pobladores de los Terrenos del Río de Costilla, Certificate of April 12, 1902, recorded in Book A-16, 267–72, Office of the Secretary, Territory of New Mexico, Santa Fe. The English translation is quoted as it appeared attached to the articles of incorporation, titled a "Free Translation." Thanks to Gregory A. Hicks for providing a copy of the Constitution for use in this book.

3. Preamble to the 1911 General Constitution, printed with the Constitución y Reglamento de la SPMDTU 1922, José A. Rivera Papers, Box 8, Folder 3, Center for Southwest Research, University Libraries, University of New Mexico, Albuquerque.

4. María Mondragón-Valdez, "Valley History in Its Plazas," La Sierra, February 14, 2003. For insightful descriptions of the Hispanic settlements of Costilla County, see the Mondragón-Valdez series of essays featured in La Sierra, "The Culebra River Villages: The Natural and Built Environments of Costilla County," from August 15 to December 5, 2003: "The Culebra's Geographic Setting," August 15, 2003; "Amerindian Occupants and Early Visitors," August 22, 2003; "Gilpin Grabs the Grant, Fails to Displace Settlers," October 24, 2003; "Blanca and Other New Towns of the Early 20th Century," November 7, 2003; "The Nisei Arrive in Costilla County," November 14, 2003; "Bigotry in the Valley," November 21, 2003; and "Concluding Phases of Development: 1946–1964," December 5, 2003.

For a multicultural history of the region, see Simmons, San Luis Valley. For a history of how various cultures utilized the land and water resources of the San Luis area in accordance with their own distinctive and opposing values, see Carlson, "Rural Settlement Patterns."

5. Mondragón-Valdez, "Valley History in Its Plazas."

6. Simmons, San Luis Valley, 24. María Mondragón-Valdez notes that Diego de Vargas referenced the landscape and wildlife of the Río Culebra in a journal entry after he camped there in 1694 ("Amerindian Occupants and Early Visitors," La Sierra, August 22, 2003). Later, from 1756 to 1785, the governors in Santa Fe commissioned cartographer don Bernardo de Miera y Pacheco to conduct inspections and draw maps of "la Provincia interna de el Nuebo México." The first and most complete

map was finished in 1758 and included the area north of Taos into the Sierra Blanca of Colorado (see Kessell, *Kiva, Cross, and Crown,* 507–12).

7. Mondragón-Valdez, "Valley History in Its Plazas."

8. Act of Possession, Conejos Grant, October 12, 1842, quoted in Brayer, *William Blackmore,* 207–9. Also see Carlson, "Rural Settlement Patterns," 114.

9. According to Marianne Stoller, some settlers lived on the Conejos Grant starting in 1847, but sustained occupation can be documented only from 1854 ("Grants of Desperation," 26, 32, 35). Also see Andrews, "Tata Atanasio Trujillo's Unlikely Tales," 6, 13–14; Simmons, *San Luis Valley,* 78–81; Swadesh, *Primeros Pobladores,* 72.

10. Brayer, *William Blackmore,* 60–63; Simmons, *San Luis Valley,* 83; Stoller, "Grants of Desperation," 28–29. A section of the petition for the Sangre de Cristo Grant by Narciso Beaubien and Louis Lee to Governor Manuel Armijo in 1843 can be found translated in Brayer, *William Blackmore,* 61, and the full text can be found in López Tushar, *People of El Valle,* 31.

11. María Mondragón-Valdez, Valdez and Associates, "The Culebra River Villages of Costilla County Colorado," National Register of Historic Places, Multiple Property Documentation Form, June 1, 2000, Section E, 9–11, U.S. National Park Service, Washington, D.C. (pdf 614 at http://www.coloradohistory-oahp.org); Mondragón-Valdez, "Valley History in Its Plazas." For a historic and contemporary review of land uses by the pobladores of the Sangre de Cristo Land Grant, see Mondragón-Valdez and Valdez, "Hispano Culture and Settlement Patterns."

12. Peña, "Cultural Landscapes and Biodiversity," 246, 267 n. 11; Karnes, *William Gilpin,* 308; Nostrand, *Hispano Homeland,* 84.

13. Mondragón-Valdez, "Valley History in Its Plazas."

14. John Nieto-Phillips notes that the railroad in partnership with the government Bureau of Immigration in the Territory of New Mexico, 1880–1912, led the campaign to attract tourists and induce immigrants to the area as a way to promote statehood. The bureau's mission was to "prepare and disseminate accurate information as to the soil, climate, minerals, resources, production and business of New Mexico, with special reference to its opportunities for development . . . and for the investment of capital" (*Language of Blood,* 118–20).

15. Blackmore, *Colorado.* See Blackmore's introduction to part II, "The Parks of Colorado," and the attached reports by Bowles, Whitsett, and Hendron, 149, 210–211, 215.

16. Taylor and Taggart, *Alex and the Hobo,* 84–85.

17. Westphall, *Mercedes Reales,* 37–40, 147, 155; Meinig, *Southwest,* 35.

18. Swadesh, *Primeros Pobladores,* 80. The most notorious of the alliances was the clique led by lawyers Stephen B. Elkins and Thomas B. Catron known as "the Santa Fe Ring"; see Rosenbaum, *Mexicano Resistance,* 27. According to Roxanne Dunbar-Ortiz, Catron owned or had an interest in thirty-four land grants in territorial New Mexico, composing a "land empire" of more than two million acres as well as homestead claims of smaller acreages located near water supplies that he controlled (*Roots of Resistance,* 101–2).

19. Stoller, "Grants of Desperation," 35.

20. Westphall, *Mercedes Reales,* 195.

21. Simmons, *San Luis Valley*, 260, 254.

22.   Weber, *Foreigners in Their Native Land*, 158. For an analysis of the effects of capitalism on land losses of hispano farmers and Pueblo Indian communities, see Dunbar-Ortiz, *Roots of Resistance*.

23.   As early as 1869, published reports on the vast resources of the Territory of Colorado appeared in London, opening the door to European emigration, investment, and opportunities for the exploitation of minerals. In 1869, Blackmore and his contributors described the abundant and profitable opportunities in mining, agriculture, ranching, and manufacturing. The Sangre de Cristo Land Grant was featured prominently as one of the major American regions accessible and desirable for emigration. A few years later, 1872, a London publisher took the trouble to condense a geological report by Professor Cyrus Thomas officially submitted in 1871 to the U.S. secretary of the interior. As with Blackmore's book, this survey described the San Luis Valley in very enticing terms. The report concluded: "This [place near Homan's Creek] is a most excellent point for a few stock ranches, as water is abundant, and as not only the valley proper, but also the little openings up into the mountains and slopes on the north and west, afford most excellent grass, and would furnish pasturage for quite a number of cattle" (Thomas, *Agricultural and Pastoral Resources*, 7).

24. Simmons, *San Luis Valley*, 215–36. Virginia Simmons notes that the entrance of Mormons into the San Luis Valley during the late 1870s and into the 1880s was facilitated by the Southern States Mission of the Latter-day Saints Church with help from church leaders in Utah. The goal was to establish colonies of Mormons from Utah and Arizona, along with new converts from the South, due to the availability of water for agriculture, the prospects for homesteading in public lands, and the advent of rail transportation. For the southerners, relocation to the West after the end of the Civil War and the hard economic times of the mid-1870s offered opportunities for a better life in towns that they and the other Mormon settlers established in places such as Manassa, Morgan, and Sanford, among others in the valley (215–23). Alvar Carlson credits the Mormons for the construction of extensive irrigation canals, facilitating the rapid growth of commercial agriculture as a lucrative endeavor for the waves of other homesteaders who came later and culminating in the "agricultural revolution in the valley" by the Japanese Americans in the 1920s and 1930s ("Rural Settlement Patterns," 123–28).

25.   Baxter, *Dividing New Mexico's Water*, viii.

26.   Swadesh, *Primeros Pobladores*, 80.

27.   The sale of the Sangre de Cristo Grant illustrates the wide range of speculators who participated in land-grabbing actions during the period of territorial status for Colorado as well as in neighboring New Mexico. A year after southern Colorado was severed from the Territory of New Mexico and Taos County itself was bisected into two counties across the new boundary, Charles Beaubien formalized deeds to 135 hispano settlers on the million-acre land grant and conveyed resource-access rights to them in the uplands commons and the commons pastures along the Río Culebra. In 1863–64, however, Beaubien and his partners sold the land grant to William Gilpin, the first territorial governor of Colorado. To raise the $41,000 needed for the purchase of the grant, Gilpin obtained a loan from New

York investment bankers and European speculators, and they, along with other partners from the eastern states, incorporated the United States Freehold Land and Emigration Company. To divide the land into estates for sale to German and Dutch emigrants as new towns, William Blackmore, an English capitalist, enlisted other investors, and, together with the Amsterdam banking firm of Wertheim and Compertz, the U.S. Freehold board of directors divided the land grant in half by forming the Costilla and Trinchera estates. To force the hispano settlers off the estates, U.S. Freehold challenged their land deeds, forcing villagers into expensive legal proceedings starting in 1871. See Brayer, *William Blackmore*, 66, 76–81; Hicks, "Memory and Pluralism," 299–304; María Mondragón-Valdez, "Gilpin Grabs the Grant," *La Sierra*, October 24, 2003.

28. Knowlton, "Land Loss as a Cause of Unrest," 29.

29. Ibid.; Weber, *Foreigners in Their Native Land*, 157.

30. Deutsch, *No Separate Refuge*, 20; Stoller, "Grants of Desperation," 26, 35; Westphall, *Mercedes Reales*, 153.

31. Gonzales, "Struggle for Survival," 306–7.

32. Ebright, *Land Grants*, 214; Westphall, *Mercedes Reales*, 256, 265.

33. Forrest, *Preservation of the Village*, 21.

34. Simmons, *San Luis Valley*, 164.

35. López, *La Historia*, 11–12.

36. Simmons, *San Luis Valley*, 163.

37. Frederick Sánchez, "Antonito Birthplace," *La Sierra*, January 3, 2003. See the series "The SPMDTU" published by Sánchez in *La Sierra*: "The Early Years," December 20, 2002; "Antonito Birthplace," January 3, 2003; "Compassion at the Heart of the Brotherhood," January 31, 2003; "Communication Essential for Society's Success," February 7, 2003; "The Acts of Charity and Mercy," February 14, 2003; "Building Fund Leads to Financial Loss," February 21, 2003; "Society Weathers Series of Crises," February 28, 2003; "The Society's Governing Body," March 7, 2003; "Society Still Has Much to Celebrate," March 14, 2003. Also see the Frederick Sánchez series in the *Alamosa Valley Courier*, September 18, 21, 27, 29, 1990, and his articles "SPMDTU Favored Aid of Poor within Society," July 21, 1997, and "SPMDTU Celebrates Centennial," August 23, 2000, both in *San Luis Valley Lifestyles*. For an earlier series, see Charles Vigil, "Largest Hispanic Fraternal Order Started Nearby," *Costilla County Citizen*, January 3, 1985.

38. Simmons, *San Luis Valley*, 178, 188.

39. Aguayo, "Los Betabeleros," 106–8.

40. María Mondragón-Valdez, "Bigotry in the Valley," *La Sierra*, November 21, 2003.

41. Meyer, "Early Mexican-American Responses," 75–77. Also see Meyer, *Speaking for Themselves*.

42. *Rocky Mountain News*, November 9, 1866, quoted in Valdez, "La Sociedad Protección Mutua," 15.

43. Hicks and Peña, "Community Acequias," 426.

44. Hicks, "Memory and Pluralism," 306. Hicks cites William Blackmore, *Southern Colorado and Its Resources* 3 (1868), copy in Folder 0130, Box 10798, and also Box 132 for the survey report by Professor F. V. Hayden, William Blackmore Land

Records, New Mexico State Records Center and Archives, Santa Fe. Also see Simmons, *San Luis Valley*, 147–48.

45. Hicks, "Memory and Pluralism," 304–6.

46. Ibid., 306; Hicks and Peña, "Community Acequias," 437.

47. Hicks, "Memory and Pluralism," 307.

48. English translation of Constitución de La Asociación Defensiva de los Pobladores de los Terrenos del Río de Costilla (see note 2 for this chapter).

49. Hicks, "Memory and Pluralism," 309–17; María Mondragón-Valdez, "Blanca and Other New Towns of the Early 20th Century," *La Sierra*, November 7, 2003.

50. The 1843 petition by Nicolas Beaubien and Stephen Louis Lee to obtain the Sangre de Cristo Grant made it clear that the land and water resources were plentiful and suitable for the development of agrarian settlements within two years after the approval of the land grant petition as required in Mexican law. At the time, the Beaubien family and Lee lived in Taos, then a major boom town in Nuevo México and the likely place from which to recruit a sufficient number of settlers to occupy and develop the land: "That desiring to encourage the agriculture of the country and place it in a flourishing condition, and being restricted in lands wherewith to accomplish said purpose, we have seen and examined with great care that embraced within the Costilla, Culebra, and Trincheras rivers . . . and finding in it the qualities of fruitfulness, fertile lands for cultivation, and abundance of pasture and water, and all that is required for its settlement, and the raising of horned and woolen cattle" (Sangre de Cristo petition to Mexican governor Manuel Armijo, 1843, quoted in Brayer, *William Blackmore*, 61). See Brayer's account of how this million-acre grant was obtained by the enterprising Charles Beaubien, already a co-owner of the Beaubien–Miranda Land Grant and later known as the Maxwell Land Grant, by guiding his twelve-year-old-son, Nicolas, and a young Stephen Louis Lee, his employee, as the official petitioners essentially in his place and thus circumventing his own legal ineligibility to petition for a second grant (*William Blackmore*, 60–61).

51. Hicks, "Memory and Pluralism," 318–19. Gregory A. Hicks, e-mail to José A. Rivera, October 22, 2007. Hicks describes the resistance by the Costilla Valley settlers of New Mexico as a "partial victory" due to the lack of a conveyance document or deeds by Charles Beaubien, unlike the case for the natives along the Río Culebra watershed in neighboring Colorado. Many early court decisions also went against the hispano landowners in the Culebra River villages, but a document and covenant signed by Beaubien upon his sale of the Sangre de Cristo Grant in 1863 described the commons rights and were finally recognized by the Colorado Supreme Court in 2002 and 2003 in *Lobato v. Taylor* (Hicks, "Memory and Pluralism," 320). For a translated text of the Beaubien document, see Hicks and Peña, "Community Acequias," 428–29.

52. Simmons, *San Luis Valley*, 239–41.

53. María Mondragón-Valdez, "The Nisei Arrive in Costilla County" and "Bigotry in the Valley," *La Sierra*, November 14, 2003, and November 21, 2003.

54. Phillip Gonzales indicates that the Spanish colonial settlement process required the development of "tightly bound social relations" among the agropastoral society. He points out that the land grant communities of the New Mexico Province attained a corporate social organization to include the formation of a local

government in order to sustain community life in a frontier environment ("Struggle for Survival," 295–98). For a history of community irrigation systems, see Rivera, *Acequia Culture*, and Rodríguez, *Acequia*.

55. Quoted in Leonard, *Role of the Land Grant*, 169.

56. La Joya Acequia of Socorro County, "Reglas y regulaciones para el gobierno y manejo de la acequia de comunidad de La Joya, N. Mex., para el año 1942," on file with José A. Rivera.

57. Rodríguez, *Acequia*, 84, 101–13.

58. Woodward, "Penitentes of New Mexico," 191–97. Mexico City in particular carried forward with the cofradía traditions of sixteenth-century Madrid, where members of these brotherhoods celebrated saints' days or other religious symbols as a path to salvation and as a way to receive the benefits of a funeral mass and burial when they passed away. See von Germeten, "Death in Black and White." By 1790, the agrarian province of Nueva Vizcaya in northern Mexico (now Durango and Chihuahua) was home to more than 150 cofradías that controlled farms, orchards, and livestock while ensuring both the material and spiritual welfare of rural parishioners affiliated with the local Catholic churches. See Lamadrid, "Rutas del Corazón," 437.

59. Buxó i Rey, "El paisaje cosmológico," 93; Lamadrid, "Rutas del Corazón," 436–40.

60. Buxó i Rey, "El paisaje cosmológico," 95–96.

61. Weigle, *Penitentes of the Southwest*, 20.

62. Woodward, "Penitentes of New Mexico," 11–12.

63. Knowlton, "Changing Spanish-American Villages," 462.

64. See "Rules for the Nurse" in Steele and Rivera, *Penitente Self-Government*, 148–49.

65. "Morada de Los Pinos Journal," in Archuleta, *Land of the Penitentes*, 83. Also see Archuleta's *Penitente Renaissance* (vii, 27, 38, 43, 45–46, 48–49, 55) for photographs of penitente ceremonies, meeting halls, artifacts, and memorabilia. Like other mutualistas, the local penitent cofradías issued devisas to their members, and they recorded their minutes and other financial transactions in journals.

66. Archuleta, *Land of the Penitentes*, 210; Barker, "Los Penitentes," 180, quoted in Hernández, *Mutual Aid for Survival*, 16; Kutsche and Gallegos, "Community Functions of the Cofradía," 92.

67. Policy Symposium on Voluntary Support Systems and Vehicles for Community Empowerment, draft transcript of proceedings, Southwest Hispanic Research Institute, University of New Mexico, Summer 1984, José A. Rivera Papers, Box 8, Folder 27, 6–7; Steele and Rivera, *Penitente Self-Government*, 24. Like other mutualistas, the penitent brotherhoods experienced a decline in membership during the second half of the twentieth century owing to the rural outmigration patterns and other demographic changes in the upper Río Grande villages where they had once proliferated. Scores of moradas were left abandoned and fell into disrepair or were razed when no longer used. Others, however, continue to function, and there appears to be a resurgence to maintain the traditions and ceremonies at many local cofradías and to restore and utilize the meeting halls once again. Examples of recent restoration projects include the morada in San Francisco funded by the Colorado Historical Society, the active morada at Fort Garland, and the morada at Garcia,

Colorado. In New Mexico, the moradas at Arroyo Seco, Talpa, Abiquiu, Tierra Amarilla, and other communities continue to function and have been utilized and maintained continuously, as have the moradas of San Luis, San Antonio, and Trinidad,
Colorado. For a list of seventy-three moradas that are still active and photo documentation of processions, structures, religious artifacts, and devisas, see Archuleta,
Penitente Renaissance.

68. Obituary for Onofre Lobato, *El Nuevo Mexicano*, March 31, 1927. A similar
event occurred in La Madera, New Mexico, when the local SPMDTU, the Club de
Protección de Servilleta, and the Cofradía de Nuestro Padre Jesús Parroquia de San
Antonio en Servilleta unified their support and jointly published resolutions of condolences addressing their "hermano y consocio Don Rafael Peña" upon the death
of his wife, Adelina S. de Peña (obituary, *El Nuevo Mexicano*, March 17, 1927). These
cases serve as examples of the overlapping membership across penitente and mutualista societies and the degree to which they coordinated their mutual aid services.
Written agreements were sometimes developed between the penitente cofradías and
SPMDTU concilios. In 1922, for example, the members of the Morada de Los Pinos,
New Mexico, passed a resolution in support of an agreement for mutual benefit
between the Concilio Superior of the SPMDTU and the counterpart Cuerpo del Centro de los Hermanos de la Penitencia (see minutes of January 25, 1922, in Archuleta,
Land of the Penitentes, 231). Similarly, the minutes of the SPMDTU Velarde Concilio
No. 40 in 1938 make reference to a commission appointed to develop an agreement
with the cofradía, presumably in Velarde as well, with positive results: "La comisión
que fue nombrada para tomar arreglo con la Cofradía de Nuestro Padre Jesús reporta
que todo pasó en buena orden" (Minutes, Velarde Journal, July 20, 1938, SPMDTU
Records, Box 24). The details of the agreements are not recorded in either the Los
Pinos or Velarde minutes, but the coordination of mutual help with funeral arrangements for deceased hermanos and benefits for survivors may have been among the
items of common interest. Precedence for the pooling of resources existed across
penitente moradas, as in the case of a joint Fondo para Beneficio established in 1907
by the moradas of Los Pinos and San Miguel to handle any emergency needs their
members might have had (Minutes, "Morada de Los Pinos Journal," April 12, 1907, in
Archuleta, *Land of the Penitentes*, 166–67).

Chapter Two

1. Celedonio Mondragón came from humble parents, José Antonio Mondragón
and María Leonor Luján, and was baptized at Our Lady of Guadalupe Church in
Conejos, Colorado (Our Lady of Guadalupe Baptismal Registry, 1861–68, compiled
and translated by David H. Salazar, per e-mail from Manuel Salazar, archivist and
genealogist, Colorado Society of Hispanic Genealogy, Denver, to José Rivera, October 15, 2008). As a young adult, he made a living as a jewelry maker, with supplemental income from farming and ranching. Mondragón's occupation as a platero
took him to Santa Fe, New Mexico, until around 1895, when he returned to Conejos
County first as a rancher and then as a jewelry maker once again in 1900 after he
moved to the town of Antonito. He remained a jewelry maker until his death in
Lobatos, Colorado, in 1923. In a decree adopted in 1910, the Superior Council stipulated that his photograph must be framed and displayed in the meeting halls of

all the local councils, with a caption recognizing him as the organizer and founder of the SPMDTU (López, *La Historia*, 36–39, 43). His legacy as a visionary and an early civil rights pioneer endures, and he is at times described as the Martin Luther King Jr. of his era. See Jim Sagel, "Workers Society Traces Its Roots to Turbulent Era" *Albuquerque Journal*, Journal North edition, April 16, 1987, citing SPMDTU superior president Esequiel Salazar.

2. López, *La Historia*, 13–14.

3. Arellano, "The People's Movement," 63–66; Gonzales, "Struggle for Survival," 305.

4. The Mondragón brothers advertised their work as exquisite Mexican jewelry art and gave their business address in Santa Fe: "N. Mondragón y Hno. Manufactureros de Joyería Mexicana. En este ramo especial y exquisito del arte mexicano garantizamos dar completa satisfacción. Toda aquella persona que visite nuestro establecimiento quedará satisfecho del trabajo ejecutado por nosotros. Calle de San Francisco, Santa Fe, NM" (*La Voz del Pueblo*, May 25, 1889). The partners in the business included Celedonio's brother, Narciso Mondragón, and possibly one or both of the other brothers, Román and Pilar. Narciso was mentioned by name in an advertisement that appeared in the March 2, 1889, issue of the *La Voz del Pueblo*, a regional newspaper published in Las Vegas. A subsequent issue of *La Voz del Pueblo* (September 6, 1890) mentioned don Celedonio's lucrative business travels to Las Vegas and counties in northeastern New Mexico as well as his plans to open a branch store in Mexico City: "Don Celedonio Mondragón de la apamada firma de Mondragón y Hermanos, de Santa Fe, manufactureros de joyas de filigrana, pasó por esta de regreso a la capital después de un viaje lucrativo a los condados del nor-oeste. La companía de Mondragón Hermanos establecerá dentro de poco tiempo un sucursal de su establecimiento en la Ciudad de México al cargo de Don Celedonio." The Mondragón brothers again advertised their business in *El Nuevo Mexicano* (April 11, 1891): "N. Mondragón y Hnos. Joyería de Filigrana Mexicana en Oro y Plata." Around 1895, Celedonio and his brothers closed the jewelry shop in Santa Fe and returned to Conejos County. Celedonio's first marriage was to Estanislada Salazar Mondragón, but he was left a widower after they had one child, Francisca, born 1891 in Mexico City. In 1899, he married his second wife, María Elena Casias Mondragón, and they had seven children (López, *La Historia*, 43, 36; see also note 4 of chapter 4 for the names of the seven children from the second marriage).

5. The impetus for the establishment of the Orden de Caballeros de Protección Mutua in December 1890 came from Republican conservatives with land and mercantile interests in northeastern New Mexico who did not condone the use of armed resistance and attacks on private property in the manner conducted by the Gorras Blancas. As a counterforce organization, the Caballeros de Protección Mutua was headquartered in Las Vegas, New Mexico (Concilio No. 1), and competed for members by establishing additional chapters in West Las Vegas and in Mora, Santa Fe, Bernalillo, and San Miguel counties. Some of the order's leaders founded a newspaper, *El Sol de Mayo*, in 1891, which served as its official organ: "Periódico consagrado a los intereses del pueblo de Nuevo México, y órgano de la Orden de Caballeros de Protección Mutua de Ley y Orden del Territorio" (*El Sol de Mayo*, May 1, 1891). The Gorras Blancas movement initially gained broad political support from Democrats

and progressive Republicans in the region but dissipated in the late 1890s after a series of court trials and the jailing of some of its leaders. See Arellano, "The People's Movement," 61–62, 79; Gonzales, "Struggle for Survival," 305; Rosenbaum, *Mexicano Resistance*, 130–31. There are some discrepancies in the exact name of the counter-society due to variations printed in subsequent issues of *El Sol de Mayo* (May 7, May 14, May 21, May 28, June 12, June 18, November 24, 1891). José Timoteo López and other authors who cite his book *La Historia* call it "La Sociedad Protección Mutua por Ley y Orden"; Rosenbaum identifies the organization as the "Sociedad de los Caballeros de Ley y Orden y Protección Mutua"; and Arellano calls it "Los Caballeros de Protección Mutua," its abbreviated form.

A letter to the editor of *El Sol de Mayo* in November 1891 referred to the organization as "La Orden de Caballeros de Protección Mutua." The letter was written on behalf of Council No. 2, located in West Las Vegas, to oppose Agua Pura, a private company of capitalists and shareholders with ties to New York banks who intended to monopolize and profit from the distribution of water at the expense of "los hijos del país" (natives of the land). Instead, the members of Council No. 2 proposed the reconstruction of the Acequia de Nuestra Señora de los Dolores, employing local labor, in order to expand irrigated agricultural lands and at the same time provide water for domestic uses (*El Sol de Mayo*, November 24, 1891, translated by Anselmo Arellano). The position taken by this council indicates that the usually conservative Caballeros de Protección Mutua adapted to changing conditions and linked the issue of resources monopoly by outsiders to the exploitation of native landowners and the local labor force, a theme that would surface in Conejos County again when Celedonio Mondragón took steps to organize a society for the mutual protection of united workers in the San Luis Valley.

6. López, *La Historia*, 37–38.

7. Ibid., 36–39.

8. Ibid., 14–15, 38–39.

9. Ibid., 7–13, 48. In addition to the seven members elected to the board of directors, several other Conejos County residents joined the society and took the oath of loyalty at the inaugural meeting of November 26, 1900. The elected tesorero, José Ramón Quintana (1865–1951), recalled at La Sociedad's golden anniversary in 1950 that his two brothers, Tomás and Apolonio Quintana, attended the first organizational meeting and were elected to other officer posts (see account of fiftieth anniversary in López, *La Historia*, 7–9, 48–49; and for the resoluciones de condolencia when José Ramón Quintana passed away on November 11, 1951, as the last surviving member of the founding board of directors, see pages 73–74).

10. López, *La Historia*, 11; Simmons, *San Luis Valley*, 264.

11. Valdez, "La Sociedad Protección Mutua," 13.

12. All told, there were about sixty-five local councils. An exact count is difficult to confirm because of the periodic decommissioning of councils in locations where the membership declined or went inactive. The Superior Council would on occasion commission new councils under a number previously assigned to another community but no longer in use. Hence, the list of the documented concilios in appendix 4 contains numbers that appear more than once. Similarly, the total enrollment of the SPMDTU can only be estimated because attendance records were kept by the

secretary-treasurer of each local council and were not forwarded to the Superior Council in Antonito. The longtime superior secretary-treasurer, Tomás Romero, estimated some three thousand members at peak enrollment from the 1930s to about 1950 (Frederick Sánchez, "The SPMDTU: The Early Years," *La Sierra*, December 20, 2002). This figure, however, may have included all members during the peak period and not membership figures in any single year. For example, the Report of Examination conducted by the Insurance Department of Colorado indicated that only 1,439 life insurance certificates were in force at the end of 1954 (SPMDTU Records, Box 1, Folder 3). At the time López published *La Historia* in 1958, he estimated some 1,600 members (p. 8).

13. Article I, Constitución de La Orden de Protección Mutua de Trabajadores Unidos por la Ley y Orden, c. 1909, SPMDTU Records, Box 1, Folder 1, and in Box 20, pasted into the Reglamento de Capulín, Treasurer's Ledger, for 1915–19. No other published article or book about the SPMDTU has cited this document, and most instead refer to the revised General Constitution and preamble of 1911 cited in López, *La Historia*. This earlier Constitución General appears to have been written for adoption at the inaugural convention of 1909 (described in López, *La Historia*, 16). The document ends with a certification of approval by the Concilio Superior and is signed with seals by the executive officers: Manuel Chávez, regidor superior; Bonifacio Gonzales, vice regidor; and Pedro A. Valdez, secretario superior, as witness. Manuel Chávez served as the society's fourth superior president, and his term in office coincides with the 1909 approval date of the General Constitution. The following year, 1910, the articles of incorporation filed with the Colorado secretary of state changed the name of the organization to "Sociedad de Protección Mutua de Trabajadores Unidos" (see note 17 for this chapter).

14. Article I, reglamento section, Constitución de la Orden de Protección Mutua, 1909, SPMDTU Records, Box 1, Folder 1.

15. Article II in ibid.

16. Articles VI and VII in ibid.

17. SPMDTU articles of incorporation, filed on September 26, 1910, Office of the Secretary of State, State of Colorado, certified copy on August 13, 1948, SPMDTU Records, Box 1, Folder 2.

18. Constitución y Reglamento de la SPMDTU, 1922, José A. Rivera Papers, Box 8, Folder 3; Frederick Sánchez, "Compassion at the Heart of the Brotherhood" and "The Society's Governing Body," *La Sierra*, January 31, 2003, and March 7, 2003.

19. Preamble to the 1911 General Constitution, printed with the Constitución y Reglamento de la SPMDTU, 1922, José A. Rivera Papers, Box 8, Folder 3.

20. The Alamosa Council was first organized in 1904 but was subsequently decommissioned until 1919. See SPMDTU Records, Box 1, Folder 1.

21. Frederick Sánchez, "Communication Essential for Society's Success," *La Sierra*, February 7, 2003.

22. Journal of Minutes, Concilio Superior, Ledger 1914–25, SPMDTU Records, Box 18, years 1915 and 1917.

23. Journal of Minutes, Concilio Superior, Ledger 1914–25, SPMDTU Records, Box 18, years 1916, 1917, and 1920. Petitions for the organization of new local councils often came by way of inquiries to the superior secretary, as in 1916, when a letter from

Mr. Eloy Vigil, Ranchos de Taos, requested more information about the society with the aim of organizing a council there. The Superior Council instructed the secretary to reply to Mr. Vigil's request: "Se presentó una carta del Señor Eloy Vigil, de Ranchos de Taos, pidiendo detalles más particulares concernientes a nuestra Sociedad, a fin de procurar organizar un Concilio en ese lugar. El Secretrario se instruyó corresponder con este señor" (minutes, November 27, 1916).

24. Demetrio Trujillo was the first organizer approved under the revised articles of the SPMDTU, as noted in Journal of Minutes, Concilio Superior, May 19, 1928, SPMDTU Records, Box 16. Also see Tomás Romero, remarks, Policy Symposium, 15, José Rivera Papers, Box 8 Folder 27; López, *La Historia*, 52, 61–62.

25. Journal of Minutes, Capulín Council No. 2, 1913–19, SPMDTU Records, Box 21. See especially the minutes for 1915. Other concilios that made small loans to members included Montrose Council No. 36 in Colorado and Velarde Council No. 40 in New Mexico (Treasurer's Ledger, Montrose Council No. 36, 1936–37; Journal of Minutes, Velarde Council No. 40, 1937–39, SPMDTU Records, Boxes 23 and 24).

26. Reglas Locales, Concilio No. 2, Capulín, Colo., adopted by the Asamblea Legislativa and approved in force by local president on September 14, 1929, SPMDTU Records, Box 22.

27. Reglamento de Capulín, minutes of March 6, 1915, SPMDTU Records, Box 20; Acta de Ley adopted in the minutes of November 4, 1916, Journal 1913–19, and "Reglas locales, Concilio No. 2," March 31, 1928, in Treasurer's Ledger, 1926–30, SPMDTU Records, Box 21. For the Antonito Council No. 1 Special Funeral Fund, see SPMDTU Records, Box 1, Folder 4: "Leyes pasadas por el Cuerpo Legislativo Local aprobadas por Concilio Número Uno, hoy 27 de enero A.D., 1923."

28. Thomas Krainz studied the implementation of public assistance in six diverse counties of Colorado from about 1890 to the late 1920s to include Costilla County, one of Colorado's poorest counties during the Progressive Era of welfare relief. He found that local economies, settlement patterns, ethnic composition, religious backgrounds, and other cultural factors strongly determined how "poor relief" was distributed across the counties. The Costilla County commissioners had little reason to provide high levels of assistance because the kinship networks, the vara strips of land ownership, subsistence agriculture dependent on irrigation ditches, access to natural resources in the communal lands, a barter economy, and the relative isolation of the San Luis Valley from outside markets combined to form a safety net for the tightly knit clusters of neighbors and family (*Delivering Aid*, 11, 18, 34–42).

29. Journal of Minutes, Concilio Superior, 1925–48, SPMDTU Records, Box 16, February 1925.

30. Constitución y Reglamento de SPMDTU, 1922, Article XXIX, José A. Rivera Papers, Box 8, Folder 3. Also see the revised Constitution of 1942 in the same folder for reference purposes.

31. Ibid., Article XXXVIII.

32. Sánchez, "A History of the SPMDTU," 9.

33. For the use of ad hoc commissions and attempts to settle disputes in the community, see the minutes of the Velarde Council No. 40, May 16, 1936, and May 9, 1937, SPMDTU Records, Box 24, and Journal of Minutes, Concilio Superior, 1917, SPMDTU Records, Box 18. For the case in 1923 involving a member of Capulín

Council No. 2 and money owed him by a member of the local penitente cofradía, see minutes of May 5 and 19, 1923, Journal of Minutes, 1923–24, Capulín Council, SPMDTU Records, Box 21.

34. Journal of Minutes, Concilio Superior, January 12, 1916, SPMDTU Records, Box 18.

35. Journal of Minutes, Concilio Superior, March 29, 1917, SPMDTU Records, Box 18.

36. Journal of Minutes, Concilio Superior, June 12, 1920, SPMDTU Records, Box 18.

37. Journal of Minutes, Concilio Superior, February 19, 1921, SPMDTU Records, Box 18; Sánchez, "A History of the SPMDTU," 6–7; Frederick Sánchez, "Building Fund Leads to Financial Loss," *La Sierra*, February 21, 2003.

38. See Journal of Minutes, Concilio Superior, August 21 and November 27, 1926, SPMDTU Records, Box 16, regarding the $10,000. For more details about this case, see Sánchez, "A History of the SPMDTU," 6–7, and his article "Building Fund Leads to Financial Loss." Sánchez's grandfather, Fred Sánchez Sr., served as the superior treasurer of the SPMDTU for twenty-four years, from 1941 to 1965.

39. Arnold Valdez and María Valdez, Valdez and Associates, "SPMDTU Concilio Superior, Conejos County, Colorado," National Register of Historic Places Registration Form, September 29, 2000, U.S. National Park Service, SPMDTU Records, Box 1, Folder 32. Thanks to Arnold Valdez for detailed descriptions of the architectural features, e-mail message to José A. Rivera, September 17, 2008. The Concilio Superior meeting hall has served many generations of members in hosting the SPMDTU conventions as well as the public by providing affordable rental space for large gatherings such as wedding receptions, graduation celebrations, *quinceañeras* (traditional birthday parties for girls turning fifteen years of age), and, in more recent history, summer craft fairs sponsored by Arco Iris, a local collective for artists and crafts production and marketing ("SPMDTU Concilio Superior Receives Rehab Funding," *La Sierra*, January 28, 2005).

40. Arnold Valdez, e-mail to José A. Rivera, September 17, 2008. See figures 9 and 10 for the Ojo Caliente meeting hall.

41. See DayBook Journal and other ledgers, Arroyo Seco Council No. 42, SPMDTU Records, Box 5. Also see figures 28a and 28b as well as Treasurer's Ledger of 1931 in appendix 2.

42. See minutes, Arroyo Seco Council No. 42, Ledger 1930–35, SPMDTU Records, Box 5. The members of Capulín Council No. 2 also favored the idea of organizing debates. Topics presented there during 1912–13 included: "El trigo y el dinero: ¿Cúal es de más utilidad al hombre?" (Wheat versus money: Which is of greater utility to a man?); and "¿Cúal hace más beneficio a la humanidad, el doctor o el abogado?" (Which occupation is more beneficial to humanity, a doctor or a lawyer?). See minutes, Capulín Council No. 2, Libro del Presidente Day Book, March 3, 1912, and Journal of Minutes, Concilio Superior, 1913–19, May 31, 1913, SPMDTU Records, Boxes 20 and 21.

43. Journal of Minutes, Concilio Superior, February 18, 1933, SPMDTU Records, Box 16.

44. Journal of Minutes, Concilio Superior, November 27, 1933, SPMDTU Records, Boxes 16 and 18; Frederick Sánchez, "Society Weathers Series of Crises," *La Sierra*, February 28, 2003.

45. Diario Legislativo de la Asemblea General, 1931–35, SPMDTU Records, Box 18.

46. Edad y Fecha de Entrada de Miembros de la SPMDTU, March 17, 1937, SPMDTU Records, Box 1, Folder 4.

47. Certificate no. 1306 issued to Manuel A. Valdez with signatures of the SPMDTU president and secretary, Sociedad de Vida Mutua, November 19, 1938, courtesy of Valdez's granddaughter Vickie Fresquez, e-mail to José A. Rivera, April 22, 2009, with attachment of certificate in electronic image.

48. López, *La Historia*, 65–73.

49. Preamble, Constitución y Reglamento de la Sociedad AMB, 1937, revised 1964; copy made for José A. Rivera by Ruben Archuleta.

50. The August 13, 1938, minutes of the Velarde Council No. 40 in New Mexico describe a request by the "hermanas" from the community to organize themselves as an auxiliary (AMB) of the SPMDTU, leading to approval by the Velarde Council at two subsequent meetings in October of that same year. This auxiliary in Velarde was presumably part of the AMB system of local affiliates or at least shared the same name as the women's councils authorized for Colorado. Other details in the minutes seem to indicate that each SPMDTU council could organize auxiliaries for women of the community simply by establishing a rule at the local council level, as happened in Velarde. See minutes, August 13 and 24, October 22 and 29, 1938, Velarde Journal 1937–39, SPMDTU Records, Box 24. The SPMDTU Constitution was later revised to recognize the contributions of the ladies auxiliaries and officially approve the establishment of women's auxiliary councils. See Article XL, Constitución y Reglamento de la SPMDTU, revised 1980, SPMDTU Records, Box 1, Folder 1. This amendment was adopted at the 1978 general convention.

51. See Constitución y Reglamento de la Sociedad AMB, 1937, revised 1964. The AMB Constitution authorized the establishment of twelve local councils, but it is not known how many were ultimately commissioned, other than the ones at Antonito and Denver in Colorado and likely in Velarde, New Mexico.

52. Article XLVII, Bandera de la Sociedad, and Article XLVIII, Vestidos y Estandartes, Constitución y Reglamento de la Sociedad AMB, 1937, revised 1964; copy supplied to José A. Rivera by Ruben Archuleta.

53. Journal of Minutes, Concilio Superior, February 17, 1936, SPMDTU Records, Box 16. In a similar case, the Concilio Superior named a commission in 1942–43 to review the rules and regulations of the already established AMB in order to determine if there were any conflicts with the SPMDTU's General Regulations, resulting in a report of no conflict while affirming the AMB's autonomy (Journal of Minutes, Concilio Superior, February 10, 1943, SPMDTU Records, Box 16).

54. Himno oficial, La Sociedad Femenil de Protección; copy made for José A. Rivera by Ruben Archuleta.

55. SPMDTU Constitution, revised 1952, SPMDTU Records, Box 1, Folder 1.

56. Trigésima Octava Celebración, November 26, 1938 program brochure, SPMDTU Records, Box 1, Folder 1.

57. See 1976 anniversary poster, SPMDTU Records, Box 25. Brief mention is made of a "Ladies Society" in 1984, but only to say that the women were meeting at the same time as the SPMDTU Superior Council and invited the men to join them for lunch: "Las señoras tienen su junta Superior y ellas van a servir comida a medio día y extienden invitación a los hermanos" (Journal of Minutes, Concilio Superior, August 14, 1984, SPMDTU Records, Box 19).

58. Feloniz Trujillo, telephone communication with José A. Rivera, November 6, 2008, and Carmen Velarde, telephone communication with José A. Rivera, November 20, 2008. Also see Journal of Minutes, Concilio Superior, April 28, 1984, SPMDTU Records, Box 2, Folder 12. Thirteen women were initiated as charter members of Concilio No. 20 at the April 28, 1984, special meeting, which concluded with an election and the installation of officers conducted by the officers of the SPMDTU Concilio Superior: Carmen Velarde (presidente), Feloniz Trujillo (vice presidente), Bella Mondragón (secretaria), Aurora Archuleta (tesorera), Pam Baca (consejera), Rita Martínez (calificador), Angie Vigil (mariscal), Lena DeVargas (guardia), Lesbia Rodríguez (portero), Valerie Vigil, Barbara Romero, Diana Mondragón, and Elena C. Cárdenas (titles given as presented in the minutes). Diana Durán, Aurora Montoya, and Elena DeVargas, among others, joined shortly after the initiation meeting. Carmen Velarde is a folk artist with national recognition for her work in the making of adobe fireplaces, *hornos*, *retablos*, *bultos*, tinwork, morada altar screens, and *colchas*. At the invitation of the Smithsonian Institution and the U.S. National Park Service, she represented New Mexico in the Festival of American Folklife in 1981 and again in 1992.

59. Minutes of general conventions, October 1984, Ogden, Utah, and October 1986, Ranchos de Taos, N.Mex., SPMDTU Records, Box 1, Folder 20.

60. For an account of the merger, see petition letter dated July 13, 1987, by Feloniz Trujillo to SPMDTU secretary-treasurer Tomás Romero and the latter's reply letter of August 7, 1987, SPMDTU Records, Box 2, Folder 12; and Journal of Minutes, Concilio Superior, August 1, 1987, SPMDTU Records, Box 19. The step to form a separate concilio for women of the Taos area turned out to be an alternative and temporary measure until more spouses and other women not previously affiliated with the SPMDTU could be recruited to join Council No. 18 with the men, as happened in 1987 and later years.

61. Journal of Minutes, Concilio Superior, August 5, 1989, SPMDTU Records, Box 17. By 2008, women made up about 20 percent of the total membership, approximately 33 out of 165 members. Women were eligible to join by virtue of a constitutional amendment adopted by a unanimous vote of thirty-five to zero at the general convention of 1978, which deleted the requirement of masculine gender as the basis of membership (part A of Article XL, Constitución y Reglamento de La Sociedad, revised 1980, SPMDTU Records, Box 1, Folder 1). Part C was also adopted in 1978 to recognize the contributions and service performed by the ladies auxiliaries in past years, with an endorsement for the formation of new auxiliaries eligible for SPMDTU rights and benefits. In 1984–85, Concilio No. 57 of Nambé enrolled about sixteen women as new members with an initial group of five on July 5, 1984: Florinda Luján, Mabel Trujillo, Norma Jean García, Marlene Luján, and Celina Ortiz.

62. López, *La Historia*, 20–23, 82.

63. Annual SPMDTU statement to the Colorado Commissioner of Insurance for the year ending December 31, 1936, SPMDTU Records, Box 39.

64. López, *La Historia*, 81–82. For the transfer of the Mutual Life Association to the SPMDTU, see Journal of Minutes, Concilio Superior, May 13, 1942, SPMDTU Records, Box 19.

65. Certificado y Artículos de Incorporación de Union Cooperativa Mutual, 1954, Constitución y Reglamento de la SPMDTU, revised 1952, SPMDTU Records, Box 1, Folder 1. For the 1965 financial report, see Sánchez, "Society Weathers Series of Crises."

66. SPMDTU pamphlets from the 1970s and 1980s, and Journal of Minutes, Concilio Superior, October 1, 1983, SPMDTU Records, Box 1, Folder 1, and Box 19. Also see David Roybal, "SPMDTU: Has Hispanic Rights Group Outlived Need?" *The New Mexican*, Section C, October 2, 1992, SPMDTU Records, Box 1, Folder 1.

67. See report of the Cuerpo Legislativo, September 9–10, SPMDTU 1994 general convention; letter from Plácido G. Goméz, University of New Mexico School of Law, to Rogelio Briones, September 9, 1994, on file with José A. Rivera; and Rogelio Briones e-mail to José A. Rivera, July 16, 2009.

68. Western Slavonic Association, *WSA Fraternal Life*, 6–7, 10–14. As of the annual report for 2008, the total WSA membership was 6,397. Also see the association's Web site at http://www.wsalife.com.

69. Randy Fuss, president and chief executive officer, Western Fraternal Life, remarks to delegates at the SPMDTU convention, Lakewood Elks Lodge, Lakewood, Colorado, September 6, 2008, from José A. Rivera's notes.

70. López, *La Historia*, 31.

Chapter Three

1. Nambé Council No. 57 anniversary program, November 15, 2003, on file with José A. Rivera. Volunteers from the Nambé Council plan each anniversary program, and members provide entertainment; for example, Roberto Mondragón, a former New Mexico lieutenant governor who joined the SPMDTU in 1972, plays the guitar and sings New Mexican tunes that are widely popular in northern New Mexico and southern Colorado. At the seventy-fifth anniversary of Nambé Council No. 57 in 2004, Mondragón addressed the members: "No olviden las creencias (Don't forget your heritage). . . . De donde vinimos, donde estamos y a donde vamos" (Where we come from, where we are, and where we are going). See news article and photos of anniversary ceremonies in Marrisa Stone, "Brotherly Love," *The Santa Fe New Mexican*, Pojoaque Valley edition, November 24, 2004.

2. Translation of meeting agenda topics: opening ceremony; official prayer; reading of minutes from the previous meeting; communications and claims; reports from commissions; ceremony for the initiation of new members; business items on the president's table; discourses and debates for the welfare of the society; report of collections, expenditures, and delinquencies of members; and closing ceremonies. See the Código Ritualístico de Régimen Interior, 1922, revised 1980, SPMDTU Records, Box 1, Folder 1.

3. José A. Rivera's notes from the meeting of Nambé Council No. 57, November 6, 2003. The Nambé Council collects small amounts yearly at the time dues are paid

as earmarked funds for a defunción, a special assessment for death benefits in the amount of $300 paid to survivors. These assessments are in addition to the general dues paid for maintenance of the meeting hall and the administrative fees forwarded to the Superior Council (receipts for dues issued to José A. Rivera, Nambé Council No. 57, January 2004 and 2005, on file with José A. Rivera).

4. Constitución y Reglamento de la SPMDTU, revised 1952, 1980, SPMDTU Records, Box 1, Folder 1.

5. Valdez, "La Sociedad Protección Mutua," 20. For the composition and duties of the Cuerpo Regulador, see minutes of the special meeting held by the Concilio Superior, October 1, 1983, per the resolution adopted at the 1982 general convention as Article II, section 15, Constitución y Reglamento de la SPMDTU, SPMDTU Records, Box 1, Folder 20.

6. See "SPMDTU Fraternity Celebrates 100 Years of service," *La Sierra*, September 8, 2000, and Frederick Sánchez, "SPMDTU: Society Still Has Much to Celebrate," *La Sierra*, March 14, 2003. The March 14 Sánchez account captures the solemnity and drama of the centennial event: "The members marched two-by-two into the Hall and stood inside, from the front to the back, facing their partners, all the time under the spell of an ancient Hispanic march of triumph and mesmerized the presence of all with their hymn and the musical trance of the American Civil War tune of 'Rally Round the Flag, Boys.' Musicians with the violin, the Spanish guitar and the accordion flooded the Hall with melody and musical euphoria, which only the human heart and mind could create. They stretched out their hands to each other as they chanted the official hymn of union and strength, with the tune of the marching band of the American Civil War soldiers. 'We swear to be free, long live the Union. Let us stretch out our hands to each other with charity and love, let us stretch out our hands,' the members chanted the official hymn in Spanish."

7. Valdez and Valdez, Valdez and Associates, "SPMDTU Concilio Superior, Conejos County, Colorado." Also see the Web site for the Directory of Colorado State Register Properties at http://www.coloradohistory-oahp.org. In addition to the nomination report of 2000, Valdez and Associates also authored the proposal to secure an initial grant of $10,000 from the Colorado Historical Society for a preliminary assessment of the repairs and restoration work that would be needed to preserve the building. The SPMDTU had contracted out the work for this proposal to Valdez and Associates following approval of $1,500 in expenditures at the 1996 general convention in Española, New Mexico.

8. Delapp Engineering Corporation, "SPMDTU Concilio Superior Structure Assessment and Preservation Plan," September 2002, p. 6, SPMDTU Records, Box 1, Folder 33.

9. Celedonio Mondragón's presence continues to be felt by SPMDTU members, as was evident during the one hundredth anniversary celebration when his spirit permeated the day's events. A photo of the revered founder hangs on a wall of the Superior Council office in Antonito, and photos of him are usually provided to newspapers when they report organization activities. In his later years, he continued his relationship to the society as the calificador superior in 1919–20 and then as an honorary member until his death in June 1923. In 1924, SPMDTU members from the Antonito Council No. 1 donated a special monument and placed it at his gravesite

at the Conejos Cemetery to memorialize him as the *fundador* of the organization. The Superior Council raised additional funds for the monument by requesting voluntary contributions from the other concilios in a carta circular drafted by a special commission (Journal of Minutes, Concilio Superior, February 16, 1924, SPMDTU Records, Box 18).

10. SPMDTU minutes of the general convention, September 14, 2002, Lakewood Elks Lodge, Lakewood, Colorado; both official minutes and notes on the convention on file with José A. Rivera.

11. José A. Rivera's notes from the SPMDTU general convention, September 14, 2002.

12. Delapp Engineering Corporation, "SPMDTU Concilio Superior Structure Assessment."

13. SPMDTU minutes of general convention and resolution number 2 presented in the report of the Cuerpo Legislativo Superior, September 11, 2004, Rusty Spur meeting hall, Antonito, Colorado. Rogelio Briones, e-mail to José A. Rivera, September 26, 2009; minutes on file with José A. Rivera.

14. "SPMDTU Concilio Superior Receives Rehab Funding," *La Sierra*, January 28, 2005; Zac Wiggy, "SPMDTU Building on the Mend," *Conejos County Citizen*, Hispanic Times insert, September 14, 2005; see also Zac Wiggy, "SPMDTU Becoming Active Again," *Conejos County Citizen*, November 30, 2005.

15. SPMDTU minutes of general convention, September 9, 2006, Sagebrush Convention Center, Ranchos de Taos, New Mexico; both minutes and notes on the convention on file with José A. Rivera.

16. José A. Rivera's notes from the SPMDTU general convention, September 6, 2008, Lakewood Elks Lodge, Lakewood, Colorado.

Chapter Four

1. Vickie Frésquez, president of Concilio No. 7, Denver, e-mail to José A. Rivera, April 22, 2009. Frésquez was raised by her grandfather Manuel A. Valdez, a member of Alamosa Council No. 19. He was issued a life insurance certificate by "S.P.M.D.T.U. Sociedad de Vida Mutua" on November 19, 1938.

2. Rivera, "Self-Help as Mutual Protection," 394, based in part on the findings of Lieberman and Borman, "Self-Help and Social Research," 455–56.

3. Márquez, *LULAC*, 1–15.

4. Don Celedonio Mondragón married his second wife, María Elena Casias, in 1899 and had seven children: Florencio, Raquel, Cristóbal, Hortancia, Rosa, Celina, and Eliria (Colorado Marriages 1858–1939, compiled by the Colorado Genealogical Society, Denver; 1920 Federal Census of Colorado, Conejos County; copies of these documents e-mailed to José A. Rivera by Manuel Salazar, archivist and genealogist, Colorado Society of Hispanic Genealogy, Denver, October 15, 2008). His descendants who are currently SPMDTU members include several grandchildren and great-grandchildren: Eppie C. Perea Jr., James A. Perea, Billy Perea, Bernadette Perea Armenta, Leroy Teofilo Mondragón, Augustine Robert Mondragón, Eppie C. Perea III, Dominic A. Perea, Ray García Jr., and the wives of Eppie C. Perea Jr., James A. Perea, and Augustine Robert Mondragón. Eppie C. Perea Jr. followed his grandfather's footsteps when he too was elected to serve as the presidente superior almost a

century later, at the 1996 La Sociedad convention. Like other descendants, Eppie C. Perea Jr. credits don Celedonio Mondragón for his vision of unity as the means to end discrimination in the San Luis Valley while ensuring family survival during times of illness or unexpected catastrophe (interview of Eppie C. Perea Jr. by Ernest Gurulé, "An Organization Is Born," *La Voz Nueva*, November 25, 2009).

5. The SPMDTU organizational records (MSS 696 BC, Center for Southwest Research, University Libraries, University of New Mexico, Albuquerque) include forty-five boxes of files, twenty-five cubic feet of materials, and document the society from about 1914 to 2002 with ledgers, journals, minutes of meetings, convention proceedings, annual statements, bank records and receipt books, treasurer's reports, business correspondence, constitutions and other booklets, membership forms, life insurance certificates, memorabilia, and miscellaneous papers. This inventory was made possible in part due to the long tenures of two secretary-treasurers who maintained the records at the Superior Council's headquarters' office: Fred Sánchez, who served in that position from about 1942 to 1965, and Tomás Romero, who took over the records just a few years later, in 1969, and remained in this key position until he passed away in 2005. Also see the SPMDTU folders, José A. Rivera Papers, Box 8.

6. Buxó i Rey, "El mutualisme com a narració de la identitat."

7. For a brief review of the social science literature on this point, see the analysis by Gonzales, *Forced Sacrifice*, 23.

8. Olzak, "A Competition Model of Ethnic Collective Action," 17–21; Olzak, *Global Dynamics*, 59–62.

9. For a discussion of the Mexican-American War and the impact of the annexation of Mexico's northern frontier, now the American Southwest, see Mario T. García's foreword to Sánchez, *Forgotten People*, xviii, as well as the rest of the book.

10. See Rosenbaum, *Mexicano Resistance*, 145–48.

11. Alejandro Portes and Robert Manning note that unskilled workers from southern Italy, Poland, and other eastern European countries who immigrated to the United States prior to World War I for the most part followed the assimilation path of acculturation and economic mobility. The two groups that did not follow this pattern, according to Portes and Manning, were the Jews of Manhattan and the Japanese on the West Coast. For a time, these immigrant enclaves managed to retain their original languages, religions, and values as a means of achieving economic advancement along a path different from acculturation. Charitable mutual aid societies, private schools, social networking, rotating credit associations, cooperative business associations, and other forms of ethnic solidarity helped successive generations of Jews and Japanese to enter the labor force, acquire property and other resources, establish successful business and farm ventures, and gradually integrate into the mainstream economy in advantaged positions ("Immigrant Enclave," 47–55).

12. See the Web site at http://www.slvheritage.org.

13. Dr. Antonio Esquibel and Reverend Stan Perea, remarks to delegates at the SPMDTU convention, Lakewood Elks Lodge, Lakewood, Colorado, September 6, 2008; from José A. Rivera's notes of the 2008 convention.

14. Propuesta/Resolución No. 4, Cuerpo Legislativo Superior, presented to the convention delegates by Lucas Trujillo, presidente, and Rogelio Briones, secretario-

tesorero superior, SPMDTU general convention, September 6, 2008, from José A. Rivera's notes and a convention handout (on file with José A. Rivera).

15. *Noticias* 2, no. 9 (October 2008), SPMDTU Council No. 7, Denver.

16. Lusk and Simon, preface and afterword to *Building to Endure*. In the chapters and case examples in this illuminating book, the editors and chapter authors examine ancient, historical, and contemporary designs for creating sustainable communities that are equitable and adaptable and that will endure for the twenty-first century. For strategies, they turn to lessons we can learn from the process of community as the most basic of adaptive tools exemplified in the cultures of the American Southwest, notably the prehistoric Anasazi settlements at Chaco Canyon, the contemporary Pueblo Indians on the Pajarito Plateau to the east of Chaco, and the land grant colonies of Hispanic pobladores north of Taos into Costilla County in the San Luis Valley of Colorado. See especially chapter 2: Mondragón-Valdez and Valdez, "Hispano Culture and Settlement Patterns."

17. Kropotkin, *Mutual Aid*, 300.

GLOSSARY

acequias: Community irrigation ditches of the upper Río Grande region in southern Colorado and New Mexico.

alabados: Religious hymns of praise associated with the penitente brotherhoods.

árbitros o mediadores en la causa: Referees or mediators appointed to help settle disputes within the membership or that involved others in the local community.

auxiliarias: Women's auxiliaries affiliated with the SPMDTU but with independent rules and constitutions.

auxilio: Help or assistance to others in circumstances of any special or extraordinary need, such as sharing irrigation water from the community acequia in times of drought or providing emergency funds to SPMDTU members in hospitals or with catastrophic illnesses.

ayuda mutua: Forms of mutual help provided by mutualista societies according to benefits and services stipulated in each organization's rules, regulations, and policies.

ayuda voluntaria: Voluntary contributions raised by local councils to supplement benefits paid by La Sociedad.

bandera: Banner or flag of a society such as the SPMDTU. Also known as the *estandarte*, or standard.

bastoneros: Managers who were charged with keeping order and performing tasks such as collecting money at the SPMDTU dances.

beneficio de enfermedad: An illness benefit paid to eligible members when they were unable to work.

beneficio de indigencia: An emergency fund to assist members in times of critical care in the hospital.

175

beneficio de muerte: A death benefit paid to widows and survivors, a prede-
cessor of the life insurance program.

beneficios de funeral: A burial fund available to the beneficiaries of deceased
members.

calificador/calificador superior: The local council or Superior Council officer
who administers oaths to incoming SPMDTU officers and new members
at the time of initiation, literally a "qualifier."

camposanto: Local cemetery, meaning "holy ground."

caridad: Charity, as in *obras de caridad*; charitable works performed by penitential societies and mutualistas alike.

carta circular: A letter circulated to local councils soliciting voluntary financial contributions, distributed with the Superior Council's permission.

certificado de juramento: A certificate of oath administered to new
SPMDTU members during the initiation rituals.

Código Ritualístico de Régimen Interior: The Code of Rituals and Internal Regulations for the SPMDTU local councils to follow for the conduct
of meetings, prayers, initiation of new members, burial ceremonies,
and other functions.

cofradías de penitentes: Confraternities or religious societies, such as the
Cofradía de Nuestro Padre Jesús Nazareno (Brotherhood of Our Father
Jesus the Nazarene), known also as the "penitente brotherhoods" of
southern Colorado and New Mexico. Some chapters of the same orga-
nization use a slightly different name—for example, the Fraternidad
Piadosa de Nuestro Padre Jesús Nazareno.

comisión sobre trabajadores: An SPMDTU commission appointed to help
members look for employment.

concilios locales: Local councils or lodges.

Concilio Superior: The SPMDTU's Superior Council and executive body.

consejero/consejero superior: The local council or Superior Council counselor who interprets parliamentary rules and by-laws during SPMDTU
meetings and deliberations.

contraseña: A secret countersign among SMPDTU members to gain
entrance into meetings or other functions.

corridos: Traditional narrative ballads sung in Mexico and the U.S.
Southwest.

Cuerpo Judicial Superior: The SPMDTU's Superior Judicial Body.

Cuerpo Legislativo Superior: The SPMDTU's Superior Legislative Body.

Cuerpo Regulador: An SPMDTU committee that serves as the financial
regulating body and acts in an advisory capacity to the Superior Council

president on the investment of funds and how best to manage other reserves.

cuotas, cuotas especiales, and cuotas de defunción: Dues paid by members to the local council's treasurer on a yearly basis; special assessments to raise funds for projects such as buildings; and assessments to pay a death benefit.

deberes mutuos: Mutual assistance duties binding on the society and on each of the members: to attend meetings faithfully; exhibit high moral standards; display courteous behavior; respect one another at all times regardless of diverse social opinions, politics or religious beliefs; and help one another in times of need, especially in cases of poverty or illness that led to unemployment and indigence.

defunción: Death of a member.

devisa: A SPMDTU badge or ribbon pinned on clothing for identification of members.

enfermero: The nurse appointed to visit members who are reported ill to determine if the circumstances warrant mutual assistance benefits and to make recommendations accordingly.

Fondo de Caridad: A special fund to help with charitable projects in the community.

Fondo de Edificio: Building Construction Fund.

Fondo de Indigencias: A special fund to issue payments in times of economic hardship or emergencies.

Fondo de Pólizas: A fund created to pay death and funeral benefits to survivors of deceased members. Also called the Fondo de Defunción.

giro: A draft order instructing the treasurer of a local council to issue a payment in the amount specified to a designated member or beneficiary usually as an illness or death benefit, similar in function to a money order.

Gorras Blancas: A vigilante group active in San Miguel County, New Mexico, in the late nineteenth century who resisted Anglo incursions into community land grants. They obscured their identities by wearing *gorras blancas*, white caps, as they rode on horseback.

gran baile: Grand ball or dance usually held during SPMDTU anniversaries.

guardia/guardia superior: The local council or Superior Council guard who admits only members to meetings and who prevents entrance of intruders.

hermano/hermandad: "Brother" and "brotherhood."

himno oficial: La Sociedad had its own official hymn, as did the women's auxiliaries.

hispano americano: A term used in the SPMDTU Constitution to describe persons of Hispanic American descent eligible to become members. At the 2002 biannual convention, the SPMDTU Constitution was amended to admit persons of any ethnicity or race as members.

hispanos: Persons of Spanish-Mexican heritage in New Mexico and southern Colorado. This book uses the terms *hispanos*, *hispano americanos*, *mexicanos*, and *natives* interchangeably to reflect the common usage spanning the territorial periods at the turn of the twentieth century. The more recent terms *Indo-Hispanos* and *Mexican Americans* are also used to coincide with the literature of self-identity in contemporary times from about the 1960s to the present.

mariscal/mariscal superior: The local council or Superior Council marshal who maintains order at meetings and special ceremonies, safeguarding the society's honor and decor and mediating disputes between and among members.

mercedes: Land grants issued to settlers by the Spanish and Mexican governments prior to U.S. jurisdiction starting in 1848.

mexicanos: In territorial New Mexico, Spanish-language newspapers often used this term to describe the native peoples of Mexican-Spanish background.

moradas: The chapels and meeting halls of the penitentes, as they are popularly called—such as the Fraternidad Piadosa de Nuestro Padre Jesús Nazareno.

multas: Fines assessed on members for violation of rules or for not attending meetings.

La Mutua: "Mutualist Society," a short reference to the SPMDTU.

mutualismo: The practice of mutual help in the spirit of reciprocal cooperation.

mutualistas/mutuas: Mutual aid societies of the American Southwest with roots in Mexico and Spain.

nuestro pueblo: Literally "our community" and often a reference to the hispano homeland in the upper Río Grande; also called *el país* or in some cases *patria chica*.

obras de caridad: Mutual aid services of La Sociedad, literally "acts of charity."

oración de apertura: Opening prayer at local council meetings.

oración de clausura: Closing prayer at local council meetings.

Orden de Caballeros de Protección Mutua por la Ley y Orden: The Order of Knights for Mutual Protection in Law and Order, a society organized in Las Vegas, New Mexico, during the early 1890s in opposition to the armed resistance tactics of the vigilante group Gorras Blancas.

Orden de Protección Mutua de Trabajadores Unidos por la Ley y Orden: The Order of Mutual Protection of United Workers in Law and Order, the SPMDTU's temporary name established in the Constitution of 1909 prior to the society's legal incorporation, when the permanent name "La Sociedad de Protección Mutua de Trabajadores Unidos" was adopted.

paso de reconciliación: A process of reconciliation in which disputes between La Sociedad members or between members and nonmembers in the community were mediated.

paso semianual: Semiannual password to gain entrance to SPMDTU meetings.

penitentes: A popular term used to identify members of the religious penitent brotherhoods. Members prefer the term *hermanos*.

platero: Jewelry maker or silversmith, the main occupation of SPMDTU founder don Celedonio Mondragón.

pobladores: Initial settlers of a community, especially in the case of Spanish and Mexican land grants.

póliza de vida: Life insurance policy offered to SPMDTU members.

portero/portero superior: The local council or Superior Council doorkeeper who stands guard at the entrance of the buildings where SPMDTU meetings are held.

querencia: An attachment to place in the hispano homeland of northern New Mexico and southern Colorado.

regidor/regidor superior: The local council director or SPMDTU superior director up until 1916, after which the titles were changed to *presidente* and *presidente superior.*

Reglas Mutuas: SPMDTU's Rules of Mutual Aid.

reina del aniversario: SPMDTU anniversary queen during the 1960s and 1970s.

repartimiento: The cultural practice of sharing or partitioning essential resources such as water for the irrigation of agricultural fields.

resoluciones de condolencia: Resolutions of condolence drafted by a commission of members and submitted to surviving family members.

respeto: One of the SPMDTU's key principles, meaning respect for others, especially elders in the community and those who have passed on to a better life.

sacar el gallo: Literally, "taking out the rooster to crow." The promotion of social events, meetings, dances, and other functions in rural or small towns by way of a horse-drawn wagon and later by pickup trucks, with speakers and musicians making public announcements as members paraded the main streets in the community.

salas: Meeting halls of local councils. The meeting hall of the Superior Council in Antonito, Colorado, is called the Sala Superior.

secretario/secretario superior: The local council or Superior Council secretary who documents the council's proceedings in a journal of minutes and reads all correspondence, reports, and petitions during the meetings. The secretario and tesorero positions were later combined into secretario-tesorero/secretario-tesorero superior.

secretario-tesorero/secretario-tesorero superior: The local council or Superior Council secretary-treasurer, two positions that were initially separate. See *secretario* and *tesorero*.

siempreviva: An evergreen leaf used as a symbol of eternal life by SPMDTU members at gravesite ceremonies to honor deceased members. Wearing the SPMDTU devisas with the black side showing, the members form a circle, and each one tosses a siempreviva leaf into the grave as the coffin is lowered.

La Sociedad: A short reference to La Sociedad Protección Mutua de Trabajadores Unidos (Society for the Mutual Protection of United Workers).

Sociedad de Vida Mutua: A description of the SPMDTU as a mutual life association during the late 1930s.

SPMDTU: The common initials for La Sociedad Protección Mutua de Trabajadores Unidos (Society for the Mutual Protection of United Workers) founded in Antonito, Colorado, in 1900.

tesorero/tesorero superior: The local council or Superior Council treasurer who serves as the financial officer and custodian of all funds, maintaining a ledger of income and expenses and reporting these transactions at meetings or conventions. The secretario and tesorero positions were later combined into secretario-tesorero/secretario-tesorero superior.

Unión Católica del Sagrado Corazón de Jesús: The Catholic Union of the Sacred Heart of Jesus, a religious mutual aid society in Nambé, New Mexico.

velorio: A funeral wake or prayer vigil.

vice regidor/vice regidor superior: The local council or Superior Council assistant director until 1916, after which the titles were changed to *vice presidente* and *vice presidente superior*.

BIBLIOGRAPHY

Archives and Documents

Articles of Incorporation of the Association for Mutual Protection and Mutual Benefit of the Town of Cerro de Guadalupe, April 7, 1888, May 24, 1930, County of Taos, State of New Mexico, no. 0624. State Corporation Commission, File no. 918, Santa Fe.

Colorado Marriages 1858–1939. Colorado Genealogical Society, Denver. Copies e-mailed to José A. Rivera by Manuel Salazar, archivist and genealogist, Colorado Society of Hispanic Genealogy, Denver, October 15, 2008.

Constitución de La Asociación Defensiva de los Pobladores de los Terrenos del Río de Costilla. Certificate of April 12, 1902, recorded in Book A-16, 267–72, Office of the Secretary, Territory of New Mexico, Santa Fe.

Federal Census of Colorado, 1920. Conejos County, Colorado. Copies e-mailed to José A. Rivera by Manuel Salazar, archivist and genealogist, Colorado Society of Genealogy, Denver, October 15, 2008.

La Joya Acequia of Socorro County. "Reglas y regulaciones para el gobierno y manejo de la acequia de comunidad de La Joya, Nuevo México, para el año 1942." On file with José A. Rivera.

National Register of Historic Places. U.S. National Park Service, Washington, D.C.

Rivera, José A. Papers. MSS 587 BC. Center for Southwest Research, University Libraries, University of New Mexico, Albuquerque.

Sociedad de Protección Mutua de Trabajadores Unidos (SPMTDU) Records. MSS 696 BC. Center for Southwest Research, University Libraries, University of New Mexico, Albuquerque.

Newpapers

Alamosa Valley Courier, Alamosa, Colo.

Albuquerque Journal, Journal North edition, Albuquerque, N.Mex.

Conejos County Citizen, Monte Vista, Colo.

Costilla County Citizen, San Luis, Colo.

The New Mexican, Santa Fe, N.Mex.

El Nuevo Mexicano, Santa Fe, N.Mex.
San Luis Valley Lifestyles, Alamosa, Colo.
The Santa Fe New Mexican, Pojoaque Valley edition, Santa Fe
La Sierra, San Luis, Colo.
El Sol de Mayo, Las Vegas, N.Mex.
La Voz del Pueblo, Las Vegas, N.Mex.
La Voz Nueva, Denver

Articles and Books

Aguayo, José. "Los Betabeleros." In *La Gente: Hispano History and Life in Colorado*, edited by Vincent C. De Baca, 105–19. Denver: Colorado Historical Society, 1998.

Andrews, Thomas G. "Tata Atanasio Trujillo's Unlikely Tales of Utes, Nuevomexicanos, and the Settling of Colorado's San Luis Valley." *New Mexico Historical Review* 75, no. 1 (2000): 5–41.

Archuleta, Ruben E. *Land of the Penitentes, Land of Tradition.* Pueblo West, Colo.: El Jefe, 2003.

———. *Penitente Renaissance: Manifesting Hope.* Pueblo West, Colo.: El Jefe, 2007.

Arellano, Anselmo F. "The People's Movement: Las Gorras Blancas." In *The Contested Homeland*, edited by Erlinda Gonzales-Berry and David Maciel, 59–82. Albuquerque: University of New Mexico Press, 2000.

Arellano, Anselmo F., and Julián Josué Vigil. *Las Vegas Grandes on the Gallinas, 1835–1985.* Las Vegas, N.Mex.: Editorial Telaraña, 1985.

Arellano, Juan Estevan. "*La Querencia*: La Raza Bioregionalism." *New Mexico Historical Review* 72, no. 1 (1997): 31–37.

Arrieta, Olivia. "La Alianza Hispano-Americana, 1894–1965: An Analysis of Collective Action and Cultural Adaptation." In *Nuevomexicano Cultural Legacy: Forms, Agencies, and Discourse*, edited by Francisco A. Lomelí, Víctor A. Sorell, and Genaro M. Padilla, 109–26. Albuquerque: University of New Mexico Press, 2002.

Atencio, Ernest. *Of Land and Culture: Environmental Justice and Public Lands Ranching in Northern New Mexico.* A report by the Quivira Coalition and the Northern New Mexico Group of the Sierra Club. Santa Fe, N.Mex.: Quivira Coalition, 2001; 2d printing, December 2004.

Barker, S. Omar. "Los Penitentes." *Overland Monthly* 82, no. 10 (1924): 180.

Baxter, John O. *Dividing New Mexico's Water: 1700–1912.* Albuquerque: University of New Mexico Press, 1997.

Bills, Garland D., and Neddy A. Vigil. *The Spanish Language of New Mexico and Southern Colorado: A Linguistic Atlas.* Albuquerque: University of New Mexico Press, 2008.

Blackmore, William. *Colorado: Its Resources, Parks, and Prospects as a New Field for Emigration.* London: Sampson Low, Son and Marston, 1869.

Brayer, Herbert O. *William Blackmore: The Spanish-Mexican Land Grants of New Mexico and Colorado, 1863–1878.* 1949. Reprinted in *The Mexican American: Spanish and Mexican Land Grants*, paginated as an individual document in the book. New York: Arno Press, 1974.

Briegel, Kaye Lynn. "Alianza Hispano-Americana, 1894–1965: A Mexican American Fraternal Insurance Society." Ph.D. diss., University of Southern California, 1974.

Buxó i Rey, María Jesús. "El mutualisme com a narració de la identitat: La Societat de Protecció Mútua de Treballadors Units a Nou Mexic (EAU)." *Revista d'etnologia de Catalunya*, no. 11 (1997): 68–77.

———. "El paisaje cosmológico de la arquitectura en el Suroeste de Norteamerica." *Revista Española de Antropología Americana*, special issue (2003): 85–98.

Carlson, Alvar Ward. "Rural Settlement Patterns in the San Luis Valley." *Colorado Magazine* 44, no. 2 (1967): 111–28.

Deutsch, Sarah. *No Separate Refuge: Culture, Class, and Gender on the Anglo-Hispanic Frontier in the American Southwest, 1880–1940*. New York: Oxford University Press, 1987.

Dunbar-Ortiz, Roxanne. *Roots of Resistance: A History of Land Tenure in New Mexico*. Norman: University of Oklahoma Press, 2007.

Ebright, Malcolm. *Land Grants and Lawsuits in Northern New Mexico*. Albuquerque: University of New Mexico Press, 1994.

———. "New Mexican Land Grants: The Legal Background." In *Land, Water, and Culture: New Perspectives on Hispanic Land Grants*, edited by Charles L. Briggs and John R. Van Ness, 15–64. Albuquerque: University of New Mexico Press, 1987.

Engstrom, David W., Alvin O. Korte, and Katie McDonough. "Understaffed, Underfunded: The Emergence of Social Welfare in New Mexico, 1940s–1950s." *New Mexico Historical Review* 79, no. 4 (2004): 459–88.

Forrest, Suzanne. *The Preservation of the Village: New Mexico's Hispanics and the New Deal*. Albuquerque: University of New Mexico Press, 1989.

Foster, George M. "Cofradía and Compadrazgo in Spain and Spanish America." *Southwestern Journal of Anthropology* 9, no. 1 (1953): 1–28.

Gist, Noel P. "Fraternal Societies." In *Development of Collective Enterprise*, edited by Seba Eldridge and Associates, 171–81. Lawrence: University of Kansas Press, 1943.

———. *Secret Societies: A Cultural Study of Fraternalism in the United States*. In the series University of Missouri Studies: A Quarterly of Research 15, no. 4. Columbia: University of Missouri, 1940.

Gonzales, Phillip B. *Forced Sacrifice as Ethnic Protest*. New York: Peter Lang, 2001.

———. "Struggle for Survival: The Hispanic Land Grants of New Mexico, 1848–2001." *Agricultural History* 77, no. 2 (2003): 293–324.

Gutiérrez, David G. *Walls and Mirrors: Mexican Americans, Mexican Immigrants, and the Politics of Ethnicity*. Berkeley and Los Angeles: University of California Press, 1995.

Hernández, José Amaro. *Mutual Aid for Survival: The Case of the Mexican American*. Malabar, Fla.: Krieger, 1983.

Hicks, Gregory A. "Memory and Pluralism on a Property Law Frontier: The Contested Landscape of the Costilla Valley." *New Mexico Historical Review* 81, no. 3 (2006): 299–355.

Hicks, Gregory A., and Devon G. Peña. "Community Acequias in Southern Colorado's Rio Culebra Watershed: A Customary Commons in the Domain of Prior Appropriation." *University of Colorado Law Review* 74, no. 2 (2003): 387–486.

Karnes, Thomas L. *William Gilpin: Western Nationalist.* Austin: University of Texas Press, 1970.

Katz, Alfred H., and Eugene I. Bender. "Self-Help Groups in Western Society: History and Prospects." *Journal of Applied Behavioral Science* 12, no. 3 (1976): 265–82.

Kessell, John L. *Kiva, Cross, and Crown: The Pecos Indians and New Mexico, 1540–1840.* Albuquerque: University of New Mexico Press, 1987.

Knowlton, Clark S. "Changing Spanish-American Villages of Northern New Mexico." *Sociology and Social Research* 53, no. 4 (1969): 455–74.

———. "Land Loss as a Cause of Unrest among the Rural Spanish-American Village Population of New Mexico." *Agriculture and Human Values* 2, no. 3 (1985): 25–39.

Krainz, Thomas A. *Delivering Aid: Implementing Progressive Era Welfare in the American West.* Albuquerque: University of New Mexico Press, 2005.

Kropotkin, Peter A. *Mutual Aid: A Factor of Evolution.* Boston: Extending Horizons Books, 1902; reissued 1925.

Kutsche, Paul, and Dennis Gallegos. "Community Functions of the Cofradía de Nuestro Padre Jesús Nazareno." In *The Survival of Spanish American Villages*, edited by Paul Kutsche, 91–98. Colorado College Studies no. 15. Colorado Springs: Colorado College, 1979.

Lamadrid, Enrique R. "Rutas del Corazón: Pilgrimage and Cultural Commerce on the Camino Real de Tierra Adentro." *New Mexico Historical Review* 83, no. 4 (2008): 423–49.

Leonard, Olen E. *The Role of the Land Grant in the Social Organization and Social Processes of a Spanish-American Village in New Mexico.* Albuquerque: Calvin Horn, 1970.

Lieberman, M. A., and L. D. Borman. "Self-Help and Social Research." *Journal of Applied Behaviorial Science* 12, no. 3 (1976): 455–63.

López, José Timoteo. *La Historia de la Sociedad Protección Mutua de Trabajadores Unidos.* New York: Comet Press, 1958.

López Tushar, Olibama. *The People of El Valle.* 2d. ed. rev. Pueblo, Colo.: El Escritorio, 1992.

Lusk, Paul, and Alf Simon, eds. *Building to Endure: Design Lessons of Arid Lands.* Albuquerque: University of New Mexico Press, 2009.

Márquez, Benjamín. *LULAC: The Evolution of a Mexican American Political Organization.* Austin: University of Texas Press, 1993.

Martin, Joanne M., and Elmer P. Martin. *The Helping Tradition in the Black Family and Community.* Silver Spring, Md.: National Association of Social Workers, 1985.

Meinig, D. W. *Southwest: Three Peoples in Geographical Change, 1600–1970.* New York: Oxford University Press, 1971.

Meyer, Doris L. "Early Mexican-American Responses to Negative Stereotyping." *New Mexico Historical Review* 53, no. 1 (1978): 75–91.

———. *Speaking for Themselves: Neo-Mexicano Cultural Identity and the Spanish-Language Press, 1880–1920.* Albuquerque: University of New Mexico Press, 1996.

Mondragón-Valdez, María, and Arnold Valdez. "Hispano Culture and Settlement Patterns." In *Building to Endure: Design Lessons of Arid Lands*, edited by Paul Lusk and Alf Simon, 43–59. Albuquerque: University of New Mexico Press, 2009.

"Morada de Los Pinos Journal." In *Land of the Penitentes: Land of Tradition*, by Ruben E. Archuleta, 161–237. Pueblo West, Colo.: El Jefe, 2003.

Nieto-Phillips, John M. *The Language of Blood: The Making of Spanish-American Identity in New Mexico, 1880s–1930s*. Albuquerque: University of New Mexico Press, 2004.

Nostrand, Richard L. *The Hispano Homeland*. Norman: University of Oklahoma Press, 1992.

Noticias 2, no. 9 (October 2008). Sociedad de Protección Mutua de Trabajadores Unidos (SPMDTU) Council No. 7, Denver.

Olzack, Susan. "A Competition Model of Ethnic Collective Action." In *Competitive Ethnic Relations*, edited by Susan Olzak and Joane Nagel, 17–46. Orlando, Fla.: Academic Press, 1986.

———. *The Global Dynamics of Racial and Ethnic Mobilization*. Stanford, Calif.: Stanford University Press, 2006.

Olzak, Susan, and Joane Nagel, eds. *Competitive Ethnic Relations*. Orlando, Fla.: Academic Press, 1986.

Orozco, Cynthia E. "The Origins of the League of United Latin American Citizens (LULAC) and the Mexican American Civil Rights Movement in Texas with an Analysis of Women's Political Participation in a Gendered Context, 1910–1929." Ph.D. diss., University of California at Los Angeles, 1993.

Peña, Devon G. "Cultural Landscapes and Biodiversity: The Ethnoecology of an Upper Rio Grande Watershed Commons." In *La Gente: Hispano History and Life in Colorado*, edited by Vincent C. de Baca, 241–71. Denver: Colorado Historical Society, 1998.

Perea, Stan, with Cheryl A. Smith. *The New America: The America of the Moo-Shoo Burrito*. Denver: HIS Ministries, 2004.

Pollard, William L. *A Study of Black Self-Help*. San Francisco: R&E Research Associates, 1978.

Portes, Alejandro, and Robert D. Manning. "The Immigrant Enclave: Theory and Empirical Examples." In *Competitive Ethnic Relations*, edited by Susan Olzak and Joane Nagel, 47–68. Orlando, Fla.: Academic Press, 1986.

Ramos, Henry. *The American G.I. Forum: In Pursuit of the Dream, 1948–1983*. Houston: Arte Público Press, 1998.

Rivera, José A. *Acequia Culture: Water, Land, and Community in the Southwest*. Albuquerque: University of New Mexico Press, 1998.

———. "Self-Help as Mutual Protection: The Development of Hispanic Fraternal Benefit Societies." *Journal of Applied Behavioral Science* 23, no. 3 (1987): 387–96.

Rodríguez, Sylvia. *Acequia: Water Sharing, Sanctity, and Place*. Santa Fe, N.Mex.: School of Advanced Research Press, 2006.

Rosenbaum, Robert J. *Mexicano Resistance in the Southwest: The Sacred Right of Self-Preservation*. Austin: University of Texas Press, 1981.

Sánchez, Frederick C. "A History of the SPMDTU." *San Luis Valley Historian* 3, no. 1 (1971): 1–12.

Sánchez, George I. *Forgotten People: A Study of New Mexicans.* Albuquerque: University of New Mexico Press, 1940; reprinted 1996.

Simmons, Virginia McConnell. *The San Luis Valley: Land of the Six-Armed Cross.* Niwot: University Press of Colorado, 1999.

Steele, Thomas J., and Rowena A. Rivera. *Penitente Self-Government: Brotherhoods and Councils, 1797–1947.* Santa Fe, N.Mex.: Ancient City Press, 1985.

Stoller, Marianne L. "Grants of Desperation, Lands of Speculation: Mexican Period Land Grants in Colorado." In *Spanish & Mexican Land Grants in New Mexico and Colorado,* edited by John R. Van Ness and Christine M. Van Ness, 22–39. Santa Fe, N.Mex., and Boulder, Colo.: Center for Land Grant Studies and Colorado Humanities Program, 1980.

Stuart, Merah S. *An Economic Detour: A History of Insurance in the Lives of American Negroes.* College Park, Md.: McGrath, 1940; reprinted 1969.

Swadesh, Frances Leon. *Los primeros pobladores: Hispanic Americans in the Ute Frontier.* Notre Dame, Ind.: University of Notre Dame Press, 1974.

Taylor, José Inez, and James M. Taggart. *Alex and the Hobo: A Chicano Life and Story.* Austin: University of Texas Press, 2003.

Thomas, Cyrus. *The Agricultural and Pastoral Resources of Southern Colorado and Northern New Mexico.* London: John King, 1872.

Valdez, María. "La Sociedad Protección Mutua de Trabajadores Unidos." *San Luis Valley Historian* 33, no. 2 (2001): 5–25.

Von Germeten, Nicole. "Death in Black and White: Testaments and Confraternal Devotion in Seventeenth-Century Mexico City." *Colonial Latin American Historical Review* 12 (Summer 2003): 275–301.

Weber, David J. *Foreigners in Their Native Land: Historical Roots of the Mexican Americans.* Albuquerque: University of New Mexico Press, 1973.

Weigle, Marta. *The Penitentes of the Southwest.* Santa Fe, N.Mex.: Ancient City Press, 1970.

Western Slavonic Association. *WSA Fraternal Life: A Celebration of the First 100 Years, 1908–2008.* Westminster, Colo.: WSA, 2008.

Westphall, Victor. *Mercedes Reales: Hispanic Land Grants of the Upper Rio Grande Basin.* Albuquerque: University of New Mexico Press, 1983.

Wirth, Louis. *The Ghetto.* Chicago: University of Chicago Press, 1928.

Woodward, Dorothy. "The Penitentes of New Mexico." PhD diss., Yale University, 1935. Reprinted in *The Mexican American: The Penitentes of New Mexico,* paginated as an individual document in the book. New York: Arno Press, 1974.

INDEX

Page numbers in italic type indicate illustrations. The letter *n* following a page number indicates a note on the cited page(s). The number following the *n* refers to the note number on that page.

187

92–93; Cuerpo Judicial Superior, 85; Cuerpo Legislativo Superior, 84–85; Cuerpo Regulador, 85; cultural diversity and, 108–9; current functions of, 100–101; dances and, vii–viii, 78, 114, 118; death benefits and, 56, 57–58; debates and, 67–68, 166n42; deberes mutuos and, 52; expansion into New Mexico, 56; financial assistance and, 59; financial difficulties and, 68–69; Fondo de Indigencias and, 58–59, 69; Fondo de Pólizas and, 69; formation of local councils and, 48–49; Founder's Day and, 75–76; founding of, xii, 21; fraternalism and, 108; General Constitution of 1909, 51; General Constitution revision of 1911, 53–55; General Constitution revision of 1980, 84; Great Depression and, 68–70; growth, expansion of, 56, 69, 100; Guardiantes de Cultura centennial celebration, 90; Himno Oficial (Official Hymn), vii, 137–39; historical social programs of, 102–3; illness benefits and, 56, 57; incorporation as mutual benefit society, 52; initial board of directors of, 48; initial services provided by, 49; legal aid and, 61; life insurance and, 70, 78–81; local church councils and, 11; local meeting halls and, 63–64, 67; Manos, *xviii*; membership of, 12, 40, 52, 62, 69, 79, 81, 91, 99–100, 163n12; Minutes of Superior Council Special Meeting 1917, 132–33; as model of self-determination and cultural retention, 104; Mortuary Fund of, 78–79, 80; motto of, 2; Mutual Life Association and, 79; names for, 2; newspapers and, 55; officers of, 52–53; Oración de Apertura (Opening Prayer) of, 123–24; Oración de Clausura (Closing Prayer) of, 124; Petition to Indigence Fund 1923: San Miguel Council No. 10, 133–34; pictorial history of, xiii–xiv; postindustrial society and, 100–101; Preámbulo (Preamble) of 1911,

124–27; purposes of, 21; qualifications for membership of, 49, 50, 54–55, 88, 91; recruitment and, 76, 79, 91; Reglas Mutuas, 50–51; revolving loan funds and, 57; sacar el gallo and, viii; Sala Superior and, 61–63; self-government and, 99; social-welfare relief and, 4; special commissions and, 59–61; structure of, 5, 84–85; Superior Council of, *84*, 84; Treasurer's Ledger 1931: Arroyo Seco Council No. 42, 134–36; treasurer's ledger of, *64–66*; Unión Cooperativa Mutual (CMU) and, 79; women and, 76–78, 100, 168n58, 168n61. *See also specific local councils*

Sociedad Femenil de Protección, 72, 73; Himno Oficial (Official Hymn) of, 144–47

Sociedad: Guardians of Hispanic Culture along the Río Grande (Rivera): as case study of collective action, 1; chapters overview, 1; contents of, 2; as institutional biography, 3; as reference book, 3; research topics, 4

Sociedad Protectora Cooperativa (SPC), 73, 147; Cántico Nacional (National Song) of, 147–48

Sociedad Unión y Fraternidad Mexicana, 11

Taylor, Lobato v., 159n51
Territory of Colorado, 34
Territory of New Mexico, 23–24
Thomas, Cyrus, 157n23
Travelers Insurance Company, 29–30
Treaty of Guadalupe Hidalgo, 19, 23–24, 26, 34, 46, 87
Trinchera and Costilla estates, map of, *37*
Trujillo, Demetrio, 56, 137, 165n24
Trujillo, Dianna Rael, *105*
Trujillo, Feloniz, 77
Trujillo, Lucas, *105*
Trujillo, Manuel Jesús, 117–18
Trujillo, Vianes, xii
Trujillo-Archuleta, María Filomena, 72, 75, 140, 143, 144, 147

www.ingramcontent.com/pod-product-compliance
Lightning Source LLC
Chambersburg PA
CBHW031300310326
41914CB00116B/1702/J